BASIC

BASIC: A SIMPLIFIED STRUCTURED APPROACH

DALE E. NELSON
DARRELL V. BURRAS
EMMA JEAN GILLIS
RON L. KING

RESTON PUBLISHING COMPANY, INC.
Reston, Virginia
A Prentice-Hall Company

ISBN 0-8359-0337-0
ISBN 0-8359-0336-2 pbk.

10 9 8 7 6 5 4 3

Printed in the United States of America.

CONTENTS

PREFACE

This book is designed for those students who have had no previous exposure to computers. Therefore, advanced work is not included. Rather, the goal is a good foundation for continuing study in the field.

The approach in this text is student oriented. By using this text, the student could learn the subject by himself because of the step-by-step presentation of material. Examples are ample, and each chapter contains a summary and a self-test. Also, the problems are simple and are from the field of business. The authors intend for the student to concentrate on learning the fundamentals of programming rather than on sophisticated scientific or mathematical applications.

A structured programming approach is taken throughout the text. This technique, used by leading computing organizations, has been found to have several advantages: the design process is clearer, on-the-job maintenance and revision are simplified, and errors are found at an earlier stage of the program writing process.

The text is written for use with the RSTS/E operating system on the PDP-11 series of computers, which are widely used in educational institutions. A few applications, which are not general to most computers, are footnoted and alternate usages are explained in Appendix B.

ACKNOWLEDGMENTS

The authors thank James B. O'Neill of McDonnell Douglas Automation Company for his suggestions and information concerning structured programming techniques and Alan D. Pearlman for resource assistance on Chapter 12.

BASIC

1 INTRODUCTION

The computer has changed greatly over the past few years, becoming smaller, faster, and more efficient. Because it is also more inexpensive, most businesses can now afford to buy one.

The computer system is basically made up of three hardware components: the input unit, the central processing unit, and the output unit. The input and output units are called *peripheral devices*. Some of the peripheral devices used for putting data into the computer are card readers, tape readers, optical scanners, magnetic ink character readers, and terminals that use cathode ray tubes. The results may be obtained from other peripheral devices such as impact printers, nonimpact printers, line printers, card punches, paper tape punches, and terminals that use cathode reay tubes. The computer and its peripheral devices are normally referred to as computer *hardware*.

The central processing unit of the computer, called the *CPU*, is made up of three components: the main storage, the processing unit, and the control unit. The processing unit consists of two operating units—the logic and the arithmetic units. The control unit is like a policeman. Everything goes through the control unit and is directed by that unit to the main storage, to the logic area of the processing unit, or to the arithmetic area. Main storage is one of the most important parts of the computer because it stores all input and the results of the executions done by the processor.

In the earlier days of the computer, the program language was a machine-oriented language. The program was written in this language and the computer assembled, or translated, the machine-oriented language into machine-language instructions. Machine-oriented languages were difficult for the average user to learn. Many attempts have been made to develop a language that is user-oriented. FORTRAN and COBOL are two that have become standard languages. BASIC is a user-oriented language developed for the nonprofessional user.

Regardless of which language is used to communicate with the machine, the computer still executes with machine-language instructions. Therefore, every computer has a translation program, called a *compiler*. The compiler translates the user-oriented language, or high-level language, into a machine-oriented language. The machine-oriented language is also called *assembler language* or *low-level language*. The computer then translates, or assembles, the assembler language into machine-language codes that activate the computer.

The user's coded program is called the *subject program* or *source program*, and the compiled or assembled program that is derived from the source program is called the *object program*.

The computer system has auxiliary storage and core storage. Auxiliary storage is slower than core storage.

One of the results of modernizing computers and making them available to many users is the principle of time sharing. A number of users on remote input/output terminals are connected with a central terminal through a communication control unit and buffers that continually shuffle users' jobs in and out of the CPU. This control unit also sends solutions back to the user and is the connecting unit to the storage. The CPU can handle several jobs at once. Buffers are storage areas that regulate the flow of data into and out of the computer. They compensate for time lapses in the sequence of events in a program, allowing the computer to handle many jobs almost simultaneously. Because the cost of the system is shared, time sharing is less expensive than buying or leasing a computer and also allows more users to have access to a computer.

BASIC (Beginner's All-Purpose Symbolic Instruction Code) is one of the computer languages available to time-sharing users. The remainder of this book will be used to instruct the potential programmer on an extended BASIC language used with the RSTS/E operating system on the PDP-11 series of computers.

2

BASIC INFORMATION NEEDED TO WRITE A SIMPLE PROGRAM

STEPS IN WRITING A PROGRAM

A computer operator does not sit down at the computer and start typing a program. There is much more to it than that. There are four steps involved in writing a program.

Step one is defining the problem. The problem must be identified before a solution can be attempted. Some questions that might be asked are: What kind of input data are used? What must be done to get an answer? What form of output is desired?

The second step is to diagram the logical flow of the program. The programmer makes a flowchart showing step-by-step instructions that must be followed to solve the problem. A flowchart can be either general or detailed. Flowcharting will be discussed in Chapter 3.

After the program is flowcharted, it is then coded. Coding is the process of writing the specific statements that will be typed on the terminal. If a person has done his homework and has followed the first two steps, the coding (the third step) will be rather simple. The rules for coding BASIC must be followed, or the computer will be unable to execute the program. These rules will be distributed through the chapters as different types of problems are introduced.

The final step is the debugging, or the finding of errors, in a program that has been run. There are two types of errors that appear in the program: syntax errors and logic errors. The computer sends an error message, called a diagnostic, immediately after a syntax error is made, making it easier to locate. However, the computer cannot identify a logic error. This type of error occurs when the operator uses an incorrect number, an incorrect arithmetic sign, etc. The computer does not know, for example, that a number was supposed to be a 3 instead of a 4, or that a multiplication sign should have been a plus sign. Another type of logic error is an error in organization or sequence of instructions. This type of error results when a problem has not been analyzed and flowcharted properly. Because an error in planning has been made, the programmer may have difficulty in locating the mistake. Good luck in debugging—this is the step that causes lots of headaches.

STATEMENT NUMBERS

The following is an example of how a simple program looks after it is coded.

```
10  REM THIS IS AN ARITHMETIC PROBLEM
20  A = 25
30  PRINT A
40  END
```

This program illustrates some important points. The first is that every line of the program must begin with what is called a statement number. Statement numbers must be whole numbers and are used for two purposes: (1) to reference the individual lines, and (2) to determine the order in which the lines are processed. On RSTS/E[1], statement numbers may run from 1 to 32767. However, most computers will probably not accept five-digit numbers. Most computer systems will accept statement numbers up to 9999.

Every line of the program must have a line number typed at the beginning of the line. These numbers must be in order in the sequence in which the computer is to process the program. It is wise to skip numbers—e.g., 10, 15, 20, 25—so that unused numbers will be available in

[1] RSTS/E (Resource Sharing Time-Sharing System/Extended) is a time-sharing system for PDP 11/20, PDP 11/40, PDP 11/45, and PDP 11/70 computers.

case an operation must be added. If lines are placed out of numerical order, the computer will put them in numerical order when it stores the program, and it will run the program in that order. When the computer reads a line, it automatically drops down and reads the next line, unless told to go somewhere else, until it reads the complete program. That is why it is important to have the statements in sequential order.

TYPES OF STATEMENTS

Not only does each line contain a line number, but also each line contains a statement. The statement can be one of many types of expressions, including remarks, instructions, assignments, arithmetic operations, etc.

NUMBERS

Expressions can contain numbers. Numbers are often called *numeric constants* because they retain their values throughout the program. Numbers can be either negative or positive. They can be expressed in one of three forms. They can be whole numbers, called *integers*; numbers with decimals, called *real numbers*; or floating-point numbers, called *exponentials*. If an output number has more than six significant digits, the computer will print it out in E format. The E format is a floating-point form, which means to the 10th power (multiplied by 10). The number 25E6 is equal to 25,000,000 because E6 means the number times 10 to the 6th power; the decimal point is moved six points to the right. The number 222222E–4 is equal to 22.2222. The E–4 is the number times 10 to the minus 4th power; the decimal point is moved four points to the left. The following numbers are examples.

1.2254E4 would be 12254 325.67E–6 would be .00032567

VARIABLES

There are also items in the program called *variables*—items whose values are changed in the program. The variable value is stored in the computer and located by a variable name. This name is actually the address of the storage location in which the variable is stored. There are numeric variables and string variables. String variables are used to designate combinations of letters, letters and numbers, and letters and characters.

Numeric variable names consist of one of the following two combinations:

1. One character—and that character must be a letter.
2. Two characters—the first must be a letter and the second must be a number; it cannot be a letter.

ACCESS TO THE COMPUTER

Before anything can be done on the computer, it is necessary to know how to gain access to the machine. "Logging on" a computer varies from computer to computer and from institution to institution.[2] Each programmer must have an identification number and a password. For illustrative purposes, identification number 62,113 and password ABPLTU will be used. With these two pieces of information, the programmer can access the computer.

On the PDP-11, after the terminal is turned on, the operator types the word HELLO and depresses the RETURN key. The computer prints out an identification message, then a number sign at the margin—#. When the symbol # appears, the operator types his identification number and depresses the RETURN key. The computer then prints PASSWORD. The operator types in his password and depresses the RETURN key. If the password is typed correctly, it will not show on the screen and the computer will print READY. After the operator is logged on, a message similar to the following will appear on the screen.

```
HELLO

          C.S.U.L.B.  TIMESHARING  JOB 11  KB18  13-Oct-81  09:29 AM

#62,113
PASSWORD:
THE LAB WILL BE CLOSED FOR VACATION.

READY
```

See Note 3 below.

[2] The systems manual for each computer supplies access directions.

[3] Any lines following the password consist of information from the computer center and the messages continually change.

If the computer is given the incorrect password, it will print: INVALID ENTRY–TRY AGAIN. It is then necessary to retype the number and password, depressing the RETURN key after each.

ACCESS TO THE COMPUTER USING A PORT SELECTOR[4]

The following log-on procedure is for the PDP-11 using a port selector. Right above the keyboard there are five rocker switches, and these switches should be in the following positions.[5]

1. The FULL/HALF duplex should be on FULL.
2. The LOCAL/REMOTE switch should be on REMOTE.
3. The HIGH/LOW SWITCH should be on LOW.
4. The WIDE/NARROW switch should be on NARROW.
5. If the printer connect indicator light is on, the PRINTER should be switched to OFF.

The operator must depress the RETURN key and type the number 1. The machine will print a message similar to the following.

```
1
C.S.U.L.B.  TIMESHARING  JOB 11  KB18  13-OCT-81  09:29 AM
#
```

The symbol # is asking for the identification number. After the identification number is typed and the RETURN key is depressed, the following will appear.

```
#62,113
PASSWORD:
```

The computer is asking for the operator's password. The password must be typed and the RETURN key depressed. The password will not be printed; but if the proper password is typed, READY will be printed on the screen. The operator has now been accepted by the system. If an incorrect password were given, the computer would print INVALID

[4] A port selector is a hardware device that connects the terminal with the computer system.

[5] The switches cited are located on Teleray Model 3711. Other CRT models may have no switches, or may have other types of switches.

ENTRY—TRY AGAIN. The number and the password must be retyped and the RETURN key depressed after each. When the computer indicates READY, the operator should type SET TELERAY. After SET TELERAY, the operator must depress the RETURN key.

```
READY

SET TELERAY

*%                    (Garbage characters may appear)
```

The speed control should then be set to HIGH. Then the RETURN key should be depressed. *Note*: When the operator leaves, he should be sure the terminal is set on FULL, REMOTE, LOW, NARROW, and PRINTER OFF. The terminal should not be turned off.

After entry to the computer is gained, the operator must designate whether he is working on an old or a new program. To begin a new program, the word NEW is typed and the RETURN key is depressed. The computer will print the following.

```
NEW FILE NAME--
```

The computer is now ready to receive the new file name. This file name can contain no more than six characters. All characters must be letters or numbers. The program for this chapter will be called CHPT2, so CHPT2 should be typed and the RETURN key depressed. The computer will now print READY. The following should appear on the screen.

```
NEW
NEW FILE NAME--CHPT2

READY
```

PROBLEM 2-1

PROGRAM WRITING

Now that the operator is logged on, what next? Is it time to write a program? As stated earlier, a program should always be flowcharted before it is coded. However, since flowcharting has not yet been discussed, a program will be developed without the customary flowchart.

One of the most important points in programming is to know the difference between the data and the program. The program in this chapter consists of statements that instruct the computer to read in the data and print out the report. The data in this problem consist of salesmen's numbers, department numbers, and total sales.

REMARK STATEMENTS

The REMARK statement is optional and allows the programmer to insert comments throughout the program without interrupting the operation of the computer. When using this statement, the programmer types a statement number, then REM, then whatever comments he wishes to make. The computer prints the comments just as they are written—it does nothing else. If the remarks will not fit on one line, another statement number is used, then another REM, and the remarks from the previous line are continued.

Now to write the first line of the program.

```
10  REM THIS IS A LISTING OF SALEMAN'S NUMBER, DEPARTMENT
15  REM NUMBER, AND TOTAL SALES FOR EACH SALESMAN.
```

The computer will print out this information exactly as typed; but when the program is run, these lines do not affect the execution of the program.

DATA STATEMENTS

Next, data will be given to the computer and a program written to tell the computer to print out that data. To get data into the computer, the data will be typed in a DATA statement and the computer will be asked to read that data in a READ statement.

Data statements can be placed anywhere in the program but are usually placed at the end. Even though the DATA statements are not written next, they will be discussed here so that the relationship between the DATA and the READ statements can more easily be demonstrated.

```
35  REM THE FOLLOWING DATA ARE ENTERED--1ST FIELD,
40  REM S=SALEMAN'S #, 2ND FIELD--D=DEPT #, AND
45  REM 3RD FIELD--S1=SALES.
```

These REM statements appear just before the DATA statements because they are nonexecutable lines put into the program to show the operator in what order to type the data and to remind him under what variable names the data will be stored.

```
20  READ S,D,S1
```

As a result of the READ command, the computer will go down to the DATA statements and to the first data field, pick up the data there, and put it in storage, naming it "S". Then it will go to the second field and secure the data typed there, store it, and name the storage "D". Back again it will go to the third field, pick up the data, and store it under the name "S1".

If decimals are included in the input data, the decimals must be typed. The normal way to type DATA statements is shown below.

```
50  DATA 12,8,934.76
```

However, the data can be placed in the DATA statements in the following ways, and the same output will be secured.

```
50  DATA 12
51  DATA 8
52  DATA 934.76
53  DATA 13
54  DATA 51
55  DATA 1127.32
56  DATA 14
57  DATA 61
58  DATA 3215.62
59  DATA 15
60  DATA 71
61  DATA 2866.20
62  DATA 16
63  DATA 81
64  DATA 1871.43
65  DATA -9
66  DATA 0
67  DATA 0
```

```
50  DATA 12,8
51  DATA 934.76
52  DATA 13,51
53  DATA 1127.32
54  DATA 14,61
55  DATA 3215.62
56  DATA 15,71
57  DATA 2866.20
58  DATA 16,81
59  DATA 1871.43
60  DATA -9,0
61  DATA 0
```

FIELDS

The following discussion will define the word *field*, which was mentioned in the preceding section. To illustrate, Statement 50 will be listed again.

```
50  DATA 12,8,934.76
```

The commas separate the different items of data, or fields. In the first field is found the salesman's number—12. In the second field is found the department number—8. In the last field is found the sales—934.76. *Note*: Symbols such as commas, $, %, etc., must not appear in the numeric variable fields.

READ STATEMENTS

Now back to the second statement of the program, the READ statement. It should be stressed that the DATA statements are normally done last. They were discussed out of order to show what the DATA statement looks like, as the READ statement and the DATA statement are necessarily related in the program. The READ statement is shown below.

```
20  READ S,D,S1
```

It is important to use the correct order when data is stored so that the computer can pick up the proper data each time. If in the DATA statement the department were listed first and the salesman's number second, the READ statement would be incorrect. The computer would have picked up the department number and stored it in "S" and the salesman's number in "D".

The READ statement may be written in more than one way. The normal way is the way shown above. However, Statement 20 can be written in the following ways, and all of the different methods will give the same result.

```
20  READ S              20  READ S               20  READ S,D
21  READ D       or     21  READ D,S1     or     21  READ S1
22  READ S1
```

The program so far looks like this.

```
10  REM THIS IS A LISTING OF SALEMAN'S NUMBER, DEPARTMENT
15  REM NUMBER, AND TOTAL SALES FOR EACH SALESMAN.
20  READ S,D,S1
```

PRINT STATEMENTS

The computer has read and stored one line of data. Now what should the computer do? The logical thing would be to do something with that data. In this program, the computer will be commanded to print that one line.

```
25  PRINT S,D,S1
```

There are many operations that can be performed with the PRINT statement, and most of them will be discussed later. When printing data with the variables separated by commas as in this statement, the data is printed on one line in five columns, called *major print zones*, which are 15 spaces apart.[6] Numeric data will start in Space 2 because Space 1 is reserved for the negative sign. String data starts in Space 1. Commas should be put after each variable. The data in the sample program will be printed out in three columns. If there were six columns of data, the sixth column would print on the next line. There is a solution to that problem, which will be discussed later.

If the programmer desires a tighter packing of printed values, a semi-colon may be used. Using the semi-colon between numeric fields causes the numbers to be printed 2 spaces apart; one of those two spaces is for a possible negative sign.

THE GO TO STATEMENT

A data line has been read and printed. What next? If all of the lines of data are going to be read and printed, the computer must be told to read a data line and print the data. It would be poor programming and much work for the operator to keep writing the same READ and PRINT statements over and over again. Earlier it was mentioned that the computer drops down to the next line when it has completed a line, unless it is told to go somewhere else. Now is the time to tell it to go somewhere else—back to the READ statement.

```
30  GO TO 20
```

The computer has just been told to go back and do Statement 20, which is the READ command. It will repeat the process of READ and PRINT until it has read all of the data in the DATA statements. Then it will print a message OUT OF DATA AT LINE XX (20 in this program).

The computer does not drop to the next line after the GO TO statement because it is sent somewhere else. It is important that somewhere in the program the computer be directed to a statement under the GO

[6] On the RSTS/E operating system, the five columns begin at Spaces 1, 15, 29, 43, and 57, or 14 spaces apart.

TO statement. Otherwise, the statements following the GO TO statement will never be executed. In this program, the DATA statements that are nonexecutable follow the GO TO and REM statements and are reached by the READ statement. The program now appears as follows.

```
10  REM THIS IS A LISTING OF SALESMAN'S NUMBER, DEPARTMENT
15  REM NUMBER, AND TOTAL SALES FOR EACH SALESMAN.
20  READ S,D,S1
25  PRINT S,D,S1
30  GO TO 20
35  REM THE FOLLOWING DATA ARE ENTERED--1ST FIELD,
40  REM S=SALESMAN'S #, 2ND FIELD--D=DEPT #, AND
45  REM 3RD FIELD--S1=SALES.
50  DATA 12,8,934.76
55  DATA 13,51,1127.32
60  DATA 14,61,3215.62
65  DATA 15,71,2866.20
70  DATA 16,81,1871.43
```

NOTE: Spaces may be used between numeric fields if desired; the computer will ignore those spaces.

PROGRAM TERMINATION

Although the program will terminate when it runs out of data, there are some statements that should be included in good programming. One more DATA statement can be added as a test that all data have been read. Any of the fields may be tested, and all fields must contain at least one number. The example shown below demonstrates this technique using a -9 in the test field and zeros in all other fields.

```
75  DATA -9,0,0
```

Then another statement will be inserted between the READ and PRINT statements. Here is a good example of the reason numbers are skipped when line numbers are assigned.

```
22  IF S=-9 GO TO 80
80  END
```

After the computer reads the data in the DATA statements, it asks the question, "Is the data picked up in the S field equal to -9?" It is not equal to -9 in the first DATA statement, so the computer drops to the next line and prints data. It continues this process until it reads Statement 75. Now it does equal -9; therefore, it is told to go to Statement 80, which says END. The END is the termination of the compiled program. The END statement must be the last statement in the program.

If the coding of the program has been completed without these three statements, they could have been coded at the end of the program. When the computer read the program, it would have placed the inserted lines in their proper numeric sequence.

RETENTION OF THE PROGRAM

Each computer user is allotted a certain amount of storage space in which to save programs. If the program will be used at a later date, it should be saved. It might be a good idea to save each program until it has been run. However, the operator should delete all unnecessary programs before he leaves the computer.

To save a program, the operator may hit the RETURN and type SAVE after the END statement. After the program is run, the operator may eliminate a program by typing UNSAVE CHPT2, or whatever the program name is, after the computer says READY. The program is now eliminated.

To run the program after SAVE has been typed, the operator hits the RETURN key, types RUN, and depresses the RETURN key. The computer will now execute the program.

RETRIEVAL OF A SAVED PROGRAM

To retrieve a program, the operator types OLD when the computer says READY. The computer will then print OLD FILE NAME-- and the operator then types his old program name. In this problem, the old file name would be CHPT2.

To get the computer to list his old program so he can see what he wrote, the operator types LIST. The output shown on the screen will be all the program and data statements that make up the old program. Instead, the operator may want the computor to execute the program, in which case he types RUN. The output shown on the screen will be the data printed as directed in the program. To find what old job names have been saved, the operator can type DIR, which means "Directory," after the computor says READY and the computor will print out the names of the programs he has in storage. The desired program may be chosen, and the word OLD typed, etc.

CORRECTION OF STATEMENTS

A program can be added to or corrected. If an OLD program has been retrieved, the operator types the same statement number as the one to be corrected, types the correction, hits the RETURN, and types REPLACE.

During the typing of a statement, the operator may make errors. To eliminate the errors, he may use the DELETE key or the RUBOUT key on the right side of the keyboard. This key backs up one space every time it is depressed and eliminates one character each time. After the incorrect character or characters have been eliminated, the operator then continues with his typing.

During the typing of a NEW program, the operator may wish to replace a whole statement. To do this, he types the same statement number and the corrected statement. The computer will automatically substitute the last of two or more statements bearing the same number. To eliminate a statement, the operator types the statement number and depresses the RETURN key.

To work with a different program after finishing with another program, the operator waits for the computer to say READY, and then types NEW or OLD.

EXIT FROM THE COMPUTER

When the operator is through with the computer and wants to sign off, he types BYE. The machine will print the following.

```
BYE
CONFIRM:
```

The operator then types Y or YES and the machine will print a long message telling what storage was used, the time consumed, etc. If the operator is not interested in the amount of storage used, time consumed, etc., he may type F instead of Y and he will be logged out without any message.

THE PRINTER

After the operator on a CRT terminal has made sure he has a correct program, he may secure a printed copy of both his program and the solution. To do so, he depresses the PRINTER rocker switch on his terminal. If a link with the printer is established, the red indicator light will go on. The operator should then type the word LIST while the PRINT key is on. A printed copy of the program will be produced. Then the operator would type the word RUN to get a printed copy of the solution to his problem. After the output is printed, the PRINTER rocker switch should be depressed to turn off the printer. The printer should NOT be on while the program is being typed on the terminal.

THE COMPLETE PROGRAM

After this program has been typed on the terminal, the operator should depress the RETURN key after SAVE or END, LIST should be typed, and the computer will print the following.

```
LIST
CHPT2  09:30 AM         13-Oct-81
10  REM THIS IS A LISTING OF SALESMAN'S NUMBER, DEPARTMENT
15  REM NUMBER, AND TOTAL SALES FOR EACH SALESMAN.
20  READ S,D,S1
22  IF S=-9 GO TO 80
25  PRINT S,D,S1
30  GO TO 20
35  REM THE FOLLOWING DATA ARE ENTERED--1ST FIELD,
40  REM S=SALESMAN'S #, 2ND FIELD--D=DEPT #, AND
45  REM 3RD FIELD--S1=SALES.
50  DATA 12,8,934.76
55  DATA 13,51,1127.32
60  DATA 14,61,3215.62
65  DATA 15,71,2866.20
70  DATA 16,81,1871.43
75  DATA -9,0,0
80  END

READY
```

After RUN is typed, the computer will print the following output. The numbers in each column will be left-justified.

```
RUN
CHPT2  09:31 AM          13-OCT-81
12            8              934.76
13            51             1127.32
14            61             3215.62
15            71             2866.2
16            81             1871.43

READY

UNSAVE CHPT2
```

Note: This statement just eliminated program CHPT2 from storage.

DEBUGGING PROBLEMS

The following problems are typical of programming mistakes made by beginning programmers. Each program should be analyzed for clerical and logic errors before the solution, following the program, is consulted.

Problem 1

```
LIST
CH2A     09:16 AM           02-FEB-81
10  READ N,S
15  PRINT N,S
20  GO TO 110
25  DATA 17,12
30  DATA 12,18
35  DATA 16,3
45  END

READY

RUN
CH2A     09:16 AM           02-FEB-81
 17            12
?STATEMENT NOT FOUND AT LINE 20
```

The computer informs the programmer that there is an error in Statement 20. In checking Statement 20 the programmer finds that he has made a typing error, typing 110 instead of 10. He replaces Statement 20 to read: 20 GO TO 10. In rerunning the program, the programmer creates debugging Problem 2.

Problem 2

```
LIST
CH2A      09:18 AM              02-FEB-81
10  READ N,S
15  PRINT N,S
20  GO TO 10
25  DATA 17,12
30  DATA 12,18
35  DATA 16,3
45  END

READY

RUN
CH2A      09:18 AM              02-FEB-81
 17             12
 12             18
 16             3
?OUT OF DATA AT LINE 10
```

Though the data were correctly printed out, the programmer does not wish the diagnostic "?OUT OF DATA AT LINE 10" to appear. A test statement must be written into the program, telling the computer that when it reads the last line of data, it is to go to the END statement. The programmer puts in a Statement 12: IF N = -9 GO TO 45. He runs the program again and creates debugging Problem 3.

Problem 3

```
LIST
CH2A     09:19          02-FEB-81
10  READ N,S
12  IF N = -9 GO TO 45
15  PRINT N,S
20  GO TO 10
25  DATA 17,12
30  DATA 12,18
35  DATA 16,3
45  END

READY
```

```
RUN
CH2A     09:19 AM          02-FEB-81
 17            12
 12            18
 16            3
?OUT OF DATA AT LINE 10
```

The programmer did put in a test statement at line 12. Why does he still get the diagnostic message "?OUT OF DATA AT LINE 10"?

After carefully checking his printout, the programmer notes that he forgot to put in a trailer constant. He adds a Statement: 40 DATA -9,0. Once more he runs the program, and finally it executes correctly.

```
RUN
CH2A     09:21 AM          02-FEB-81
 17            12
 12            18
 16            3
```

Problem 4

Debugging Problem 4 is another typical programming error made by novice programmers. Why does "?OUT OF DATA AT LINE 10" appear on the printout?

```
LIST
CH2B     09:24 AM          02-FEB-81
10  READ X,Y
20  PRINT X,Y
30  GO TO 10
40  DATA 30,25
50  DATA 40,50
60  DATA 50,75
70  DATA 60,100
80  DATA -9,0
90  END

READY

RUN
CH2B     09:24 AM          02-FEB-81
 30            25
 40            50
 50            75
 60            100
-9             0
 ?OUT OF DATA AT LINE 10
```

Problem 4 contains test data, but there is no test statement. After insertion of a Statement: 15 IF X = -9 GO TO 90 into the program, the program runs correctly, as shown below.

```
RUN
CH2B     09:24 AM             02-FEB-81
 30             25
 40             50
 50             75
 60             100
```

Problem 5

```
LIST
CH2C     09:24 AM             02-FEB-81
10  READ A,B
15  IF A = -9 GO TO 50
20  PRINT A,B,
25  GO TO 10
30  DATA 11,13
35  DATA 24,23
40  DATA 32,55
45  DATA -9,0
50  END

READY

RUN
CH2C     09:24 AM             02-FEB-81
 11             13             24             23             32
 55
```

When the programmer looks at the printout shown above, he realizes he made an error in the PRINT statement because the program is not printed as he desires. In looking at the PRINT statement, Statement 20, he notes that there is a comma at the end of the statement. The comma tells the computer to go to the next major print zone. After omission of the comma at the end of the PRINT statement, the program runs as follows.

```
RUN
CH2C     09:24 AM             02-FEB-81
 11             13
 24             23
 32             55
```

Problem 6

One of the most common errors made by beginning programmers appears in the program shown below.

```
LIST
CH2D      10:37 AM              02-FEB-81
10  READ C,D,E
15  IF C=-9 GO TO 50
20  PRINT C,D,E
25  GO TO 10
30  DATA 17,30,2
35  DATA 20,15,7
40  DATA 25,40,6
45  DATA -9
50  END

READY

RUN
CH2D      10:38 AM              02-FEB-81
 17              30                2
 20              15                7
 25              40                6
?OUT OF DATA AT LINE 10
```

If the computer is told to read three fields, as in Statement 10, then it must be given three fields to read. Statement 45 has only one. After Statement 45 was changed to read 45 DATA -9,0,0 the printout ran without the error message.

```
RUN
CH2D      10:39 AM              02-FEB-81
 17              30                2
 20              15                7
 25              40                6
```

SUMMARY

1. Every line of the program must have a statement number, and the number must be a whole number.
2. Statement numbers must be in the numeric sequence in which the computer is to process the program.
3. There should be gaps in the numbering of the statement lines—

e.g., 10, 15, 20, 25—so the program need not be typed again if a statement must be inserted in the program.

4. A statement can be added anywhere in the program, even if it is out of numeric sequence. The computer will put it in numeric sequence when it stores the program.
5. Numeric constants can be positive or negative and are either integers, called *whole numbers*, or real, called *decimal numbers*.
6. If a number is larger than six digits, the computer will print out in E format. E means to the 10th power.
7. Variable names can be numeric or string. Numeric variable names can be: (1) only one character, and that character must be a letter; (2) two characters—the first character must be a letter and the second character must be a number.
8. To log in on the computer, an ID number and password are necessary.
9. If the RSTS/E operating system is connected to a port selector, the rocker switches on the Teleray Model 3711 must be on FULL, REMOTE, LOW, and NARROW before the operator attempts to log on.
10. The REMARK statement allows comments to be made throughout the program without affecting processing.
11. When a computer is finished with a line, it drops to the next line unless it is told to go somewhere else.
12. Data statements can be placed anywhere, but are normally placed at the end of the program.
13. Print statements have punctuation after all variables but the last.
14. There are 5 major print zones. If tighter packing of printed values is desired, a semi-colon instead of a comma is used after the variable names.
15. There must be a statement somewhere in the program telling the computer to go to the line directly under the GO TO statement.
16. The log-in procedures on the RSTS/E operating system with a port selector is as follows.
    a. Rocker switches must be in the positions stated in 9.
    b. RETURN and then 1 are typed.
    c. When # appears, the identification number is typed and the RETURN key is depressed.
    d. When PASSWORD appears, the password is typed and the RETURN key is depressed.

e. When READY appears, the log-in procedure is complete.

f. SET TELERAY is then typed and the RETURN key is depressed.

g. The speed is set to HIGH. Garbage characters may appear.

h. When the word READY appears, the program then may be typed.

17. The log-in procedure on the RSTS/E operating system without a port selector is as follows.

a. After the terminal is turned on, HELLO is typed, and the RETURN key depressed.

b. When # appears, the identification number is typed and the RETURN key depressed.

c. When PASSWORD appears, the password is typed and the RETURN key depressed.

d. When READY appears, logging on is complete.

18. There may be up to six characters in a program name, and all characters must be letters or numbers.

19. To work with an old program, OLD is typed after the computer says READY. Then the computer prints OLD FILE NAME--. The operator then types the name of the old program.

20. To create a new program, the operator types NEW when the computer says READY.

21. Each time the DELETE key is depressed, it backspaces one space and deletes a character at the same time.

22. To remove a file from storage, UNSAVE (program name) is typed.

SELF TEST

1. Find the errors in the following program.

```
10  REM THIS PROBLEM LISTS THE SALESMAN'S NUMBER, DEPARTMENT NUMBER
    REM AND TOTAL SALES.
20  PRINT S1,D1,T1,
25  READ S1 ,D1,T1
30  GO TO 25
35  IF S1 = -9 GO TO
40  DATA 12,41,1,233.76
45  DATA 12,51,1,176.27
50  DATA 14,61,2,365.65
```

2. Which of the following are valid variable names?

a. A	d. SS	f. B
b. A1	e. AA1	g. N2
c. S1		

3. What is an integer?
4. What is a real number?
5. What is the complete numeric expression of each of the following?
   a. 1.0076E-5
   b. 96327E4
   c. .89837E-3
6. What does E in a number mean?
7. a. How many characters are in a program name?
   b. Explain what the characters can or cannot be.
8. What does IF S1 = -9 GO TO 50 mean?
9. What are the two reasons for the statement numbers?
10. a. How are the letters in the following statement used in storage?
    b. What are they called?

```
60  READ A,B,C
```

TRUE AND FALSE

11. Statement numbers do not need to be typed in sequential order.
12. In DATA statements, the dollar sign and comma must be typed in the data.
13. The computer *always* drops to the next line when it finishes the line being executed.
14. To log in on the PDP-11 using a port selector, the rocker switches should be on FULL, REMOTE, LOW, and NARROW.
15. The program should have an END statement as the last statement in the program.
16. The following is a valid program name–2NDCH
17. The following is a valid program name–NEWCHPT
18. All lines of a program must have statement numbers.
19. All programs should be flowcharted before they are coded.
20. To work with an old program, the operator must type OLD when the computer prints READY.

ASSIGNMENTS[7]

1. The owner of a paint company wants the following inventory list run through the computer. Although the quantity is on the list first, the owner wants the paint number listed first and the quantity listed second on the printout. Data should be entered in the order given in the problem.

QTY.	PAINT NUMBER	BIN LOCATION	PRICE PER ITEM
10	1715	38	5.05
70	1732	39	6.07
157	2318	72	5.90
36	2345	78	3.76
432	6502	159	7.15
59	6511	168	4.95
68	6588	175	4.05

2. A teacher wants a list of student numbers and test scores.

STUDENT NUMBER	TEST SCORES
117632	95
213781	87
312896	92
100532	73
191863	85
141111	79

3. The annual inventory has just been completed for ROY MARKETS. The manager wants this partial list of items to be listed by the computer.

UNIT NUMBER	QTY. BY CASES	UNIT PRICE
123	38	7.20
716	92	8.95
527	176	11.27
32	58	6.30
954	110	12.50
387	48	9.67

[7]Column titles are not to be printed. Number fields will be left-justified in the printout and spacing will not be as shown in the examples.

3

THE STRUCTURED FLOWCHART AND ADDITIONAL STATEMENT TYPES

In this chapter the following topics will be discussed.

1. The flowchart
2. The structured flowchart
3. Total counters
4. The addition operator
5. String variables
6. PRINT statement uses

THE FLOWCHART

The flowchart is a chart of symbols that depict the arithmetic and logic of the sequence of steps used to solve a problem. Flowcharting makes it easy to code a program by separating the program design from the coding. There are many symbols which can be used in a flowchart, but only those shown in Figure 3-1 will be utilized in this text.

FIGURE 3-1.

Flowchart Symbols

Terminal. This symbol represents the beginning or end of the program.

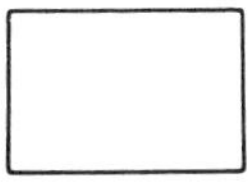

Processing. This symbol represents calculations, initializing, and other processing functions.

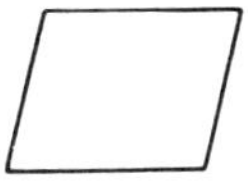

Input/Output. This symbol represents the process of putting data into storage or calling it from storage through input/output devices.

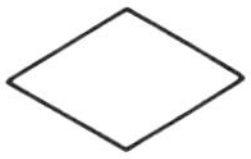

Decision. This symbol represents a decision, question, or comparison that determines which of alternate paths are to be followed.

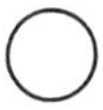

Onpage Connector. The notation inside this symbol signifies to which other symbol the program flow is moving.

Flow. This symbol connects other symbols and indicates the sequence of operations.

Offpage Connector. This symbol is to designate exit from or entry to another page.

THE STRUCTURED FLOWCHART

The flowcharts in this text are based on structured programming, which follows the basic principles listed below.

1. The flow is from the top down.
2. Three control structures make up the basic design, but extensions of these structures are often used.
   a. Sequence structure means that statements are performed one before another or sequentially, as illustrated in Figure 3-2.

b. Conditional structure means that branching occurs depending on a condition, as illustrated in Figure 3-3. An extension of this structure is shown in Figure 3-4.

c. Loop structure means that execution loops continually until exiting the loop is desired, as illustrated in Figures 3-5 and 3-6. An extension of this structure, exit from a loop, is shown in Figure 3-7.

3. Each control structure has one entry and one exit. Control structures may be nested, as illustrated in Figure 3-6.

FIGURE 3-2.
Sequence Control

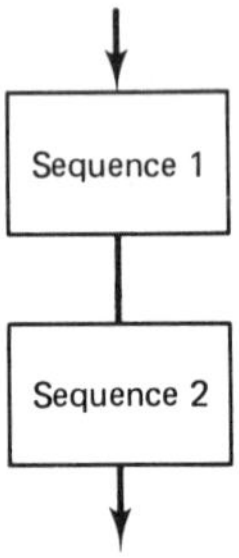

Sequence 1 is performed first.
Then Sequence 2 is performed.

FIGURE 3-3.
Conditional Control—Simple Branch

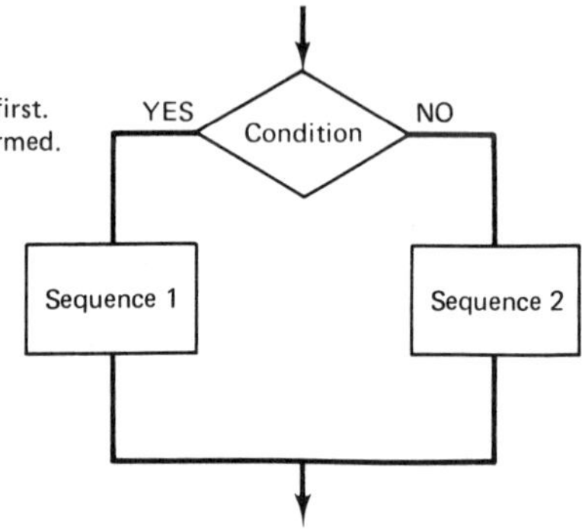

If Condition is true, then Sequence 1 is performed.
If Condition is not true, then Sequence 2 is performed.

FIGURE 3-4.
Conditional Control—Multiple Condition Branch

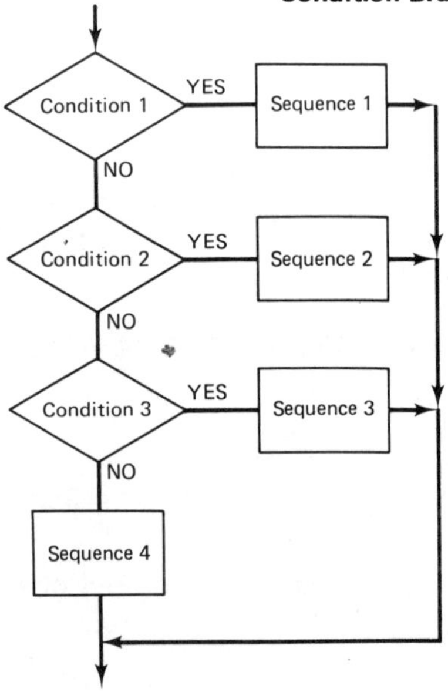

If Condition 1 is true, then only Sequence 1 is performed.
If Condition 1 is false, then Condition 2 is tested.
If Condition 2 is true, then only Sequence 2 is performed.
If Condition 2 is false, then Condition 3 is tested.
If Condition 3 is true, then only Sequence 3 is performed.
If Condition 3 is false, then only Sequence 4 is performed.
This conditional control branching is called an IF-THEN-ELSE branching and is explained in Chapter 6.

FIGURE 3-5.
Loop Control

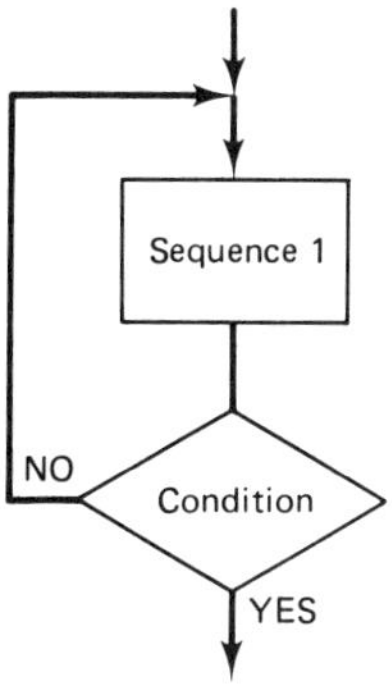

Sequence 1 is performed until the condition is true.
More explanation of looping is found in Chapter 8.

FIGURE 3-6.
Nested Control

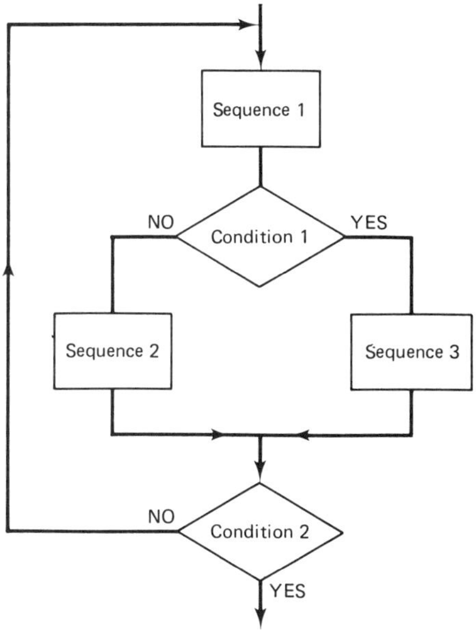

The outer control structure is a loop that is performed repeatedly until Condition 2 is met. The inner control structure is a conditional control, which is said to be "nested" within the outer control structure.

FIGURE 3-7.
Exiting from a Loop

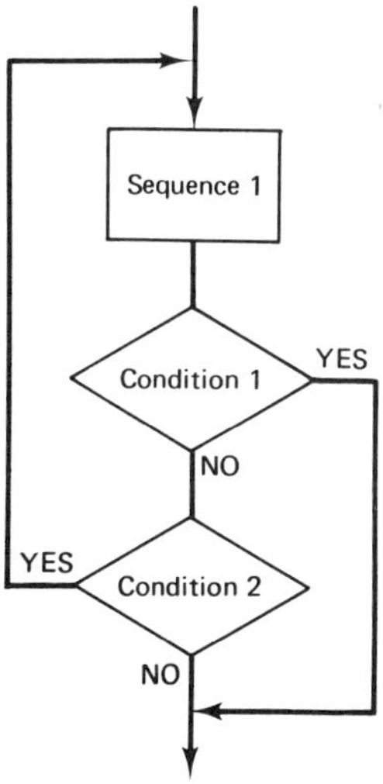

If Condition 1 is true, exit is made from the loop.
If Condition 1 is false, Condition 2 is tested.

WALKTHROUGH

After the programmer has written the flowchart, a careful "walk-through" or review should be conducted to be sure the flow of the program will cause the computer to execute the program correctly. In other words, the programmer should pretend to be a computer and do what the flowchart tells him to do.

CODING

Once the flowchart has been accepted as properly charted, the programmer then codes the program *from* the flowchart. Many neophyte programmers write the flowchart from the coded program. The purpose of the flowchart is to separate the process of designing the program from the process of coding. Although it is not necessary, the authors recommend the use of a printed form for coding. As an example, the coding of the program for Problem 2-1 is shown in Figure 3-8.

FLOWCHARTING

The flowchart for the sample program in Chapter 2 is shown in Figure 3-9. Referring to the flowchart, the programmer notes that the first step the computer takes, after starting, is to read a data line. Then a decision must be made as to whether the data line just read is the last data line. This determination is made with an IF statement, such as IF S = -9 GO TO 80. This statement tells the computer that if the value stored in S is equal to -9, the computer is to end the program. The dummy value stored in S can be zero, a positive number, or a negative number. If the value stored in S is not equal to the dummy value, the computer drops down to print a line of data. Then the computer will loop back to the READ statement.

PROBLEM 3-1

The problem shown in Figure 3-10 will be used as an exercise in flowcharting. The computer will read the department name and department sales. Then it will list these names and sales. Finally, it will leave a blank line, print TOTAL SALES $, and print the total for all of the departments.

FIGURE 3-8.

Sample Program from Chapter 2

BASIC CODING FORM

PROGRAMMER VERNA MURDOCK	DATE SEPT. 15, 1981
PROGRAM NAME CHAPTER TWO PROBLEM	CLASS MWE 10-11

STATE-MENT NO.	STATEMENT
10	REM THIS IS A LISTING OF SALESMAN'S NUMBER, DEPARTMENT
15	REM NUMBER, AND TOTAL SALES FOR EACH SALESMAN.
20	READ S, D, S1
22	IF S = -9 GO TO 80
25	PRINT S, D, S1
30	GO TO 20
35	REM THE FOLLOWING DATA ARE ENTERED--1ST FIELD,
40	REM S=SALESMAN'S #, 2ND FIELD, D=DEPT #, AND
45	REM 3RD FIELD, S1=SALES.
50	DATA 12, 8, 934.76
55	DATA 13, 51, 1127.32
60	DATA 14, 61, 3215.62
65	DATA 15, 71, 2866.20
70	DATA 16, 81, 1871.43
75	DATA -9, 0, 0
80	END

DATAPROF 1000

FIGURE 3-9.
Flowchart of Problem 2-1

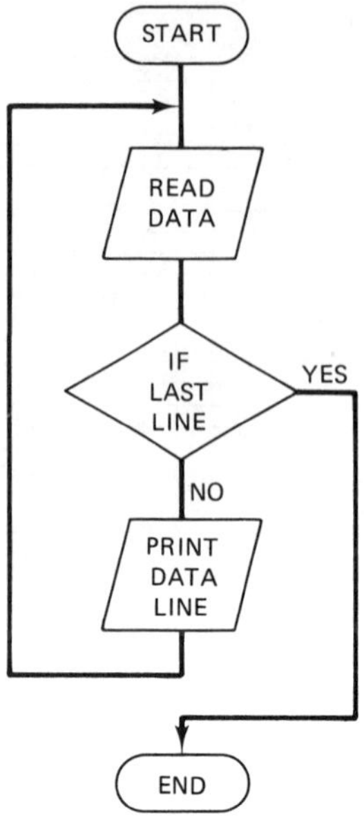

FIGURE 3-10.
Data for Problem 3-1

DEPT.	SALES
Clothing, Men	4500.76
Clothing, Women	3372.35
Clothing, Children	1572.22
Shoes, Men	955.17
Shoes, Women	1216.28
Jewelry	426.34
Sundries	513.96
Cosmetics	476.29
Linens	615.15
TOTAL SALES	$ 13648.52

The flowchart for Problem 3-1 is shown in Figure 3-11. There are items in the flowchart that will not mean anything until explanations are made later in this chapter.

After logging on, the new program is named DEPT. The first statements will be REM statements.

```
10  REM THIS IS A LISTING OF DEPARTMENT SALES AND A TOTAL
15  REM OF ALL THE SALES
```

ASSIGNMENT STATEMENTS

In BASIC language, values are assigned to variables through LET statements, such as 10 LET A = 25. On the PDP-11 and in many other systems, the LET is optional, and the statement would read 10 A = 25. The equal sign does not mean *equal*. It means *replace*. Whenever the computer reads an equal sign, it knows that the value assigned or generated on the right side of the sign replaces the value stored at the variable address cited on the left. In the statement 10 A = 25, for example, if there had been a value of 2 stored in A, the 2 would be eliminated and replaced with the value of 25.

FIGURE 3-11.

Flowchart of Problem 3-1

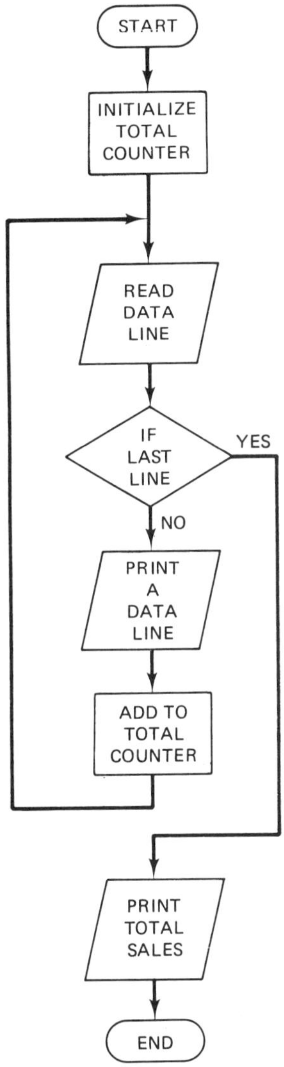

DATA STATEMENTS

As stated in Chapter 2, DATA statements can be placed anywhere in the program but normally are placed near the end. Even if DATA statements are placed in several places, the computer collects all of the data in the order in which they appear and creates a data block before the program is run. Then each time a READ statement is executed, the computer uses the items of data in the order in which they are stored in the data block.

Whenever a field contains a letter or symbol, it is called *alphanumeric*. Numbers may also appear in alphanumeric fields, e.g., A12 or #34B. A string is made up of alphanumeric characters. The variable names used to address alphanumeric data are called *string variables*. String variable names consist of a letter and a $ sign, such as A$, B$, C$.

The DATA statements in Problem 3-1 are placed at the end of the program but are listed below for further explanation. Quotes should be inserted around the names of the departments in the DATA statements; otherwise, the computer would treat the commas in the department titles as field separators in DATA statements. The quotes prevent the computer from reading the commas as separators. Whenever the programmer wishes the computer to read or to print material literally, space by space, he must enclose that material in quotes. Long Beach, California, for instance, would be treated by the computer as two fields, LONGBEACH and CALIFORNIA. No spaces between LONG and BEACH are printed because in DATA statements without quotes, the computer ignores spaces.

```
70  DATA "CLOTHING, MEN",4500.76
72  DATA "CLOTHING, WOMEN",3372.35
74  DATA "CLOTHING, CHILDREN",1572.22
76  DATA "SHOES, MEN",955.17
78  DATA "SHOES, WOMEN",1216.28
80  DATA "JEWELRY",426.34
82  DATA "SUNDRIES",513.96
84  DATA "COSMETICS",476.29
86  DATA "LINENS",615.15
88  DATA EXIT,0
```

Alphanumeric data need not always be put in quotes, but quotes are necessary to accomplish the following output.

1. To get punctuation marks in the data, including commas.
2. To get spaces between words.

Also, string data that do not begin with letters *must* be placed in quotes.

After initializing the counter, which will be explained in *The Total Counter* section, the next step is to read data. The data in this problem consist of two fields, the department name and the sales. The first field is alphanumeric and must be given a string variable name, D$, and the second field is numeric and is named S, as shown below.

```
25  READ D$, S
```

THE LAST DATA STATEMENT TEST

After the READ statement, the last DATA statement test, or IF statement, should be used to determine whether the last DATA field has been read. Although programmers usually use the first field for testing purposes, any field can be used. In Chapter 2 the last DATA statement contained a negative number (-9) for the test. Since the first item in the READ statement is a string variable, a string should be used in the first field to test for last data. The string "EXIT" is used here because it is descriptive. In the IF statement, a string must be in quotes. When the last DATA statement is read, the computer is directed to go to the statement commanding the computer to print the number stored in the total counter. In computer terminology, the type of data placed in DATA statements for test purposes is called a *dummy value* or a *trailer constant.*

```
30  IF D$ = "EXIT" GO TO 50
```

As a result of this statement, the computer tests to find if the word EXIT is written in the D$ field. If not, the computer drops to the next line and will print a line of data as a result of the statement shown below.

```
35  PRINT D$,S
```

If the word EXIT appears in the D$ field, control is sent to Statement 50.

THE TOTAL COUNTER

In Problem 3-1 there is to be a total of all of the department sales. This requires a total counter, which is a storage location containing the totals. The first step is to give this counter, a variable named T1, the value of zero. The setting of a variable to zero value is called *initializing*. Some computers automatically initialize variables to the value of zero, so the programmer could omit this step. However, by initializing to zero, the programmer will have a reminder of the counters he will use. In this problem the total counter is initialized to zero with the following statement, which is placed just before the READ statement.

```
20  T1 = 0
```

After the data line has been printed, the sales for the given department should be added into the total counter. This is done with the following statement.

```
40  T1 = T1 + S
```

Many principles are illustrated by this statement. The equal sign commands the computer to replace whatever is stored in the location addressed by the variable on the left side of the equal sign with the value of the expression on the right side. Therefore, if the statement had been 40 T1 = S, the previous sales total would have been *replaced* by the sales from this department. There would be no accumulation, and a final total would not be available for printing at the end of the program.

The plus sign is an addition operator and is used in math statements, as well as in adding into a counter. As a result of the statement T1 = T1 + S, the computer is commanded to retrieve whatever is in the storage location addressed T1, add what is stored in S, and replace what is in T1 with the new total.

After the sales have been accumulated in the total counter, the computer is directed by the following statement to go back and read another DATA line.

```
45  GO TO 25
```

PRINT STATEMENTS

Placing material in quotes in a PRINT statement will cause the computer to print exactly what is inside the quotes, including spaces.[1] If the programmer wishes to show output with blank lines, he merely uses a PRINT statement without anything after it. The PRINT line commands the computer to print nothing, which it does—it prints a line of nothing.

A comma at the end of one PRINT statement tells the computer to treat the information in the following PRINT statement as if it were to be printed on the same line. In other words, the data from the 101 PRINT statement shown below would be printed on the same line as the data in the 100 PRINT statement.

[1] Single quotes are not processed on the TRS-80.

```
100 PRINT "WHAT TIME IS IT?",
101 PRINT "IT IS 2 O'CLOCK"
```

The printout would be the following.

```
WHAT TIME IS IT?              IT IS 2 O'CLOCK
```

Statements 100 and 101 could be combined into one statement that would achieve the same output. The combined statement is shown below.

```
100 PRINT "WHAT TIME IS IT?", "IT IS 2 O'CLOCK"
```

In the sample problem, a blank line is needed after the body of the report is printed. The next line to be printed should include the words TOTAL SALES, a space, a dollar sign, a space, and the total sales.

The computer prints spaces before and after the dollar sign because those spaces are inside the quotes. Actually there are two spaces after the dollar sign; one is the space within the quotes and the second is a space the computer skips before a field, leaving a space for the negative sign. If the number is positive, the sign is omitted. However, if the sign is negative, the sign will be printed.

```
50  PRINT
55  PRINT "TOTAL SALES $ " T1
```

The printout will be as follows.

```
TOTAL SALES $  13648.52
```

If a comma is placed after the ending quote, the total will be in the next print zone.

```
50  PRINT
55  PRINT "TOTAL SALES $ ",T1
```

The printout will be as follows.

```
TOTAL SALES $                13648.52
```

Either single quotes or double quotes may be used to designate a string. The computer treats them as equivalent symbols. However, if a single quote is used at the beginning of a string, a single quote must be used at the end. Also, if there is a quote within a quote in a PRINT statement, the inside quotation marks will be printed as part of the string, as shown below.

```
40  PRINT '"HI"'
```

The output would be: "HI"

The complete program as listed and run by the computer is shown in Figure 3-12. When the data fills most of a print zone, the computer skips the next zone and prints the data. That is why the second and third lines of the output have the alphanumeric data in the first zone and the numeric data in the third zone. All of the other lines have the alphanumeric data in the first zone and the numeric data in the second zone.

ERRORS IN THE PROGRAM

One of the jobs of a programmer is to find errors in his program (debugging). Syntax errors, logical errors, and execution errors are types of mistakes that might be made in programming. Syntax has to do with language structure. For example, the computer will not accept PRNT for PRINT or REED for READ. Terminals have an advantage in that the computer prints an error message as soon as a syntax error is made in the typing of a program.

Execution errors are syntactically correct, but when the computer attempts to execute the statement, some incongruity is discovered. For example, the READ statement may show only numeric variable names, while the DATA statements contain string fields. The system flashes error messages, or diagnostics, on the screen after the execution of the program, telling what kind of error has been made and the line number of the statement that is in error or is connected with the error.

Logic errors reflect errors in the programmer's reasoning. The results will not be what is required to solve a problem correctly. For example, if the programmer wrote C=A–B when he wished to add A to B and store the answer in C, the computer would not detect the error. The statement, though incorrect logically, is syntactically correct and will not cause an error in execution.

FIGURE 3-12.

Problem 3-1 Listing and Printout

```
DEPT  06:48 PM          11-Jan-81
10  REM THIS IS A LISTING OF DEPARTMENT SALES AND A TOTAL
15  REM OF ALL THE SALES.
20  T1 = 0
25  READ D$,S
30  IF D$ = "EXIT" GO TO 50
35  PRINT D$,S
40  T1 = T1 + S
45  GO TO 25
50  PRINT
55  PRINT "TOTAL SALES $ " T1
70  DATA "CLOTHING, MEN",4500.76
72  DATA "CLOTHING, WOMEN",3372.35
74  DATA "CLOTHING, CHILDREN",1572.22
76  DATA "SHOES, MEN",955.17
78  DATA "SHOES, WOMEN",1216.28
80  DATA "JEWELRY",426.34
82  DATA "SUNDRIES",513.96
84  DATA "COSMETICS",476.29
86  DATA "LINENS",615.15
88  DATA EXIT,0
90  END

READY

RUN
DEPT 06:48 PM           11-Jan-81
CLOTHING, MEN  4500.76
CLOTHING, WOMEN              3372.35
CLOTHING, CHILDREN           1572.22
SHOES, MEN     955.17
SHOES, WOMEN   1216.28
JEWELRY        426.34
SUNDRIES       513.96
COSMETICS      476.29
LINENS         615.15

TOTAL SALES $  13648.52
```

Two very common errors will be shown here. These errors would cause the following messages to be printed.

```
%DATA FORMAT ERROR AT LINE 15

?OUT OF DATA AT LINE 15
```

The following program will be used to demonstrate the errors generating the above error messages, or diagnostics.

```
15  READ A,B,C
25  PRINT A,B,C
30  GO TO 15
35  DATA 97,113,10
38  DATA 76,127,11
40  DATA 55,103,18
50  END
```

```
RUN
NONAME   12:58          01-Feb-81
 97           113            10
 76           127            11
 55           103            18
?OUT OF DATA AT LINE 15
```

The reason for the error message in the example shown above is that there was no test made to check for the trailer data. This message does not give an incorrect printout; it just prints out the correct data, gives the error message, and stops.

The following changes and additions will be made to the previous program.

```
20  IF A = -9 GO TO 50
38  DATA 76,E27,11
45  DATA -9,0,0
```

After these statements were placed in the program, RUN was typed and the following printout appeared.

```
RUN
NONAME   12:58  PM         01-Feb-81
 97             113            10
%DATA FORMAT ERROR AT LINE 15
```

Why did this message appear? In checking the second DATA statement (38), the programmer noticed that the second field had alphanumeric data in it, and it was supposed to contain numeric data—thus, the error message. After the programmer corrected this error, changing E27 to 127, the program ran perfectly.

Statement 40 was changed to read 40 DATA 55 103,18. The following printout appeared.

```
RUN
NONAME  12:58 PM          01-Feb-81
 97             113             10
 76             127             11
 55103          18              -9
?OUT OF DATA AT LINE 15
```

The error message in the example shown above was caused because the comma was left out between the fields in the DATA Statement 40. The computer read the first two fields as one and the third field as the second, and then went down to the next DATA statement and picked up the -9 to fill the last field. Then when it read DATA Statement 45, it found only two fields of data where there were supposed to be three (the -9 in that statement had already been read). The programmer retyped the statement, putting in the comma, and typed RUN, and the program ran perfectly.

Another change will be made in the program to demonstrate a typical error.

```
45  DATA EXIT,0,0
```

When RUN is typed, the following printout appears.

```
RUN
NONAME  01:01 PM          01-Feb-81
 97             113             10
 76             127             11
 55             103             18
%DATA FORMAT ERROR AT LINE 15
```

The reason for the error message in this program is that the programmer had mistakenly put string data in a numeric test field. When Statement 45 was changed and -9 instead of EXIT was placed in the first field, the program ran perfectly.

Statement 45 was changed to read 45 DATA -9,0 and RUN was typed. The following printout appeared.

```
RUN
NONAME  01:01 PM          01-Feb-81
 97             113             10
 76             127             11
 55             103             18
?OUT OF DATA AT LINE 15
```

In the READ statement, the computer was instructed to read three fields, but Statement 45 contained only two fields. Therefore, the computer typed the error message.

When the programmer inserted another comma and a zero in the statement, the program ran without an error message.

DEBUGGING PROBLEMS

The following programs all have some programming error. The programs should be studied carefully to determine what the errors are before the solutions, which follow the programs, are consulted.

Problem 1

```
LIST
CH3A     10:26 AM           07-FEB-81
10  READ A,B,C
15  IF A = -9 GO TO 50
20  PRINT A,B,C
25  GO TO 10
30  DATA BILL,10,3
35  DATA DON,7,5
40  DATA JOHN,13,8
45  DATA -9,0,0
50  END

READY

RUN
CH3A     10:26 AM           07-FEB-81
%DATA FORMAT ERROR AT LINE 10
```

After he read the diagnostic, the programmer realized that he had tried to address the alphanumeric data field with a numeric variable name. He changed the first variable name from A to A$, changed the test statement to read 15 IF A$ = "EXIT" GO TO 50, and put the word EXIT instead of -9 in the first field of Statement 45. He ran the program again and obtained another incorrect solution, as shown in Problem 2.

Problem 2

```
LIST
CH3B     10:28 AM             07-FEB-81
10  READ A$,B,C
15  IF A$ = "EXIT" GO TO 50
20  PRINT A,B,C
25  GO TO 10
30  DATA BILL,10,3
35  DATA DON,7,5
40  DATA JOHN, 13,8
45  DATA EXIT,0,0
50  END

RUN
CH3B     10:38 AM             07-FEB-81
 0              10              3
 0              7               5
 0              13              8
```

Why are there zeros in the first column of the printout? The programmer made a typical error in that he corrected the variable name in the READ statement but forgot to change it in the PRINT statement. The data stored as A$ remained in storage, but data for A, which contained nothing, was obediently supplied as directed by the program. That is why the first column contains zeros. After Statement 20 was changed to 20 PRINT A$,B,C the printout finally contained the desired results, as shown below.

Problem 3

```
LIST
CH3C     10:40 AM             07-FEB-81
10  READ A$,B,C
15  IF A$ = "EXIT" GO TO 50
20  PRINT A$,B,C
25  GO TO 10
30  DATA BILL,10,3
35  DATA DON,7,5
40  DATA JOHN,13,8
45  DATA EXIT,0,0
50  END
```

```
RUN
CH3C     10:40 AM          07-FEB-81
BILL           10              3
DON            7               5
JOHN           13              8
```

Problem 4

```
LIST
CH3D     10:41 AM          07-FEB-81
10  READ D$,B,A
15  IF D$=-9  GO TO 25
?ILLEGAL MODE MIXING AT LINE 15  .
```

When the programmer saw the error message shown in Problem 4, he realized that he must replace -9 with a string, so he retyped Statement 15 to read 15 IF D$ = "EXIT" GO TO 25 and continued typing his program.

```
LIST
CH3D     10:41 AM          07-FEB-81
10  READ D$,B,A
15  IF D$="EXIT" GO TO 25
20  PRINT D$,B,A
25  T=T+N
30  GO TO 10
35  PRINT
40  PRINT "TOTAL SALES $" T
45  DATA PAINT,17,12
52  DATA HARDWARE,20,3
55  DATA ELECTRIC,25,6
60  DATA EXIT,0,0
65  END

READY

RUN
CH3D     10:41 AM          07-FEB-81
PAINT          17             12
HARDWARE       20             3
ELECTRIC       25             6
?OUT OF DATA AT LINE 10
```

Why would the program printout show out of data? Looking over the program, the programmer saw that he had typed 25 instead of 35 in Statement 15. The loop thus created does not direct control out of the main loop, the program is aborted when no further data exist, and a diagnostic message is printed. After correcting Statement 15, the program was run again and Problem 5 resulted.

Problem 5

```
LIST
CH3E        10:43 AM                07-FEB-81
05  T=0
10  READ D$,B,A
15  IF D$="EXIT" GO TO 35
20  PRINT D$,B,A
25  T=T+N
30  GO TO 10
35  PRINT
40  PRINT "TOTAL SALES $" T
45  DATA PAINT,17,12
52  DATA HARDWARE,20,3
55  DATA ELECTRIC ,25,6
60  DATA EXIT,0,0
65  END

READY

RUN
CH3E      10:43 AM                07-FEB-81
PAINT                17                 12
HARDWARE             20                 3
ELECTRIC             25                 6

TOTAL SALES $ 0
```

Why did the total line show a zero? Although Statement 25 appears to be correct, it must contain an error. Since no value is ever stored at N, it will always contain a zero. The variable A rather than N should be added into the total counter T. Statement 25 was changed, and the program ran perfectly, as shown below.

```
LIST
CH3E     10:43 AM           07-FEB-81
05  T=0
10  READ D$,B,A
15  IF D$="EXIT" GO TO 35
20  PRINT D$,B,A
25  T=T+A
30  GO TO 10
35  PRINT
40  PRINT "TOTAL SALES $" T
45  DATA PAINT,17,12
52  DATA HARDWARE,20,3
55  DATA ELECTRIC,25,6
60  DATA EXIT,0,0
65  END


RUN
CH3E     10:43 AM           07-FEB-81
PAINT          17               12
HARDWARE       20               3
ELECTRIC       25               6

TOTAL SALES $ 21
```

Problem 6

The following debugging problem will demonstrate a logical method for determining where the error occurred. The program should be studied carefully to identify that method.

```
LIST
CH3F     10:45 AM           07-FEB-81
10  READ A$,B,C,D
15  IF A$ = "EXIT" GO TO 50
20  PRINT A$,B,C,D
25  GO TO 10
30  DATA BILL,10,6,8
35  DATA DON,8,59
40  DATA JIM,11,7,4
45  DATA EXIT,0,0,0
50  END

READY

RUN
CH3F     10:45 AM           07-FEB-81
BILL           10               6               8
%DATA FORMAT ERROR AT LINE 10
```

The READ and PRINT statements are correct because the first record printed out correctly. Therefore, the error is in the second DATA statement. When the programmer looked at Statement 35, he noted that there is a comma missing between the third and fourth fields. Because the number 59 was allocated to field C, the computer attempted to take the string data from DATA Statement 40 and store it in the numeric storage location D. The program ran perfectly after the comma was inserted between the fields.

```
RUN
CH3F     10:45 AM          07-FEB-81
BILL           10               6              8
DON            8                5              9
JIM            11               7              4
```

SUMMARY

1. All problems should be flowcharted. Flowcharting facilitates coding a program.
2. A flowchart is a chart of symbols representing the arithmetic and logic of a sequence of steps taken to solve a problem.
3. Flow in a structured program is from the top down.
4. In a structured program, each structure has but one entry and one exit.
5. Three control structures are used in structured programming.
   a. *Sequence control* means that one sequence is performed before another.
   b. *Conditional control* means that branching occurs only when a condition is met.
   c. *Loop control* means that execution loops continually until exiting is required.
6. Two extensions to the basic structures that are often used are (1) exit from a loop and (2) multiple branching, depending on a sequence of conditions.
7. Control structures may be nested. The nested structure must have only one entry and one exit.
8. The values used on the last DATA statement in the program are tested by the IF statement and show that the last DATA statement has been read. These values are called *dummy values* or *trailer constants.*
9. String variable names are used when storing alphanumeric data. Any string not beginning with a letter must be placed in quotes.

10. String variable names consist of a letter and a dollar sign—D$, S$.
11. In BASIC, values are assigned to variables through LET statements, such as 20 LET B = 35. The LET is optional on some systems, and the same statement could be written 20 B = 35.
12. The equal sign in assignment statements means *replace*. The value or the result of a computation on the right side of the equal sign *replaces* the value in the storage addressed by the variable on the left side of the sign. If Statement 30 B = 8 is executed, the value 8 is stored in B. Whatever value was in B would be replaced by 8.
13. To accumulate a total, a total counter is used. If a total of each department's sales is desired, the computer must take the value currently in the counter and add it to the department's sales (S) and store the sum of the two in the total counter (T). The statement to be used would be 30 T = T + S.
14. When a value of zero is assigned to a counter, it is said to be initialized to zero, as in 10 T1=0.
15. The addition operator is the plus sign.
16. To have a computer print a title, a symbol, a heading, etc., the item to be printed is placed in quotes after the word PRINT in a PRINT statement, as in 30 PRINT "TOTAL SALES $" T1. The computer will print: TOTAL SALES $ XXX.XX.
17. If a comma is placed at the end of a PRINT statement, the computer will print the string in the following PRINT statement on the same line if there is enough room.

```
100 PRINT "WHAT SCHOOL DO YOU ATTEND?",
105 PRINT "CSULB"
```

The computer will print the following.

```
WHAT SCHOOL DO YOU ATTEND?  CSULB
```

18. Statements 100 and 105 shown above could be combined into one statement that would achieve the same output. The combined statement is shown below.

```
100 PRINT "WHAT SCHOOL DO YOU ATTEND?", "CSULB"
```

19. If a blank line is needed anywhere in the printout of a program, a PRINT statement is used that places nothing after the word

PRINT, as in 30 PRINT. This statement will cause the computer to print a line of nothing—a blank line.

20. When a total is to be printed, a lack of punctuation after the last quotes in the PRINT statement will cause the computer to space once and then print the data.

```
30  PRINT "TOTAL SALES $" T1
```

The output would be: TOTAL SALES $ XXX.XX. If a comma is placed after the last quotation mark, the data will be printed in the next print zone.

```
30  PRINT "TOTAL SALES $",T1
```

The printout would be as follows.

```
TOTAL SALES $                 XXX.XX
```

21. Single quotes or double quotes are considered equivalent. However, if a single quote is used at the beginning of a string, a single quote must also be used at the end. The same applies to the double quotes.
22. If there are both a single quote and a double quote around a string, the inside quote is part of the string.

```
40  PRINT '"WHAT IS THE QUESTION?"'
```

The output would look like this:

```
"WHAT IS THE QUESTION?"
```

23. In the DATA statements, quote marks should always be placed around string data that begin with a numeral or in which there are punctuation marks or spaces. Otherwise, the computer will treat string data with commas as if each string separated by a comma were a different field. It also ignores spaces; therefore, strings not placed in quotes will be printed with no spacing.

LONG BEACH would be printed LONGBEACH.

"LONG BEACH" would be printed LONG BEACH.

If a string field were given a variable name N$ and the programmer typed in the DATA statement JENKINS, BOB, the computer would read JENKINS and store it in N$. Then it would attempt to store BOB in the location addressed by the next variable name. "JENKINS, BOB" would be printed correctly as JENKINS, BOB because of the quote marks.

SELF TEST

1. Find the errors in the following program:

```
10  THIS PROGRAM USES A TOTAL REGISTER
15  T = 0
20  READ A,D$,S
25  IF A = -99 GO TO 45
30  PRINT A,D$,S
35  T = S
40  GO TO 20
45  PRINT "TOTAL SALES $" S
50  END
60  DATA 112,PAINT DEPT,1131.76
65  DATA 141,HARDWARE DEPT,2963.55
70  DATA 201,FURNITURE DEPT,5767.32
75  DATA -99
```

2. Write a statement or statements that will print out the following.

```
"WHY DID YOU DO THAT?"                "BECAUSE I HAD TO!"
```

3. What are the flowchart symbols for each of the following?
   a. Input/output
   b. Terminal
   c. Processing
   d. Decision
4. What does the sign (=) mean?
5. Write a string variable name.
6. What READ statement would be used to cause the computer to read the following DATA?

SALESMAN	DEPT. NO.	DEPARTMENT	PAYROLL NUMBER	TOTAL SALES
Hibbings, Don	A10	PAINT DEPARTMENT	7327	1000.00

7. Write a statement that will add C, D, and E, and store the total in A.
8. Write a statement with a total counter (T) to which hours (H) is added every time a DATA line is printed.
9. How do you cause the computer to skip lines in the printout?

TRUE AND FALSE

10. It is necessary to use quotes in alphanumeric data in the DATA statements if there are spaces or punctuation in the string.
11. The following statement would cause a value stored in R to be added into a total counter T : 20 T = R
12. The following statement would cause a counter, B, to be initialized to zero: 20 B = 0
13. The following is a valid PRINT statement.

```
30 PRINT '"WHAT IS THE QUESTION?'"
```

14. The following is a valid variable: 3$
15. The following is a valid statement: 30 A + B = C
16. If A = 8, B = 6, and D = 5, A would have the value of 19 after the computer processed the following statement: 20 A = B + D.
17. If A = 4, B = 7, and C = 3, D would have the value of 14 after the computer processed the following statement: 20 D = A + B + C.
18. The following are valid statements.
    a. 20 IF A$ = -99 GO TO 70
    b. 20 A = 10
    c. 20 READ A$,B$,C$,
    d. 20 GO TO 80
    e. 20 END
    f. 20 REM THIS IS A PROGRAM
    g. 20 T1 = A + 3
    h. 20 DATA JOHN HENRY JONES,16,113.7
    i. 20 PRINT D,J,B,

ASSIGNMENTS

1. The owner of Maxi Dept. Store wants a printout of the department number, department name, number of items sold, and sales. He also wants two totals printed at the left margin. There

is to be a total for the number of items sold and a total for the sales of all of the departments. A flowchart, a computer listing of the problem, and the running of the program should be prepared.[2] The data are listed below.

DEPT. NO.	DEPT. NAME	ITEMS SOLD	SALES
27	Paint	1200	8200
35	Hardware	1575	12376
42	Furniture	347	78800
83	Sundries	3000	9000
76	Jewelry	900	8750
88	Appliances	250	77000
26	Records	1500	6000

2. The Robers Realty Company employs five salesmen. The manager wants a printout of the salesmen's names, the number of houses they have sold, and their total sales. He also wants a total of all of the houses sold, as well as a total of all the sales. A flowchart, a computer listing of the problem, and the running of the program should be prepared.[2] The data are listed below.

ROBERS REALTY COMPANY

SALESMAN	NO. OF HOUSES SOLD	SALES
B. J. Cunningham	4	240000
Ron Roberts	3	140000
Bill Jessel	4	210000
Mary Jane Hopkins	2	105000
Theresa Jury	3	155000

3. Bill Barney was hired to stand on a corner for an 8-hour period and tally all of the General Motors cars that passed that corner. He was told to prepare a computer printout showing each make, how many passed during the day by make, and the total num-

[2] The titles should not be printed. A blank line should be left between the report and the total lines. Another blank line should be left before the second total line, and a dollar sign should precede the sales total.

ber of General Motors cars that passed. A flowchart, a computer listing, and a running of the program should be prepared.[3] The data are listed below.

MAKE OF CAR	TOTAL NO.
Chevrolet	180
Buick	49
Pontiac	45
Oldsmobile	48
Cadillac	35

[3] The titles should not be printed. A blank line should be left between the report and the total line.

4 LISTING AND COUNTING PROGRAMS AND ADDITIONAL COMMANDS

This chapter covers the following topics.

A. The TAB function
B. Right-justification of material by use of the PRINT USING statement
C. The arithmetic operators for subtraction, multiplication, division, and exponentiation (raising to powers)
D. The hierarchy of operations
E. Use of a counter
F. The TAB key

TABULATION

As was explained in Chapter 2, the computer prints material in five columns. If it is necessary or desirable to have the printout spaced in a different manner, the TAB function can be used by placing it in a PRINT statement, as in PRINT;TAB(38);N. The TAB function serves the same function as the tab key on the typewriter. The computer will go to the position designated by the number in parentheses after the word TAB. If the programmer wanted to print a string (A$) at Column 20, a numeric value (N) at Column 40, and a numeric value (K) at Column 50, the statement would appear as follows.

```
30  PRINT;TAB(20);A$;TAB(40) ;N;TAB(50);K
```

It is standard programming procedure to place a semi-colon between the words PRINT and TAB.

The TAB function has no relationship to the TAB key. Each time the TAB key is depressed, the line is indented eight spaces; however, the number of spaces may vary in different systems. Tabulating in the listing of the program does not affect the printout.

THE PRINT USING STATEMENT

PRINT USING statements vary from system to system. The statements described in this book are utilized on the PDP-11.

All of the data output to date has been left-justified. However, numeric data should be right-justified. A PRINT USING statement containing a "#" for each digit in the field and a decimal point in the proper position will cause the field to be right-justified. Examples of the statements and resulting printouts are shown below.

```
15 PRINT USING "####.##",N
```

```
Printout:                   1000.00
                             276.76
                               5.43
                            1945.23
```

```
15 PRINT USING "####",J
```

```
Printout:                   4762
                              22
                             534
                            9675
```

Note: There must be a comma after the quotation mark following the last "#" in the PRINT USING statement, except for the TRS-80 which requires a semi-colon.

```
15 PRINT USING ".##",L
```

```
Printout:                .27
                         .65
                         .03
                         .48
```

The command PRINT, which justifies to the left, and the command PRINT USING, which justifies to the right, cannot be included in the same statement. It is possible, however, to have both left- and right-justified material printed on the same line by using several PRINT and PRINT USING statements ending with semi-colons. However, since the TAB function cannot be included in a PRINT USING statement, the TAB function is placed in a PRINT line and a field designation is included in a PRINT USING line. The report shown in Figure 4-1 will be used to illustrate how the printout can be obtained.

FIGURE 4-1

Example Printout

```
                     DEPT.   TOTAL
                      NO.    SALES

Clothing Dept.        11    4571.85
Jewelry Dept.          5    1703.72
Shoe Dept.--Men's     27     976.53
```

In printing out this report, the first column should be left-justified and the other two columns should be right-justified. The Dept. No. starts at Column 38 and the Total Sales at Column 47. The fields are D$ for Department, N for Dept. No., and S for Total Sales. The print statements for printing data are shown below.

```
60  PRINT D$;TAB(38);
64  PRINT USING "##",N;
68  PRINT;TAB(47);
72  PRINT USING "####.##",S
```

Statement 60 tells the computer to print the data found in the storage location addressed D$ starting at the left margin and then to tab over to Column 38. The semi-colon is necessary at the end of Statement

60 to tell the computer that whatever is in the next statement that causes printing will go on the same line with the data printed as a result of Statement 60. Statement 64 tells the computer that at Column 38 there will be a two-digit number without a decimal point that is to be right-justified, and the information to be put into these positions is to be found in storage location addressed N. Because it is not possible to use TAB in the PRINT USING statement, a PRINT statement for the TAB function must be used. Statement 68 commands the computer to tab to Column 47. Statement 72 tells the computer that the data to be printed is found in the storage location addressed S. The field is seven spaces wide and is right-justified, and a decimal is inserted two places from the right. When a PRINT USING statement formats for only two decimal places, the computer will round all numbers with three or more decimal places if the third decimal position is five or greater.

ARITHMETIC OPERATORS

In the previous chapter, the arithmetic operator for adding was introduced. In this chapter the remaining operators will be presented. The subtraction operator is the "-" sign. The multiplication operator is the "*" sign, and the division operator is the "/" sign. The exponentiation sign (raising to powers) is shown by two asterisks, "**", or by the "∧" or "↑" sign.

The computer performs arithmetic operations in a certain order, called the *hierarchy* of operations. The computer checks each statement containing arithmetic operations and performs calculations in the following order.

1. All operations within the parentheses are calculated first. If there are parentheses within parentheses, the computer works from the inside out.
2. All exponentiation calculations are performed next.
3. Multiplication or division operations are then performed in the order in which they appear from left to right.
4. Lastly, addition and subtraction operations are executed in the order in which they appear from left to right.

```
55  N = ((C*D) - (A*B))**Y/X
```

In Statement 55, the computer performs the operations within the parentheses first, working from inside to outside. The innermost parentheses contain the operations that are performed first: C * D and A * B. After these two operations are executed, the operations inside of the next parentheses are performed—the product of A * B is subtracted from the product of C * D. That answer is then raised to the Y power because that is the next highest in the hierarchy of operations. The last operation is the division by X of the answer found by raising to the Y power. The final answer is stored in N.

A simple arithmetic operation is demonstrated below in Statement 25 to show how the arithmetic statements are written.

```
10  B = 10
15  Y = 14
20  U = 3
25  A = (B+Y)/U
30  PRINT A
```

In this example, B + Y is placed in parentheses because without the parentheses, Y would be divided by U and that answer added to B. The reason for this order of operation is that division is performed before addition. The correct answer, which is stored in A, is 8.

USE OF ARITHMETIC OPERATORS

Three problems will be used as examples of the use of arithmetic operations. These problems will be flowcharted and fully explained. The first problem is described below.

PROBLEM 4-1

Rainfall figures for Johnston, California, for the month of January for the past seven years are listed below. What would be the average January rainfall for this period?

January, 1970	4.5 in.	January, 1974	5.9 in.
January, 1971	8.8 in.	January, 1975	5.3 in.
January, 1972	7.6 in.	January, 1976	6.7 in.
January, 1973	6.9 in.		

The fields are to be printed out as follows: the month is to start in Column 25; the number of inches in Column 46. After the data is printed, the computer is to double-space and print "AVERAGE JANUARY RAINFALL IS X.XX IN."

Analysis shows that there are string data in both fields. So that the inches of rainfall (4.5 IN) may be totaled, the numeric and string data in the field must be separated. The computer will not calculate arithmetic with string data, so the string (IN) is assigned to I$ at Statement 35 and the numeric data is read from DATA statements into Variable R. As a result, the computer can perform math on the numeric data. The DATA statement now contains two fields: January, 1970 and 4.5.

The computer is to read the data, and, after each line is read, the rainfall is to be added into a total counter and each year is to be counted. Then a line is to be written. The computer must continue the loop, reading the data, counting the years, adding rainfall to the total counter, and then writing a line, until the last data line is read. Then the total in the total counter is to be divided by the total years and the answer printed out after the computer has double-spaced. The flowchart would appear as shown in Figure 4-2.

In Problem 4-1, the first lines would be REM lines. Although it is not necessary to have REM lines, they are used to document the problem by explaining what will be done. It is also sound programming to use REM statements to declare what the variable names are for each field.

```
10  REM THIS PROBLEM IS TO FIND THE AVERAGE RAINFALL FOR THE
15  REM MONTH OF JANUARY FOR THE YEARS 1970 - 1976.
20  REM M$=MONTH AND YEAR, R=RAINFALL, I$=INCHES, A=AVERAGE
25  REM RAINFALL, Y=COUNTER FOR YEARS, N1=TOTAL COUNTER
30  REM FOR RAINFALL.
32  N1 = 0
33  Y = 0
35  I$ = "IN"
40  READ M$,R
```

COUNTER STATEMENTS

A total counter appears in Statement 55. Statement 55 is used to accumulate the rainfall for January for seven consecutive years. The computer picks up whatever is stored at N1 and adds the contents of R and replaces the number at N1 with the sum of N1 and R, as shown below.

```
55  N1 = N1 + R
```

FIGURE 4-2
Flowchart for Problem 4-1

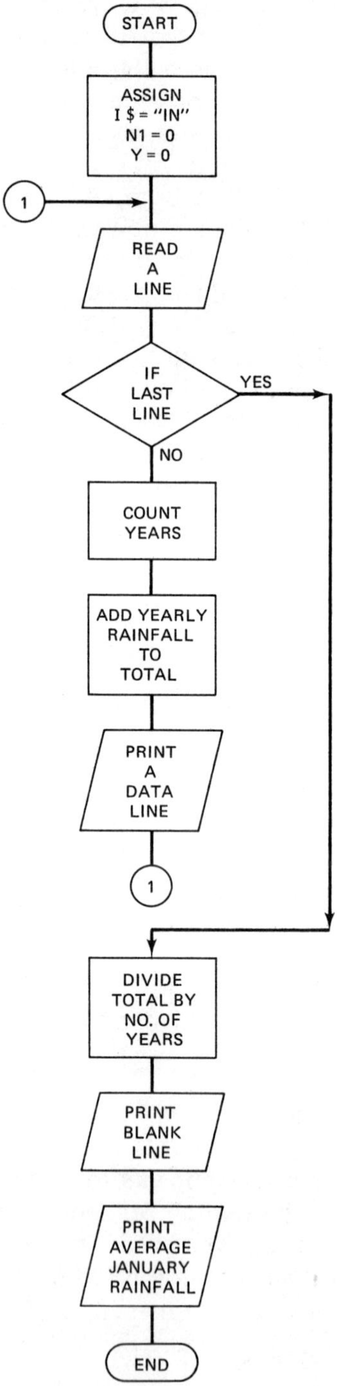

The counter statement is based on the same principle. The variable Y was made a counter of the number of years in this problem. It is used in Statement 50 in the following manner.

```
50  Y = Y + 1
```

Every time this statement is executed, the value in Y is retrieved, a 1 is added to it, and the result is placed back in Y. Thus, counting by 1 is accomplished every time the statement is executed. The counter appears after the IF statement, not before. If it appeared before the IF statement, the trailer constant "EXIT" would be counted as a year.

Statements 60, 65, and 68 are used to print the output.

```
60  PRINT;TAB(25);M$;TAB(46);
65  PRINT USING "#.#",R;
68  PRINT;TAB(50);I$
```

Statement 60 has the computer tabulate to Column 25 and print out the contents of storage addressed by M$ (the month and year). Because it is not possible to use the TAB function in the PRINT USING statement, it appears at the end of the PRINT statement, followed by a semi-colon. The semi-colon informs the computer that the printer is not to move after it goes to Column 46 until told to do so. Statement 65 tells the computer to print the contents of storage addressed by R (the rainfall) starting at Column 46, using the following format: digit, decimal, digit. Again, the semi-colon notifies the computer that after printing the last number, the printer is not to move until it receives further instructions. Statement 68 directs the printer to go to Column 50 and print the contents of the storage location addressed by I$ (IN).

To have the computer connect the loop, Statement 70 is written. It tells the computer to go to Statement 40, which is the READ statement.

```
70  GO TO 40
```

When the computer reads the trailer constant (EXIT), it is directed to Statement 75, where the average rainfall is computed.

```
45  IF M$ = "EXIT" GO TO 75
75  A = N1/Y
80  PRINT
85  PRINT "AVERAGE JANUARY RAINFALL IS ";
86  PRINT USING "#.# ",A;
87  PRINT;I$
```

The instructions state that the computer is to double-space after the last line of data is printed and then to print "AVERAGE JANUARY RAINFALL IS", followed by the answer found in Statement 75.

A statement containing only the word PRINT will result in one blank line. This statement is followed by Statement 85. The space inside the ending quote mark is included because whenever quote marks are used, the computer prints literally whatever appears inside the quote marks, even spaces. The variable I$ in Statement 87 will cause the computer to print IN after the number, so that the output will read AVERAGE JANUARY RAINFALL IS 6.5 IN.

The DATA statements follow Statement 87. The complete program and printout are shown in Figure 4-3.

Spacing in statements can vary. In Statement 50 in the program, the statement could have been written Y=Y+1. The computer ignores spacing, so it reads the material the same as if it had been written Y = Y + 1 or Y = Y + 1.

PROBLEM 4-2

The data shown Figure 4-4 contains the commissions paid to salesmen who work for various companies in the Long Beach area. Their rates of commission should be figured. The formula to find the rate is: Rate = Percentage ÷ Base. The percentage in this problem is the amount of commission; the base is the sales.

Problems 4-2 and 4-3 are very similar to Problem 4-1, except that they do a different arithmetic computation and print the answer of this computation on every line instead of at the end of the problem. Problem 4-2 is flowcharted in Figure 4-5 and the program and output listings are shown in Figure 4-6.

PROBLEM 4-3

Part of an invoice sent by Burras Grocer Wholesalers to Smither's Market is shown below. The computer is to be programmed to print out the details of the invoice, which include quantity, description, price, and amount. All data is supplied except the amount. The computer will have to be programmed to figure the amount before printing the detail

FIGURE 4-3

Listing and Printout for Problem 4-1

```
LIST
RAIN    10:15 PM         1-Feb-81
10  REM THIS PROBLEM IS TO FIND THE AVERAGE RAINFALL FOR THE
15  REM MONTH OF JANUARY FOR THE YEARS 1970 - 1976.
20  REM M$=MONTH AND YEAR,R=RAINFALL,I$=INCHES,A=AVERAGE
25  REM RAINFALL,Y=COUNTER FOR YEARS,N1=TOTAL COUNTER
30  REM FOR RAINFALL.
32  N1 = 0
33  Y = 0
35  I$ = "IN"
40  READ M$,R
45  IF M$ = "EXIT" GO TO 75
50  Y = Y + 1
55  N1 = N1 + R
60  PRINT;TAB(25);M$;TAB(46);
65  PRINT USING "#.#",R;
68  PRINT;TAB(50);I$
70  GO TO 40
75  A = N1/Y
80  PRINT
85  PRINT "AVERAGE JANUARY RAINFALL IS ";
86  PRINT USING "#.# ",A;
87  PRINT;I$
88  DATA "JANUARY,1970",4.5
90  DATA "JANUARY,1971",8.8
92  DATA "JANUARY,1972",7.6
94  DATA "JANUARY,1973",6.9
96  DATA "JANUARY,1974",5.9
98  DATA "JANUARY,1975",5.3
100 DATA "JANUARY,1976",6.7
102 DATA EXIT,0
104 END

READY

RUN
RAIN    10:15 PM         1-Feb-81
                          JANUARY,1970          4.5 IN
                          JANUARY,1971          8.8 IN
                          JANUARY,1972          7.6 IN
                          JANUARY,1973          6.9 IN
                          JANUARY,1974          5.9 IN
                          JANUARY,1975          5.3 IN
                          JANUARY,1976          6.7 IN

AVERAGE JANUARY RAINFALL IS 6.5 IN
```

FIGURE 4-4
Problem 4-2

Salesman	Amount of Commission	Sales	Rate of Commission
A. Johnson	$495	$ 9900	.XX
B. Nelson	480	8000	.XX
C. Smith	624	7800	.XX
D. Hanson	580	11680	.XX
E. Fountain	533	8200	.XX
F. Sheridan	616	8800	.XX

FIGURE 4-5
Flowchart for Problem 4-2

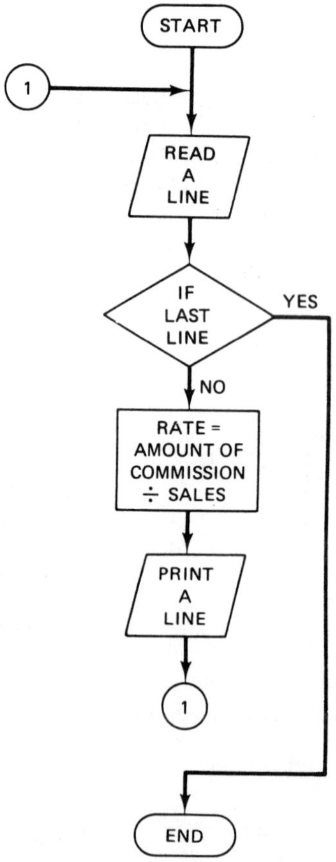

FIGURE 4-6

Listing and Printout for Problem 4-2

```
LIST
COM      07:07 PM         3-Feb-81
10  REM THE PURPOSE OF THIS PROGRAM IS TO CALCULATE THE
15  REM RATE OF COMMISSION OF LONG BEACH AREAS SALESMEN.
20  REM S$=SALESMAN,A=AMT OF COMMISSION,S=SALES,R=RATE
25  REM OF COMMISSION.
30  READ S$,A,S
35  IF S$="EXIT" GO TO 95
40  R=A/S
45  PRINT;TAB(8);S$;TAB(29);
48  PRINT USING "###",A;
50  PRINT;TAB(40);
53  PRINT USING "#####",S;
55  PRINT;TAB(55);
58  PRINT USING ".##",R
65  GO TO 30
70  DATA "A. JOHNSON",495,9900
72  DATA "B. NELSON",480,8000
74  DATA "C. SMITH",624,7800
76  DATA "D. HANSON",580,11680
78  DATA "E. FOUNTAIN",533,8200
80  DATA "F. SHERIDAN",616,8800
90  DATA EXIT,0,0
95  END

READY

RUN
COM      07:07 PM         3-Feb-81
         A. JOHNSON        495          9900          .05
         B. NELSON         480          8000          .06
         C. SMITH          624          7800          .08
         D. HANSON         580         11680          .05
         E. FOUNTAIN       533          8200          .07
         F. SHERIDAN       616          8800          .07
```

line. The programmer used an assignment statement (P$ = "A CASE") to eliminate the string data from the price field in order to use the price in calculations.

Problem 4-3 is flowcharted in Figure 4-8, and the program and output listings are shown in Figure 4-9.

DEBUGGING

The computer cannot detect some kinds of errors because coding of the program is technically correct. The kind of errors it cannot detect are

FIGURE 4-7

Problem 4-3

Quantity	Description	Price	Amount
2 cases	Burton's Green Lima Beans	8.78 a case	XX.XX
1 case	Burton's Butter Beans	4.26 a case	XX.XX
2 cases	Burton's Golden Wax Beans	4.98 a case	XX.XX
5 cases	Burton's Cut Green Beans	7.89 a case	XX.XX
4 cases	Burton's Peeled Whole Tomatoes	5.98 a case	XX.XX
3 cases	Burton's Whole Beets	5.50 a case	XX.XX

FIGURE 4-8

Flowchart for Problem 4-3

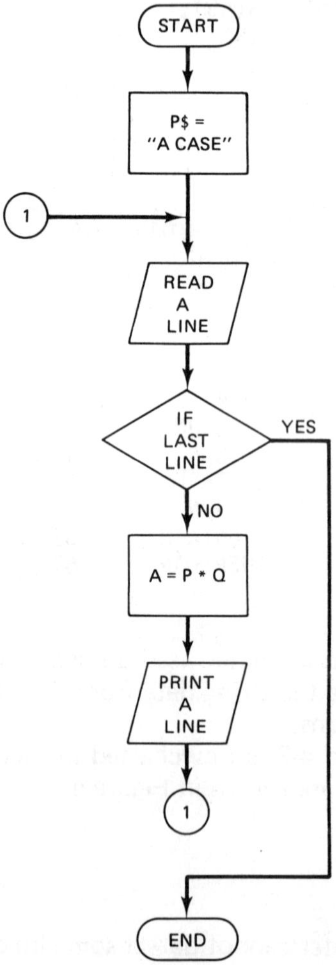

FIGURE 4-9

Listing and Printout for Problem 4-3

```
LIST
EXT      07:31 PM        28-Jan-81
10  REM THIS PROBLEM CONSISTS OF EXTENDING THE INVOICE BILLED
15  REM TO SMITHER'S MARKET.
20  REM Q=QTY,C$=CASES,D$=DESCRIPTION,P=PRICE,P$=A CASE,
25  REM AND A=AMOUNT.
27  P$ = "A CASE"
30  READ Q,C$,D$,P
35  IF Q=-9 GO TO 76
40  A=P*Q
45  PRINT Q;TAB(3);C$;TAB(11);D$;TAB(49);
47  PRINT USING "#.##",P;
48  PRINT;TAB(54);P$;TAB(64);
50  PRINT USING "##.##",A
57  GO TO 30
60  DATA 2,CASES,"BURTON'S GREEN LIMA BEANS",8.78
62  DATA 1,CASE,"BURTON'S BUTTER BEANS",4.26
64  DATA 2,CASES,"BURTON'S GOLDEN WAX BEANS",4.98
66  DATA 5,CASES,"BURTON'S CUT GREEN BEANS",7.89
68  DATA 4,CASES,"BURTON'S PEELED WHOLE TOMATOES",5.98
70  DATA 3,CASES,"BURTON'S WHOLE BEETS",5.50
72  DATA -9,0,0,0
76  END

READY

RUN
EXT      07:31 PM        28-Jan-81
 2 CASES    BURTON'S GREEN LIMA BEANS              8.78 A CASE    17.56
 1 CASE     BURTON'S BUTTER BEANS                  4.26 A CASE     4.26
 2 CASES    BURTON'S GOLDEN WAX BEANS              4.98 A CASE     9.96
 5 CASES    BURTON'S CUT GREEN BEANS               7.89 A CASE    39.45
 4 CASES    BURTON'S PEELED WHOLE TOMATOES         5.98 A CASE    23.92
 3 CASES    BURTON'S WHOLE BEETS                   5.50 A CASE    16.50
```

logic errors. As a result, an output that the programmer did not want may be produced. For example, in Problem 4-2, if Statement 30 read as follows: 30 READ S$,A and the operator typed RUN, the terminal would have printed the following message:

```
DIVISION BY 0 AT LINE 40
       JOHNSON            495           0            %0
DATA FORMAT ERROR AT LINE 30
```

The reason for these error messages is that the programmer forgot a variable name (S) for the sales field. Therefore S = 0 and is the reason for the first error message—DIVISION BY 0 AT LINE 40. Leaving out the variable is the reason for the second error message—DATA FORMAT ERROR AT LINE 30.

In Figure 4-10 is another printout of a program of Problem 4-1 and the output. It is readily apparent that "IN" is on a line lower than it should be. Before the error is explained, the student should try to locate it. Also, at the end of the printout there is the statement OUT OF DATA AT LINE 40 instead of AVERAGE JANUARY RAINFALL IS 6.5 IN. The OUT OF DATA AT LINE 40 message would not appear if the program were properly done. The last error is that the rainfall is incorrect. For example, for January, 1970, the rainfall should be 4.5, not 5. So the programmer must look closely. The errors are not easy to spot.

What caused the computer to print "IN" on a separate line each time? Either a semi-colon or a comma must appear at the end of a PRINT line if the programmer wishes data in a following PRINT statement to appear on the preceding line. Statement 65 has no semi-colon after the R. Also the format should read "#.#" instead of "##". That is why there is only one digit for rainfall.

Also, the computer will stop when it runs out of data and will print ?OUT OF DATA AT LINE 40. For good programming, a trailer constant should be used. The programmer left out EXIT, 0 in the last DATA statement despite the fact that the test for the word EXIT appeared in the IF statement. Because it ran out of data instead of reading EXIT, the computer never went to Statement 75 (Statement 45 says IF M$ = "EXIT" GO TO 75). Statements 80, 85, 86, and 87 follow Statement 75, so they would not be executed either. Statements 85, 86, and 87 are the ones that cause the computer to print AVERAGE JANUARY RAINFALL IS 6.5 IN.

DEBUGGING PROBLEMS

Many errors in programs are those dealing with logic. They are most difficult to locate, especially if the programmer has no idea what the output should be.

Problem 1

```
RUN
CH4A      02:12 AM          16-FEB-81
 20             4                  2              25
 40             5                  2              64
 60             3                  2              400
```

FIGURE 4-10

A Faulty Program for Problem 4-1

```
RNFALL  06:50  PM          28-Jan-81
10  REM THIS PROBLEM IS TO FIND THE AVERAGE RAINFALL FOR THE
15  REM MONTH OF JANUARY FOR THE YEARS 1970 - 1976
20  REM M$=MONTH AND YEAR, R=RAINFALL,I$=INCHES,A=AVERAGE
25  REM RAINFALL,Y=COUNTER FOR YEARS,N1=TOTAL COUNTER
30  REM FOR RAINFALL.
32  N1 = 0
33  Y = 0
35  I$ = "IN"
40  READ M$,R
45  IF M$ = "EXIT" GO TO 75
50  Y = Y + 1
55  N1 = N1 + R
60  PRINT;TAB(25);M$;TAB(46);
65  PRINT USING "##",R
68  PRINT;TAB(49);I$
70  GO TO 40
75  A = N1/Y
80  PRINT
85  PRINT "AVERAGE JANUARY RAINFALL IS ";
86  PRINT USING "#.# ",A;
87  PRINT;I$
88  DATA "JANUARY, 1970",4.5
90  DATA "JANUARY, 1971",8.8
92  DATA "JANUARY, 1972",7.6
94  DATA "JANUARY, 1973",6.9
96  DATA "JANUARY, 1974",5.9
98  DATA "JANUARY, 1975",5.3
100 DATA "JANUARY, 1976",6.7
102 END

RUN
RNFALL  06:50  PM          28-Jan-81
                        JANUARY, 1970        5
                                                IN
                        JANUARY, 1971        9
                                                IN
                        JANUARY, 1972        8
                                                IN
                        JANUARY, 1973        7
                                                IN
                        JANUARY, 1974        6
                                                IN
                        JANUARY, 1975        5
                                                IN
                        JANUARY, 1976        7
                                                IN
? OUT OF DATA AT LINE 40
```

The output shown above is the correct solution to a programming problem. However, the programmer committed a logic error and an incorrectly listed program and its solution were generated, as shown below.

```
LIST
CH4A      02:12 AM          16-FEB-81
10  REM THE VARIABLE A IS TO BE DIVIDED BY THE VARIABLE B.
15  REM THE ANSWER OF  A  DIVIDED BY B IS TO BE RAISED TO THE
20  REM C POWER.  THAT ANSWER IS TO BE STORED IN F.
25  READ A,B,C
30  IF A=-9 GO TO 70
35  F = A/B**C
40  PRINT A,B,C,F
45  GO TO 25
50  DATA 20,4,2
55  DATA 40,5,2
60  DATA 60,3,2
65  DATA -9,0,0
70  END

RUN
CH4A      02:13 AM          16-FEB-81
 20            4              2              1.25
 40            5              2              1.6
 60            3              2              6.66667
```

The REM statements in the listed program tell what the program is supposed to do. However, unless one is math-oriented, he may not know whether the output is correct.

The programmer knew that the desired answers were not correct. In looking at Statement 35, he noted that he had neglected to put parentheses around A/B. The computer, following the hierarchy of operations, had raised B to the C power and then divided the answer into A, whereas it was supposed to divide A by B and raise that answer to the C power. When parentheses were placed around A/B, the correct printout resulted.

Problem 2

Why was the total line in the following problem omitted?

```
LIST
CH4B      02:13 PM          16-FEB-81
10  READ A,B,C
15  IF A=-9 GO TO 85
```

```
20  N=N+1
25  PRINT;TAB(10);
30  PRINT USING "##",A;
35  PRINT;TAB(20);
40  PRINT USING "##.##",B;
45  PRINT;TAB(35);
50  PRINT USING "##",C
55  GO TO 10
60  PRINT;TAB(10);"TOTAL NO. OF TRANSACTIONS",N
65  DATA 20,30.76,21
70  DATA 40,11.32,11
75  DATA 50,7.08,10
80  DATA -9,0,0
85  END

RUN
CH4B     02:13 PM          16-FEB-81
           20         30.76           21
           40         11.32           11
           50          7.08           10
```

The programmer noted that he had the computer go to the END statement after the last DATA statement was read. He wrote a new statement 57 PRINT to generate a blank line and changed Statement 15 to IF A=-9 GO TO 57. Then he reran the program and secured a correct printout.

```
LIST
CH4B     02:30 PM          16-FEB-81
10  READ A,B,C
15  IF A=-9 GO TO 57
20  N=N+1
25  PRINT;TAB(10);
30  PRINT USING "##",A;
35  PRINT;TAB(20);
40  PRINT USING "##.##",B;
45  PRINT;TAB(35);
50  PRINT USING "##",C
55  GO TO 10
57  PRINT
60  PRINT;TAB(10);"TOTAL NO. OF TRANSACTIONS",N
65  DATA 20,30.76,21
70  DATA 40,11.32,11
75  DATA 50,7.08,10
80  DATA -9,0,0
85  END
```

```
RUN
CH4B      02:31 PM           16-FEB-81
               20         30.76          21
               40         11.32          11
               50          7.08          10

               TOTAL NO. OF TRANSACTIONS             3
```

Problem 3

Both errors in the following program are careless errors.

```
LIST
CH4C      02:32 AM           16-FEB-81
10  PRINT
15  PRINT;TAB(9);"EMPLOYEE";TAB(30);"SALARY"
20  PRINT
25  READ E$,S
30  IF E$ = "EXIT" GO TO 80
35  PRINT,TAB(9);E$;TAB(29);
40  PRINT USING "####.##,S
45  GO TO 25
50  DATA JOHNSON, 1200.73
55  DATA MOORE, 1475.25
60  DATA OLSON,1320.88
70  DATA TALBERT,1515.62
75  DATA EXIT,0
80  END

RUN
CH4C      02:32 AM           16-FEB-81

              EMPLOYEE              SALARY

                    JOHNSON
                    MOORE
                    OLSON
                    TALBERT
```

The first error is in Statement 35. The programmer should use a semi-colon after PRINT to ensure that the computer does not space until it receives instructions. If a comma is placed after PRINT, the computer is instructed to go to the next print zone at Space 15 before it is given the TAB instruction. The programmer rewrote Statement 35, placing a semi-colon after the word PRINT.

The reason the second field of data did not print was that a quote was missing at the end of the formatted area in the PRINT USING statement in Statement 40. He rewrote the statement, placing the ending quote in the statement, and ran the program. The output then was correct, as shown below:

```
RUN
CH4C     02:34 AM             16-FEB-81

         EMPLOYEE                SALARY

         JOHNSON               1200.73
         MOORE                 1475.25
         OLSON                 1320.88
         TALBERT               1515.62
```

Problem 4

When a program that will process a great quantity of data is written, the programmer usually will test the program to be certain it does what it is supposed to do. A printout containing a typical programming error is shown below. What is the error and what caused it?

```
LIST
CH4D      08:40 AM            28-MAR-81
5   T1=0
10  READ A$,B,C
20  IF A$ = "EXIT" GO TO 100
30  T1=T1+D
40  D=B*C
50  PRINT A$,B,C,D
60  GO TO 10
100 PRINT
110 PRINT;TAB(15);"TOTAL",,T1
120 DATA A,2,4
130 DATA B,3,6
140 DATA C,4,8
150 DATA D,5,10
160 DATA EXIT,0,0
170 END

RUN
CH4D      08:40 AM            28-MAR-81
A                2              4             8
B                3              6             18
C                4              8             32
D                5              10            50

                 TOTAL                        58
```

The programmer would first check to see that the arithmetic statement is performing properly. It is in this program. Then he would check the total to see that it is correct. In this program it is not. The answer should have been 108, but it was 58. For some reason the last amount was not added to the counter. In checking the program, the programmer noted that he had the total counter before the computer calculated the amount to be counted. After the statement number was changed from 30 to 55, the program ran correctly.

```
LIST
CH4D     08:41 AM            28-MAR-81
5   T1=0
10  READ A$,B,C
20  IF A$ = "EXIT" GO TO 100
40  D=B*C
50  PRINT A$,B,C,D
55  T1=T1+D
60  GO TO 10
100 PRINT
110 PRINT;TAB(15);"TOTAL",,T1
120 DATA A,2,4
130 DATA B,3,6
140 DATA C,4,8
150 DATA D,5,10
160 DATA EXIT,0,0
170 END
```

```
RUN
CH4D     08:41 AM            28-MAR-81
A              2              4              8
B              3              6              18
C              4              8              32
D              5              10             50

                TOTAL                        108
```

Problem 5

If the programmer happens to be an experienced typist, he may make an error that a nontypist would not make. This type of error is extremely difficult to locate. What error was made in the program shown below?

```
LIST
CH4E     09 :36  PM              14-MAR-81
10  READ A,B,C
15  IF A=-9 GO TO 95
20  D=B*A
25  PRINT;TAB(10);
30  PRINT USING "##",A;
35  PRINT ;TAB(25);
40  PRINT USING ".##",B;
45  PRINT ;TAB(40);
50  PRINT USING "###",C;
55  PRINT;TAB(55);
60  PRINT USING "##.##",D
65  GO TO 10
70  DATA 24,.07,135
75  DATA 36,.15,2L2
80  DATA 17,.05,147
85  DATA 25,.07,118
90  DATA -9,0,0
95  END

RUN
CH4E     09:36  PM              14-MAR-81
              24                  .07            135             1.68
%DATA FORMAT ERROR AT LINE 10
```

If the programmer had been using lower-case letters, he might have spent a long time in locating the error. Because it was typed in capital letters and the error had to be in the second DATA statement, the programmer easily located his error. He had typed an "L" instead of a "1" in Statement 75. He corrected that error and obtained the following printout, which still contained an error message, as shown below:

```
RUN
CH4E     09:37  PM              14-MAR-81
              24                  .07            135             1.68
              36                  .15            212             5.40
              17                  .05            147             0.85
%DATA FORMAT ERROR AT LINE 10
```

This error is more difficult to locate, but the programmer knew it had to be in the fourth DATA statement. Finally he guessed that he had typed the letter "O" rather than the numeral zero. After Statement 85 was changed, the program ran correctly.

```
RUN
CH4E     09:39 PM            14-MAR-81
              24               .07            135             1.68
              36               .15            212             5.40
              17               .05            147             0.85
              25               .07            118             1.75
```

Problem 6

The problem shown below contains a very common error.

```
LIST
CH4F     10:20 PM            14-MAR-81
5    N=0
10   READ N$,A
15   IF N$="EXIT" GO TO 40
20   N=N+A
25   PRINT;TAB(10);N$;TAB(30);
30   PRINT USING "##.##",A
35   GO TO 10
40   PRINT
45   PRINT;TAB(10);"TOTAL";TAB(29);
50   PRINT USING "###.##",N
55   DATA JOHNSON,28.76
60   DATA  MOORE,97.32
65   DATA NELSON,33,27
70   DATA SMITH,47.62
75   DATA EXIT,0
80   END
```

```
RUN
CH4F     10:20 PM            14-MAR-81
              JOHNSON               28.76
              MOORE                 97.32
              NELSON                33.00
%DATA FORMAT ERROR AT LINE 10
```

The programmer knew the error had to be in the fourth data statement because the computer had printed out three lines of data. After spending quite awhile trying to locate the error and not finding it, he looked at the third statement, Statement 65. In Statement 65, he had placed a comma where a decimal should have been. The computer, therefore, found three fields instead of two. It used the first two to fill fields N$ and A. Because the next storage location to be filled is for string data and the third field in Statement 65 is numeric, the error message was printed. After Statement 65 was changed, the program printed out properly, as shown below.

```
RUN
CH4F      10:21 PM          14-MAR-81
              JOHNSON                  28.76
              MOORE                    97.32
              NELSON                   33.27
              SMITH                    47.62

              TOTAL                   206.97
```

Problem 7

The program shown below contains an error that appears in many programs. What is the error and how is it to be corrected?

```
LIST
CH4G      09:45 AM          06-APR-81
5   N=0
10  READ A,B,C
15  IF A=-9 GO TO 60
20  N=N+C
25  PRINT;TAB(10);
30  PRINT USING "###.##",A;
35  PRINT;TAB(30);
40  PRINT USING "##.##",B;
45  PRINT;TAB(50);
50  PRINT USING "$###",C
55  GO TO 10
60  T=N/3
63  PRINT
65  PRINT;TAB(30);"AVERAGE";TAB(50);"$";T
75  DATA 121.85,22.57,121
80  DATA 217.63,17.63,217
90  DATA 312.51,81.72,315
100 DATA -9,0,0
105 END
```

```
RUN
CH4G      09:45 AM          06-APR-81
              121.85              22.57              $121
              217.63              17.63              $217
              312.51              81.72              $315

                                  AVERAGE            $ 217.667
```

The programmer realized that the average of a money amount should not be printed with three decimal places. Also, the programmer did not want a space after the dollar sign in the total line. The computer always leaves a space for the minus sign in PRINT statements, but does not leave a space when a PRINT USING statement is used. To correct both of these errors, the programmer rewrote Statement 65 and added Statement 67, a PRINT USING statement.

```
65  PRINT;TAB(30);"AVERAGE";TAB(50);
67  PRINT USING "$###.##",T
```

When the program was rerun, the printout appeared correctly, as shown below.

```
RUN
CH4G      09:46 AM           06-APR-81
            121.85                22.57                $121
            217.63                17.63                $217
            312.51                81.72                $315

                                  AVERAGE              $217.67
```

SUMMARY

1. To output numeric data that is right-justified, a PRINT USING statement is used.
2. The PRINT USING statement uses a # sign to indicate how many digits in the statement and in what format.

   a. 30 PRINT USING "##.##",B prints out:
   ```
   12.76
    1.86
     .33
   11.95
   ```

   b. 30 PRINT USING "##",C prints out:
   ```
   17
    5
   32
    6
   ```

   c. 30 PRINT USING ".##",L prints out:
   ```
   .11
   .05
   .53
   .09
   ```
3. There must be a comma after the last quote mark in the PRINT USING statement.
4. The PRINT command, which justifies to the left, and the

PRINT USING command, which justifies to the right, cannot be used in the same statement.

5. The TAB function cannot be included in a PRINT USING statement.
6. Both left- and right-justified material may be printed out on the same line by using both PRINT and PRINT USING statements followed by semi-colons.

```
60  PRINT D$;TAB(38);
64  PRINT USING "##",N;
68  PRINT;TAB(61);
72  PRINT USING "####.##",S
```

7. The line is indented eight spaces when the TAB key is depressed.
8. The subtraction operator is "–".
9. The multiplication operator is "*".
10. The division operator is "/".
11. The symbol to raise to a power is "**", as in B**5, or "∧", as in B∧5, or "↑", as in B↑5.
12. The hierarchy of arithmetic operations is listed below.
    a. All operations within the parentheses are calculated first. If there are parentheses within parentheses, the computer works from the inside out.
    b. All exponentiation calculations are performed next.
    c. Multiplication or division operations are then performed in the order in which they appear from left to right.
    d. Lastly, addition or subtraction operations are executed in the order in which they appear from left to right.
13. A counter can be used in programming. An example would be:

```
10  Y=Y+1.
```

SELF TEST

TRUE AND FALSE

1. The following is a valid statement.

```
30  PRINT USING "#.##" B
```

2. When the TAB key is depressed, the line is indented 18 spaces.
3. The following is a valid statement.

```
30  PRINT;TAB(10);B;TAB(30);PRINT USING "##",C
```

4. The following is a valid statement.

```
35  PRINT USING "######",B$
```

5. The first operation the computer will perform in a math statement is that which is inside the parentheses.
6. The computer performs division before multiplication.
7. To raise B to the A power, the following statement could be used:

```
30  C = B ** A
```

SHORT ANSWER

8. What symbols in BASIC are used to denote the following?
   a. Addition
   b. Subtraction
   c. Multiplication
   d. Division
9. What statement would store an answer in B and would tell the computer to multiply C times D, raise that answer to the F power, add to that answer the number 10, and then divide that answer by 4?
10. What PRINT statements would start a customer name in Column 10, account number in Column 30, amount of sale in Column 50, and balance in Column 60? Amounts are to be right-justified.

Customer	Acct No	Amt of Sale	Balance
B. A. Johnson	BA37-5	XXXX.XX	XXXXX.XX

11. List the hierarchy of arithmetic operations.

12. What statement (10) using the counter N would count customers?
13. What statement (30) would store sales (S) in the total counter (S1)?

ASSIGNMENTS

1. A flowchart, a computer listing, and a printout for the following problem should be prepared. Dollar signs should not appear in the data lines but should appear in the total line.

   Mrs. Hobart's electrical bills for last year were as follows:

   January, $14; February, $13.50; March, $12.75; April, $11.24; May, $9.99; June, $7.32; July, $7.66; August, $7.25; September, $7.75; October, $8.59; November, $9.75; and December, $13.87.

   a. Print out all of the data.
      - The month is to be printed starting in Column 20, the amount of the bill in Column 35.
      - The amount is to be right-justified.

   b. The printer is to print a blank line after printing the body of the report and print, starting at Column 11, the following: AVERAGE MONTHLY BILL IS. The answer, including a dollar sign, is to be printed at Column 40. The printer is to print another blank line and then at Column 11, the following: AVERAGE DAILY AMOUNT IS (use 365 days in the math statement). The answer, including a dollar sign, is to be printed at Column 40.

2. A flowchart, a computer listing, and a printout for the following problem should be prepared.

   The following members of the bowling team posted the scores listed below. What were their averages for the nine lines? Also, print the team bowling average.

Bob Johnson	198	217	183	195	202	175	182	209	215	XXX
Bill Avery	165	172	159	151	162	179	154	191	180	XXX
Jack Nelson	179	201	183	172	191	195	168	179	192	XXX
Jim Thompson	199	191	189	210	201	185	193	189	207	XXX
Randy Thomas	175	182	163	178	185	171	169	181	179	XXX

TEAM AVERAGE XXX

Their names, all of their scores, and their averages (in the last column) should be printed out. The spacing must be determined by the programmer.

3. A flowchart, a computer listing, and a printout for the following problem should be prepared. Titles should not be printed.

   The 49ers baseball team played the Spartans yesterday in a league game. The 49er line-up appears below, along with the times at bat and the number of hits. The computer is to calculate the batting percentage to three decimal places for each member. The percentage is found by dividing the number of hits by the number of times at bat. The team batting average should also be computed. The program is to be printed out as shown below, with the four fields in the detail lines beginning in Columns 13, 31, 42, and 53.

```
                    49ers vs Spartans

                      49er Line-up
                          and
                   Batting Statistics

                                  Times     Batting
   Player            Hits         At Bat   Percentage

  Almquist             1            5         X.XXX
  Jacobson             2            5         X.XXX
  Rawlings             2            4         X.XXX
  Harrison             3            5         X.XXX
  Moore                1            4         X.XXX
  Garcia               2            5         X.XXX
  Smith                1            4         X.XXX
  Franks               1            5         X.XXX
  Pickard              1            3         X.XXX
  Barnes               1            1         X.XXX
  Johnson              1            2         X.XXX

  TEAM BATTING AVE.                           X.XXX
```

5

TITLES AND TOTALS

In this chapter the following material will be covered.

A. The printing of neatly arranged reports with headings, columnar titles, and total lines
B. Additional uses of the PRINT USING statement

To secure centered headings, columnar titles, and columns in the printout, the programmer should use the principles in the following section.

CENTERING

Because of the limited number of horizontal spaces on the CRT screen, it is recommended that 68 spaces be assumed. Some systems allow a different number of spaces; but in this text, the principle of centering will be explained using a 68-space line.

Many programmers seem to have difficulty trying to figure out where to start columns, columnar titles, and headings. The problem in Figure 5-1 will be used to show where to place columns and headings.

FIGURE 5-1

Centering Problem

```
                    Johnson and Sons

                       Appliances

     Salesman               Dept        Sales       Commissions

Wilson, Bill                 A1        1234.67        308.67
Nelson, Frank                B2        2378.95        594.74
Eagles, Joe                  C3        1835.64        458.91
Sorenson, George             D5        2838.96        709.74
```

Step 1. There are 16 letters and spaces in the title. That number should be subtracted from the number available (68), and the number of spaces remaining are 52. As there should be an equal number of spaces on both sides of the title, the spaces remaining (52) are divided by 2 and the answer (26) is the number of blank spaces that should be left on each side of the title. Therefore, the title should start at Column 27.

```
10  PRINT;TAB(27);"JOHNSON AND SONS"
```

Step 2. There are 10 letters and spaces in the second line of the title. That number should be subtracted from the total spaces available (68). The answer (58) is divided by 2. That answer (29) is the number of blank spaces left on each side of that line of the title. The tab should be set at 30.

```
15  PRINT;TAB(30);"APPLIANCES"
```

Step 3. As the columns must be equally spaced and the columnar titles centered over the columns, the total number of characters in all columns are then computed.

a. A diagram of the columns may be plotted in a rectangle, as shown below.

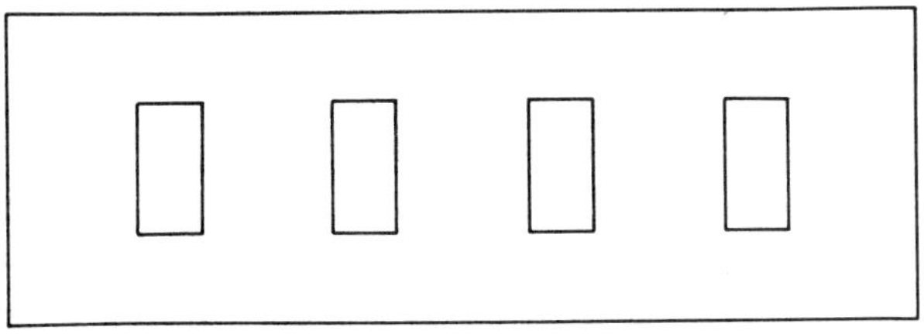

b. The longest line in each column should be counted. This number will be the column width. The number of characters in the column should be placed in the corresponding column. If column titles are abnormally long, then the width of the column title should be counted rather than the width of the column.

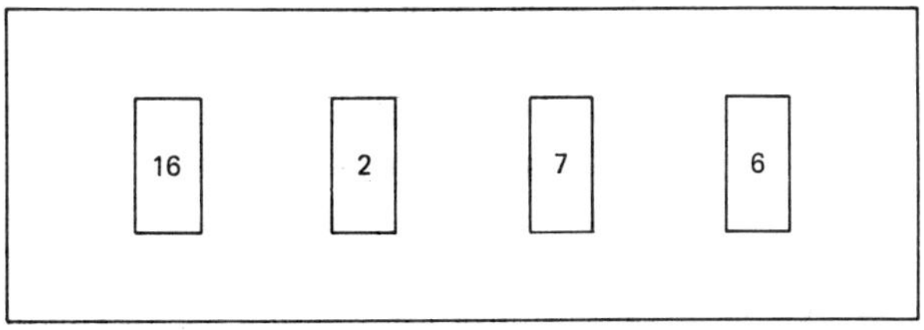

c. The number of characters in the columns should be added together, as shown below.

16 + 2 + 7 + 6 = 31

d. That answer (31) should be subtracted from the number of spaces available (68). The answer is 37. Thirty-seven is the number of spaces left for the columns of spaces. There is always one more column of spaces than there are columns of characters. There are 4 columns of characters, so there are 5 columns of spaces.

e. Now the spaces remaining (37) should be divided by 5 and the number of spaces between the columns will be 7, with 2 left over. In this problem it is logical to add the extra spaces to the outside columns of spaces.

f. The tabs are now established for the columns.

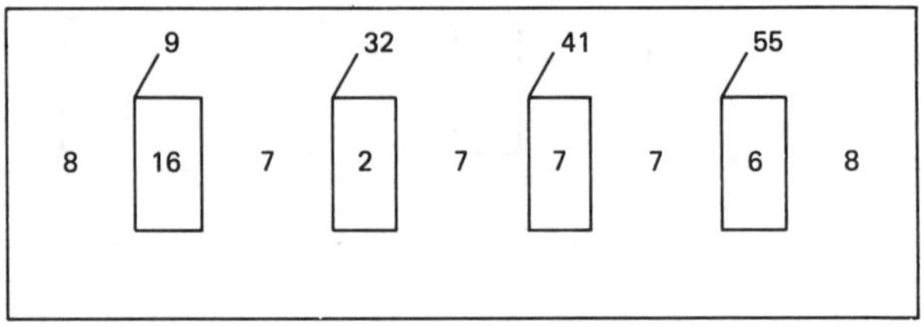

Step 4. In determining where to start columnar titles, another rule applies. If the title is wider than the column, the number of characters in the column should be subtracted from the number of characters in the title. That number is then divided by 2 and the operator should back up that number of spaces to find the proper place to begin the title. This is true of two of the columnar titles in this problem, the second and the fourth.

a. In Column 2 the title "Dept" is 4 spaces wide and the column is only 2 spaces wide. Applying the rule, 2 should be subtracted from 4 and the answer (2) divided by 2. The column started at 32, so by backing up from the beginning of the column the 1 space found by dividing 2 by 2, "Dept" will start at Column 31.

b. The columnar title for the fourth column "Commissions" is 11 spaces wide. The number of spaces in the column (6) should be subtracted from 11 and the answer divided by 2. The answer is an uneven number. The operator should always back up 1 for the odd space or he never should. In this book, the extra space will not be used. The column starts at 55, so by backing up 2 spaces, the word "Commissions" will be placed at Column 53.

Step 5. If the columns are wider than the titles, the number of characters in the title are subtracted from the number of characters in the columns. The answer is divided by 2 and that number is added to the beginning of the column to determine where the title begins.

a. Column 1 is 16 spaces wide and its columnar title is 8 spaces wide. The 8 should be subtracted from 16. That answer (8) is divided by 2 and the answer (4) is added to the beginning of the column (9), so the title, "Salesman," starts at Column 13.

b. In the third column the title "Sales" is 5 spaces wide and the column is 7 spaces wide. The operator should subtract 5 from 7 and divide the answer (2) by 2. That answer (1) should be added to the beginning of the column (41), and the title, "Sales", will begin at 42.

The remaining statements of the program are listed below.

```
17  PRINT
19  PRINT
21  PRINT;TAB(13);"SALESMAN";TAB(31);"DEPT";TAB(42);"SALES";TAB(53);
23  PRINT;"COMMISSIONS"
25  PRINT
27  READ S$,D$,S1,C1
30  IF S$ = "EXIT" GO TO 65
35  PRINT;TAB(9);S$;TAB(32);D$;TAB(41);
40  PRINT USING "####.##        ###.##",S1,C1
45  GO TO 27
50  DATA "WILSON, BILL",A1,1234.67,308.67
52  DATA "NELSON, FRANK",B2,2378.95,594.74
54  DATA "EAGLES, JOE",C3,1835.64,458.91
56  DATA "SORENSON, GEORGE",D5,2838.96,709.74
58  DATA EXIT,0,0,0
65  END
```

PROBLEM 5-1

The example problem used in this chapter is shown in Figure 5-2.

To aid in plotting the flowchart for this problem, the following facts are established: There are three lines in the heading, a blank line between the main heading and subheading, no blank lines between subheadings, two blank lines between subheading and columnar headings, and one blank line between columnar headings and the body of the report. The body of the report is single-spaced. Each year is to be totaled, which creates the need for six total counters—T1, T2, T3, T4, T5, and T6. The totals for each year are to be divided by 12 to find the average monthly sales. The variables for the averages will be A1, A2, A3, A4, A5, and A6. The total of the sales for the six years is to be divided by 6 to find the average yearly sales. The variables for the fields will be M$ for the months, Y1 for 1971 sales, Y2 for 1972 sales, Y3 for 1973 sales, Y4 for 1974 sales, Y5 for 1975 sales, and Y6 for 1976 sales. The flowchart for this problem appears in Figure 5-3.

FIGURE 5-2

Problem 5-1

THE GEORGIA COMPANY

Monthly Sales in Dollars
1971 - 1976

	1971	1972	1973	1974	1975	1976
January	20222	21543	21876	22931	23171	23536
February	25176	26325	27321	26976	27473	27853
March	31832	31943	43187	32876	33276	33953
April	33117	33400	33760	34176	34231	34957
May	38132	39541	39726	40153	40117	41325
June	36325	36132	36815	36543	32713	37431
July	39532	40132	39971	40732	41655	41327
August	40723	40137	41315	41417	42935	42131
September	38327	38415	38913	38950	40117	40231
October	31543	32115	32314	32415	32713	33154
November	27325	27500	27936	28137	28476	28513
December	25476	25913	26137	26431	26715	26813
Total	387730	393096	409271	401737	403592	411224

Average Monthly Sales in Dollars

1971	32310.80
1972	32758.00
1973	34105.90
1974	33478.10
1975	33632.70
1976	34268.70

Yearly Average for Period 1971 - 1976 Is $401108.33

The REM statements will be done first, as shown below.

```
10  REM THIS PROBLEM LISTS THE MONTHLY SALES OF THE GEORGIA
12  REM COMPANY BY YEARS FROM 1971 THROUGH 1976.  THE TOTAL
14  REM SALES FOR THE YEAR ARE LISTED, AS WELL AS THE AVERAGE
16  REM MONTHLY SALES FOR EACH YEAR AND THE AVERAGE YEARLY
18  REM SALES FOR THIS PERIOD.
20  REM M$=MONTHS, THE TOTAL COUNTERS FOR THE MONTHLY SALES
22  REM ARE T1=1971, T2=1972, T3=1973, T4=1974,T5=1975,
24  REM T6=1976.  THE VARIABLES ARE Y1 FOR 1971 SALES, Y2 FOR
26  REM 1972 SALES, Y3 FOR 1973 SALES, Y4 FOR 1974 SALES, Y5
28  REM FOR 1975 SALES, AND Y6 FOR 1976 SALES.  THE TOTAL
```

FIGURE 5-3

Flowchart for Problem 5-1

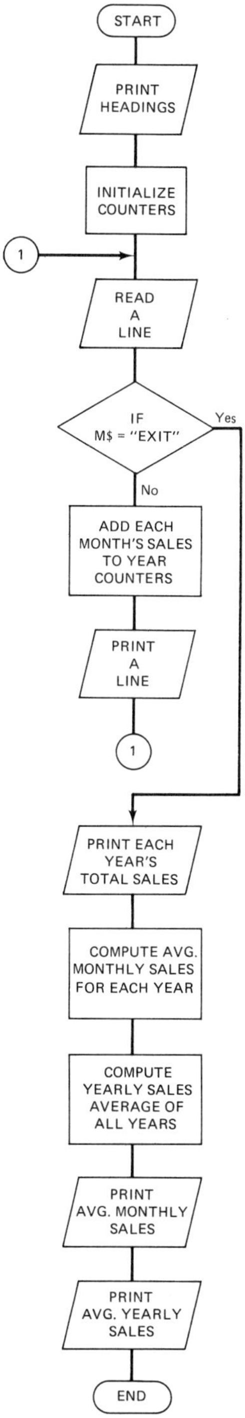

```
30  REM COUNTERS FOR THE AVERAGE MONTHLY SALES WILL BE--
32  REM A1=1971,A2=1972,A3=1973,A4=1974,A5=1975,A6=1976.
34  REM YEARLY AVERAGE WILL BE Y.
```

The titles are to be printed next. The computer never leaves spaces between the listing of the RUN command and the printout. Because it is desirable to have spaces before the printout, the next two statements will be PRINT statements that will leave two blank lines before the first line of the heading.

```
36  PRINT
38  PRINT
```

HEADINGS

In determining where to start the first line of the heading, the operator should follow the guidelines explained in the centering section. The characters in the heading should be counted (19) and subtracted from the 68 spaces available. Because half the spaces left over must go on one side and half on the other, the answer must be divided by 2. The answer is 24, so the title starts in Column 25. There are 24 characters in the second line, so 24 should be subtracted from 68 and the answer divided by 2. The second line will start in Column 23. There are 11 characters in the third line, so 11 should be subtracted from 68 and the answer divided by 2. The third line starts in Column 29. In the columnar title line, 1971 starts in Column 19.

```
40  PRINT;TAB(25);"THE GEORGIA COMPANY"
41  PRINT
42  PRINT;TAB(23);"MONTHLY SALES IN DOLLARS"
43  PRINT;TAB(29);"1971 - 1976"
44  PRINT
45  PRINT
46  PRINT;TAB(19);"1971     1972     1973     1974     1975     1976"
47  PRINT
```

The PRINT statement in Statement 47 causes a blank line after the columnar headings. The PRINT line should not appear after the READ statement. In this problem if the PRINT statement appeared after the READ statement, the report would be double-spaced.

THE IF TEST

In previous chapters, a trailer constant was used in the first field of the last DATA statement and the remaining fields were filled with zeros. There is an easier way to use trailer constants. If only the first field of a DATA statement is read in one READ statement, the decision statement would ask if that one variable is equal to the trailer constant. If the variable is not equal to the trailer constant, the remaining fields are read in a following READ statement. That is the way it will be done in this problem.

```
54  READ M$
57  IF M$="EXIT" GO TO 85
60  READ Y1,Y2,Y3,Y4,Y5,Y6
```

ADDING TO COUNTERS

The year counters are initialized in Statements 48 through 53, and Statements 62 through 72 are used to add each month's sales to these counters.

```
48  T1 = 0              62  T1 = T1 + Y1
49  T2 = 0              64  T2 = T2 + Y2
50  T3 = 0              66  T3 = T3 + Y3
51  T4 = 0              68  T4 = T4 + Y4
52  T5 = 0              70  T5 = T5 + Y5
53  T6 = 0              72  T6 = T6 + Y6
```

When a number is added to a counter, the original number in the counter is replaced by the sum of the original number plus whatever is added to it, as is explained in Chapter 3.

A NEW PRINT USING STATEMENT[1]

The following statements are the print statements for printing a line of data. There is a way of using the PRINT USING statement that is ideally

[1] Appendix B contains information on PRINT USING statements used on systems other than the PDP-11.

suited to this program and that is demonstrated below. Several field formats can be printed with spaces in between, as shown in Statements 80 and 81.[2]

```
76  PRINT;TAB(7);M$;TAB(19);
80  PRINT USING "#####   #####   #####   #####",Y1,Y2,Y3,Y4;
81  PRINT USING "   #####   #####",Y5,Y6
84  GO TO 54
85  PRINT
```

TOTALS

As was explained in Chapter 4, the number sign (#) is used in a PRINT USING statement to format numbers and to right-justify them. Statement 86 causes the word TOTAL to be printed, and the semi-colon following the tab position commands the computer to wait for further instructions. These instructions are given in Statements 88 and 89, which print the totals on the same line with the word TOTAL.

```
86  PRINT;TAB(7);"TOTAL";TAB(18);
88  PRINT USING "######  ######  ######  ######",T1,T2,T3,T4;
89  PRINT USING "  ######  ######",T5,T6
```

COMPUTING AND PRINTING AVERAGES

Next, several statements are needed to do the computations to arrive at the average monthly sales and the yearly average. Each time the computer reads a line, the fields Y1 through Y6 are added to the appropriate counters, T1 through T6, which are the years' total counters. The variables for the average monthly sales are A1, A2, A3, A4, A5, and A6. The computer is to divide the year's total sales by 12 and store it in the average monthly sales variable.

```
94  A1 = T1/12
96  A2 = T2/12
98  A3 = T3/12
100 A4 = T4/12
102 A5 = T5/12
104 A6 = T6/12
```

[2] The note on page 55 pertains to the TRS-80.

To secure the average yearly sales, the totals of each year's sales are added together, divided by 6, and stored in Y.

```
106 Y = (T1+T2+T3+T4+T5+T6)/6
```

If the parentheses had not been placed around the addition, the computer would have divided T6 by 6 first and then added the other variables to that answer.

The PRINT statements to print out the average monthly sales and the average yearly sales are shown below.

```
108 PRINT;TAB(7);"AVERAGE MONTHLY SALES IN DOLLARS"
109 PRINT
110 PRINT;TAB(15);"1971      ";
112 PRINT USING "#####.##",A1
114 PRINT;TAB(15);"1972      ";
116 PRINT USING "#####.##",A2
118 PRINT;TAB(15);"1973      ";
120 PRINT USING "#####.##",A3
122 PRINT;TAB(15);"1974      ";
124 PRINT USING "#####.##",A4
126 PRINT;TAB(15);"1975      ";
128 PRINT USING "#####.##",A5
130 PRINT;TAB(15);"1976      ";
132 PRINT USING "#####.##",A6
137 PRINT
139 PRINT;TAB(7);"YEARLY AVERAGE FOR PERIOD 1971 - 1976 IS $";
141 PRINT USING "######.##",Y
150 DATA JANUARY,20222,21543,21876,22931,23171,23536
152 DATA FEBRUARY,25176,26325,27321,26976,27473,27853
154 DATA MARCH,31832,31943,43187,32876,33276,33953
156 DATA APRIL,33117,33400,33760,34176,34231,34957
158 DATA MAY,38132,39541,39726,40153,40117,41325
160 DATA JUNE,36325,36132,36815,36543,32713,37431
162 DATA JULY,39532,40132,39971,40732,41655,41327
164 DATA AUGUST,40723,40137,41315,41417,42935,42131
166 DATA SEPTEMBER,38327,38415,38913,38950,40117,40231
168 DATA OCTOBER,31543,32115,32314,32415,32713,33154
170 DATA NOVEMBER,27325,27500,27936,28137,28476,28513
172 DATA DECEMBER,25476,25913,26137,26431,26715,26813
174 DATA EXIT
176 END
```

The complete listing and printout of the sample problem are found below.

```
LIST
GRGIA  10:53 PM          26-Jan-81
10  REM THIS PROBLEM LISTS THE MONTHLY SALES OF THE GEORGIA
12  REM COMPANY BY YEARS FROM 1971 THROUGH 1976.  THE TOTAL
14  REM SALES FOR THE YEAR ARE LISTED, AS WELL AS THE AVERAGE
16  REM MONTHLY SALES FOR EACH YEAR AND THE AVERAGE YEARLY
18  REM SALES FOR THIS PERIOD.
20  REM M$=MONTHS, THE TOTAL COUNTERS  FOR THE MONTHLY SALES
22  REM ARE T1=1971, T2=1972, T3=1973, T4=1974, T5=1975,
24  REM T6=1976.  THE VARIABLES ARE Y1 FOR 1971 SALES, Y2 FOR
26  REM 1972 SALES, Y3 FOR 1973 SALES, Y4 FOR 1974 SALES, Y5
28  REM FOR 1975 SALES, AND Y6 FOR 1976 SALES.  THE TOTAL
30  REM COUNTERS  FOR THE AVERAGE MONTHLY SALES WILL BE--
32  REM A1=1971,A2=1972,A3=1973,A4=1974,A5=1975,A6=1976.
34  REM YEARLY AVERAGE WILL BE Y.
36  PRINT
38  PRINT
40  PRINT;TAB(25);"THE GEORGIA COMPANY"
41  PRINT
42  PRINT;TAB(23);"MONTHLY SALES IN DOLLARS"
43  PRINT;TAB(29);"1971 - 1976"
44  PRINT
45  PRINT
46  PRINT;TAB(19);"1971     1972     1973     1974     1975     1976"
47  PRINT
48  T1 = 0
49  T2 = 0
50  T3 = 0
51  T4 = 0
52  T5 = 0
53  T6 = 0
54  READ M$
57  IF M$="EXIT" GO TO 85
60  READ Y1,Y2,Y3,Y4,Y5,Y6
62  T1 = T1 + Y1
64  T2 = T2 + Y2
66  T3 = T3 + Y3
68  T4 = T4 + Y4
70  T5 = T5 + Y5
72  T6 = T6 + Y6
76  PRINT;TAB(7);M$;TAB(19);
80  PRINT USING "#####    #####    #####    #####",Y1,Y2,Y3,Y4;
81  PRINT USING "    #####    #####",Y5,Y6
84  GO TO 54
```

```
85  PRINT
86  PRINT;TAB(7);"TOTAL";TAB(18);
88  PRINT USING "######  ######  ######  ######",T1,T2,T3,T4;
89  PRINT USING "  ######  ######",T5,T6
90  PRINT
94  A1 = T1/12
96  A2 = T2/12
98  A3 = T3/12
100 A4 = T4/12
102 A5 = T5/12
104 A6 = T6/12
106 Y = (T1+T2+T3+T4+T5+T6)/6
108 PRINT;TAB(7);"AVERAGE MONTHLY SALES IN DOLLARS"
109 PRINT
110 PRINT;TAB(15);"1971      ";
112 PRINT USING "#####.##",A1
114 PRINT;TAB(15);"1972      ";
116 PRINT USING "#####.##",A2
118 PRINT;TAB(15);"1973      ";
120 PRINT USING "#####.##",A3
122 PRINT;TAB(15);"1974      ";
124 PRINT USING "#####.##",A4
126 PRINT;TAB(15);"1975      ";
128 PRINT USING "#####.##",A5
130 PRINT;TAB(15);"1976      ";
132 PRINT USING "#####.##",A6
137 PRINT
139 PRINT;TAB(7);"YEARLY AVERAGE FOR PERIOD 1971 - 1976 IS $";
141 PRINT USING "######.##",Y
150 DATA JANUARY,20222,21543,21876,22931,23171,23536
152 DATA FEBRUARY,25176,26325,27321,26976,27473,27853
154 DATA MARCH,31832,31943,43187,32876,33276,33953
156 DATA APRIL,33117,33400,33760,34176,34231,34957
158 DATA MAY,38132,39541,39726,40153,40117,41325
160 DATA JUNE,36325,36132,36815,36543,32713,37431
162 DATA JULY,39532,40132,39971,40732,41655,41327
164 DATA AUGUST,40723,40137,41315,41417,42935,42131
166 DATA SEPTEMBER,38327,38415,38913,38950,40117,40231
168 DATA OCTOBER,31543,32115,32314,32415,32713,33154
170 DATA NOVEMBER,27325,27500,27936,28137,28476,28513
172 DATA DECEMBER,25476,25913,26137,26431,26715,26813
174 DATA EXIT
176 END

READY

RUN
```

FIGURE 5-4

Printout of Problem 5-1

```
GRGIA     10:54 PM       26-Jan-81


                          THE GEORGIA COMPANY

                        MONTHLY SALES IN DOLLARS
                              1971 - 1976


                1971    1972    1973    1974    1975    1976

JANUARY         20222   21543   21876   22931   23171   23536
FEBRUARY        25176   26325   27321   26976   27473   27853
MARCH           31832   31943   43187   32876   33276   33953
APRIL           33117   33400   33760   34176   34231   34957
MAY             38132   39541   39726   40153   40117   41325
JUNE            36325   36132   36815   36543   32713   37431
JULY            39532   40132   39971   40732   41655   41327
AUGUST          40723   40137   41315   41417   42935   42131
SEPTEMBER       38327   38415   38913   38950   40117   40231
OCTOBER         31543   32115   32314   32415   32713   33154
NOVEMBER        27325   27500   27936   28137   28476   28513
DECEMBER        25476   25913   26137   26431   26715   26813

TOTAL          387730  393096  409271  401737  403592  411224

AVERAGE MONTHLY SALES IN DOLLARS

        1971     32310.80
        1972     32758.00
        1973     34105.90
        1974     33478.10
        1975     33632.70
        1976     34268.70

YEARLY AVERAGE FOR PERIOD 1971 - 1976 IS $401108.33
```

"!" IN THE PRINT USING STATEMENT[3]

For emphasis, a programmer might place asterisks after totals or other items, as in the example shown below.

```
TOTAL SALES $13456.78*
```

[3] The "!" is used on the PDP-11 and the TRS-80.

The "!" in the PRINT USING statement can be used to format one column of alphanumeric data. The field formatted (in this case the "*") must be placed in quotes. If more than one asterisk is desired, one "!" is used for each asterisk and each asterisk is placed in quotes.

```
30  PRINT USING "#####.##!",T1,"*"
```

or

```
30  PRINT USING "#####.##!!",T1,"*","*"
```

Another way of solving this problem would be to use another print statement for the asterisks, as shown below.

```
30  PRINT USING "#####.##",T1;
32  PRINT "*"   or   32  PRINT "**"
```

Spacing can be done before and after a field in the PRINT USING statement. If two spaces were desired after a field and before three plus signs, the following statements will accomplish the following spacing:

```
20  PRINT;TAB(20);"TOTAL SALES $";
25  PRINT USING "###.##  !!!",B,"+","+","+"
```

The printout would be:

```
TOTAL SALES $123.45  +++
```

Any character or characters may be placed within quotes in the PRINT USING statement between the fields of number signs and the printout will appear exactly as given within the quotes. An example of the PRINT USING statement and the printout are shown below.

```
100 PRINT USING "AGE ##  NET WORTH  $###,###",A,N

AGE 55  NET WORTH  $800,000
```

Also, the dollar sign may be placed in a unique manner in the PRINT USING statement. It can be used literally before any or all of the variables. The comma may be placed within the field to designate thousands if no space is left around the comma. An example is shown below.

```
20  PRINT USING "      $##       ###        $#,###.##",N,M,S

         $71       376       $3,987.65
```

UNDERFORMATTING

In the following program if A = 114.725, the computer will round the number to 114.73. If A = 1134.72, the computer will place a "%" before the number and will not line the number up with the other numbers. In other words, the "%" in the output designates that the field was underformatted, not leaving enough room for the data.

```
10  READ A
12  IF A = -9 GO TO 40
15  PRINT USING "###.##",A
20  GO TO 10
25  DATA 114.725,23.25,195.777,1134.72,-9
40  END
```

The output will appear as follows.

```
RUN
UNDER      04:45 PM          01-MAR-81
 114.73
  23.25
 195.78
 % 1134.72
```

DEBUGGING THE PROGRAM

In Chapter 4, the subject of debugging a program was discussed because even the most experienced programmer makes errors. In this chapter more debugging will be done. The next section will demonstrate the errors made by a programmer when he first ran the program for Problem 5-1. Needless to say, he was flabbergasted at the output shown in Figure 5-5.

At first glance, it appeared that the title and columnar titles were correct. Experience had taught the programmer two things about the way data had printed out. One of these is that a semi-colon probably

FIGURE 5-5

Incorrect Output of Problem 5-1

```
                         THE GEORGIA COMPANY

                       MONTHLY SALES IN DOLLARS
                              1971 - 1976


                1971     1972     1973     1974     1975     1976

      JANUARY
 % 20222     % 21543     % 21876     % 22931     % 23171     % 23536
      FEBRUARY
 % 25176     % 26325     % 27321     % 26976     % 27473     % 27853
      MARCH
 % 31832     % 31943     % 43187     % 32876     % 33276     % 33953
      APRIL
 % 33117     % 33400     % 33760     % 43176     % 34231     % 34957
      MAY
 % 38132     % 39541     % 39726     % 40153     % 40117     % 41325
      JUNE
 % 36325     % 36132     % 36815     % 36543     % 32713     % 37431
      JULY
 % 39532     % 40132     % 39971     % 40732     % 41655     % 41327
      AUGUST
 % 40723     % 40137     % 41315     % 41417     % 42935     % 42131
      SEPTEMBER
 % 38327     % 38415     % 38913     % 38950     % 40117     % 40231
      OCTOBER
 % 31543     % 32115     % 32314     % 32415     % 32713     % 33154
      NOVEMBER
 % 27325     % 27500     % 27936     % 28137     % 28476     % 28513
      DECEMBER
 % 25476     % 25913     % 26137     % 26431     % 26715     % 26813
      TOTAL          316473   347254   368850   380538   371671   239906

      AVERAGE MONTHLY SALES IN DOLLARS
                1971      32310.80
                1972 ;
32758.00
                1973      34105.90
                1974      33478.10
                1975      33632.67
                1976      34268.67

      YEARLY AVERAGE FOR PERIOD 1971 - 1976 IS $% 401108.33
```

was left off the end of a print statement, leaving two lines where there is supposed to be one. The other point is that every time there is a "%" in the output, it signifies that the field was underformatted—not enough room was specified for the data.

Looking at his rough-coded program (the handwritten copy from which he typed at the terminal), the programmer noticed that the PRINT statements that printed out the data were 76, 80, and 81. The computer can be asked to list specific lines, one line at a time. By typing LIST 76, the programmer commands the computer to print out that line as it was programmed. The lines can be specified all at one time by writing LIST 76,80,81. The computer then would print out the three lines as programmed. Another way, especially if many statements are involved, is to write LIST 76-81. The computer would print out lines 76 through 81.

In this problem the programmer used the last method; he typed LIST 76-81. The computer printed out the following lines of the program.

```
GRGIA     09:45 AM          27-Jan-81
76  PRINT;TAB(7);M$
80  PRINT USING "    ####    ####    ####     ####",Y1,Y2,Y3,Y4;
81  PRINT USING "    ####    ####",Y5,Y6
```

Just as the programmer had surmised, he had left out the semi-colon after "M$" and had formatted the fields for only four digits. He was especially exasperated because in his handwritten program he had included the semi-colon and had formatted for five digits.

Although normally an attempt is made to correct all errors at one time, with a long program with many errors it is advisable to correct a few at a time. To correct the errors, the line is retyped correctly, the return is depressed, and the word REPLACE is typed if the program has been saved. If the program has not been saved, just retyping the lines is all that is necessary. The new lines will then replace the old ones.

```
76  PRINT;TAB(7);M$;
80  PRINT USING "    #####    #####    #####     #####",Y1,Y2,Y3,Y4;
81  PRINT USING "    #####    #####",Y5,Y6
REPLACE
```

The programmer then typed the word RUN. The output showed the elimination of some of the errors but also showed that there were still errors in alignment of the columns. Rather than to show the complete program again, just the columnar headings and the first three lines of the data will be shown.

```
               1971    1972    1973    1974    1975    1976

JANUARY    20222    21543    21876    22931    23171    23536
FEBRUARY    25176    26325    27321    26976    27473    27853
MARCH    31832    31943    43187    32876    33276    33953
```

Alignment errors are rather common. In trying to line up columns properly, a person sometimes makes a logic error. The programmer had allowed three spaces after all of the names of the months, forgetting that the names of the months ranged from three letters through nine letters. He can handle that problem by tabbing after "M$" and dropping the initial spaces before the first field in the PRINT USING statement, changing the lines as follows.

```
76  PRINT;TAB(7);M$;TAB(19);
80  PRINT USING "#####    #####    #####    #####",Y1,Y2,Y3,Y4;
81  PRINT USING "    #####    #####",Y5,Y6
```

Fairly certain that the columns were lined up properly, the programmer typed the RUN command. A partial printout follows.

```
               1971    1972    1973    1974    1975    1976

JANUARY       20222   21543   21875   22931   23171   23536
FEBRUARY      25176   26325   27321   26976   27473   27853
MARCH         31832   31943   43187   32876   33276   33953
```

This alignment is not uncommon either. It is rather difficult at times to line up headings. The programmer next commanded the computer to list the subheading statement by typing LIST 46. The computer responded with the following printout.

```
46  PRINT;TAB(19);"1971    1972    1973    1974    1975    1976"
```

The programmer rewrote Statement 46 as shown below.

```
46  PRINT;TAB(19);"1971     1972     1973     1974     1975     1976"
REPLACE
```

When the program was rerun, the columns and subheadings were lined up. But there remained some more problems. As shown in Figure 5-5, there was something wrong with 1972 under Average Monthly Sales in Dollars, and not enough room was allowed in the Yearly Average line. To find the problem, the programmer commanded the computer to list lines 114 and 141.

```
LIST 114,141
GRGIA    09:50 AM          27-Jan-81
114 PRINT;TAB(15);1972       ";
141 PRINT USING "#####.##",Y
```

A quick look at the listing showed that the beginning quote was omitted before 1972 and that there should be six digits left of the decimal point in Statement 141 instead of the five that were formatted.

The programmer also wanted a blank line between December and Total, one after Average Monthly Sales, and two blank lines after Yearly Average so that READY would not follow immediately after the printout. Because consecutive numbers were not used in the statement numbers, there was room to insert PRINT lines where needed. The changed statements are listed below.

```
114 PRINT;TAB(15);"1972      ";
141 PRINT USING "######.##",Y
85  PRINT
109 PRINT
142 PRINT
143 PRINT
57  IF M$="EXIT" GO TO 85
```

The last statement (57) had to be changed because the original IF statement directed the computer to go to 86. If 57 had been left as it was, the computer would never have executed Statement 85. After Statement 57 is changed, the computer executes Statement 85, prints a blank line, and drops down to line 86.

The programmer once more typed RUN, and the computer printed the output shown in Figure 5-4.

One more point. The END statement should always be the last line of the program. If it is anywhere else and the program is saved, everything after the END statement will be purged when the program is called out of auxiliary storage.

SUMMARY

1. The PRINT USING statement can be used to print out more than one field.

```
20  PRINT USING "##.##    #.##     ##",A,B,C
```

2. Alphanumeric data may be formatted in the PRINT USING statement with the "!" symbol. Each "!" symbolizes a one-column field of alphanumeric data. Each column of an alphanumeric field is represented by *one* "!" and each one column of data must be placed in quotes after the PRINT USING statement.

```
20  PRINT USING "##.##!!!",A,"*","*","*"
```

3. Placing alphanumeric data after a PRINT USING statement can also be accomplished by using a PRINT statement.

```
20  PRINT USING "##.##",A;
25  PRINT "***"
```

4. If spacing is desired between headings and data, a PRINT line must be placed before the READ statement. If placed after the READ statement, the PRINT command will affect the spacing of the body of the report.
5. The END statement should be the last statement in the program.
6. The "%" before data in the printout signifies that not enough space was formatted for the data.
7. If a one-line data line prints out as a two-line data line, a comma or semi-colon was left off the end of the PRINT statement.

SELF-TEST

1. What statements, using variable B for the field, would output the following line?

```
Start at Column 20     TOTAL SALES $12376.89 ***
```

2. What statements are required to start a heading at Column 20, allow a blank line, print one subheading at Column 16 and another subheading at Column 19, and allow two blank lines before printing the body of the report? The headings and subheadings to be printed are the following.

C.S.U.L.B.

FOOTBALL SCHEDULE
1981 SEASON

3. What statement will add sales (variable S) to total sales (variable T)?
4. What statements are required to secure the printout shown below? The program is to have a total counter into which sales are added. The columns of data should have six spaces between them.

```
                JOHNSON INC.

            MONTHLY SALES REPORT
               February, 1981


             Salesman      Sales

            Brinkley       160069
            Hendrikson      95763
            Jones          125427
            Murray         108632

            TOTAL SALES   $489891 ***
```

ASSIGNMENTS[4]

1. A flowchart, computer listing, and printout are to be prepared showing a partial list of employees for the KING NUT FACTORY, with their names, weekly gross salaries, amounts deducted for pension, and the amounts deducted for FICA. The pension is 2.75% of the gross salary. The FICA tax is 5.85% of the gross salary. The printout should appear similar to the example below, including the title, subtitle, and columnar headings.

```
                    KING NUT FACTORY

          Record of Weekly Gross Salary,
                 Pensions, and FICA


                  Wkly Gross
   Employee         Salary        Pension       FICA

  Bellman          239.86          X.XX        XX.XX
  Berry            224.54          X.XX        XX.XX
  Cartwright       205.78          X.XX        XX.XX
  Carson           196.93          X.XX        XX.XX
  Dillon           216.45          X.XX        XX.XX
  Doyle            231.78          X.XX        XX.XX
```

[4] The rules for centering explained in this chapter should be applied.

2. The Gillis Department Store wants a printout of all of the departments, their sales in hundreds, and their percentage of total sales, which are $761,100. The percentage of sales is found by dividing the department's sales by the total sales. A flowchart, a computer listing, and a printout should be prepared.

GILLIS DEPARTMENT STORE

Listing of Total Sales
and
Percentage of Sales
First Quarter of 1980

Department	Sales in Hundreds	Percent of Total Sales
A	342	XX.XX
B	210	XX.XX
C	819	XX.XX
D	711	XX.XX
E	1121	XX.XX
F	650	XX.XX
G	1280	XX.XX
H	418	XX.XX
I	990	XX.XX
J	1070	XX.XX
Total	7611	

3. A flowchart, computer listing, and printout of the following program should be prepared. The total quantity, the extensions, and the total of the extensions must be computed.

BAYLOR & SONS HARDWARE

Long Beach, California

Qty.	Item	Rate	Extension
33	Commodity 109	22.17 ea.	XXXX.XX
27	Commodity 105	17.75 ea.	XXXX.XX
14	Commodity 111	33.35 ea.	XXXX.XX
25	Commodity 107	12.76 ea.	XXXX.XX
46	Commodity 103	24.23 ea.	XXXX.XX
18	Commodity 112	11.75 ea.	XXXX.XX
27	Commodity 104	9.82 ea.	XXXX.XX
XXX			$ XXXX.XX

6 THE CONDITIONAL TRANSFER STATEMENT AND ITS USES

In this chapter, a statement will be presented that was used in a simpler form in Chapter 2. The new statement is called by a number of names: conditional transfer, conditional IF, logical IF, etc. It is a comparison made by use of one of the following statements.

> If some condition exists, then (command), or
> If some condition exists, go to (statement number), or
> If some condition exists, then (statement number).

RELATIONAL OPERATORS

The characters used for comparison in the logical IF statement are the following.

>	greater than
> =	greater than or equal to
<	less than
< =	less than or equal to

<> not equal to
= equal to
== approximately equal to

THE IF-THEN STATEMENT

Some examples of the use of relational operators are shown below.[1] Explanations of the meanings of the statements are given at the right.

10 IF A > B THEN C = D	If A greater than B, then make C equal to D.
20 IF A > = B THEN STOP	If A greater than or equal to B, then stop.
30 IF A > 700 AND A <= 1200 THEN 70	If A greater than 700 and A less than or equal to 1200, then go to Statement 70.
40 IF A < B THEN D = B * C	If A less than B, then make D equal to B times C.
50 IF A <> B THEN 30	If A not equal to B, then go to Statement 30.
60 IF A >= B OR C > D THEN 110	If A greater than or equal to B, or C greater than D, then go to Statement 110.
70 IF A <= B AND B = D THEN 80	If A less than or equal to B, and B equal to D, then go to Statement 80.

These statements amount to a true and false test. If the condition stated in the statement is true, then the directions in the statement are followed. If the conditions do not exist (the statement is false), the computer ignores the statement and drops down and executes the following line.

PROBLEM 6-1

The following problem will be used to demonstrate the logical IF. The City of Paduka pays mileage to all of its employees who use their own cars for city business. The city pays 15 cents a mile for all mileage up to and including 700 miles. Every mile over that figure is paid at the rate of 7 cents a mile.

[1] Dual comparisons, using the word AND or the word OR, are allowed on the RSTS/E operating system, but not on all other systems.

The business manager of one of the city institutions was asked to submit a report showing employees claiming mileage, their employee numbers, the number of miles driven, and the amounts claimed. A listing was to be made of the total miles and the total amount claimed for all employees. The output form is shown in Figure 6-1, and the flowchart is shown in Figure 6-2.

FIGURE 6-1

Problem 6-1

CITY OF PADUKA

DEPARTMENT OF EDUCATION
Mileage Claims

B. Dawson	11-12-3596	1500	161.00
C. Grogan	12-85-4121	800	112.00
D. Hows	11-73-3763	650	97.50
A. Hamilton	06-42-2195	1200	140.00
L. Jackson	19-29-1183	500	75.00
E. Klift	21-75-2197	2100	203.00
G. Moore	17-23-7250	480	72.00
H. Sorenson	15-56-6505	1070	130.90
TOTAL		8300	$ 991.40

The business manager programmed the following REM, heading, and columnar statements.

```
10  REM THIS PROGRAM PRINTS THE NAME OF THE EMPLOYEE, HIS
15  REM NUMBER, THE NUMBER OF MILES TRAVELED, AND THE AMOUNT
20  REM CLAIMED.  THE EMPLOYEE IS PAID 15 CENTS A MILE
25  REM FOR THE FIRST 700 MILES, 7 CENTS FOR ALL MILES IN
30  REM EXCESS OF 700.
35  REM E$=EMPLOYEE, N$=EMPLOYEE NO., M=MILES, A=AMOUNT, T=
37  REM TOTAL AMOUNT, M1=TOTAL MILES.
38  PRINT
40  PRINT;TAB(28);"CITY OF PADUKA"
42  PRINT
44  PRINT;TAB(23);"DEPARTMENT OF EDUCATION"
46  PRINT;TAB(28);"MILEAGE CLAIMS"
48  PRINT
50  PRINT
52  T = 0
53  M1 = 0
```

FIGURE 6-2
Flowchart for Problem 6-1

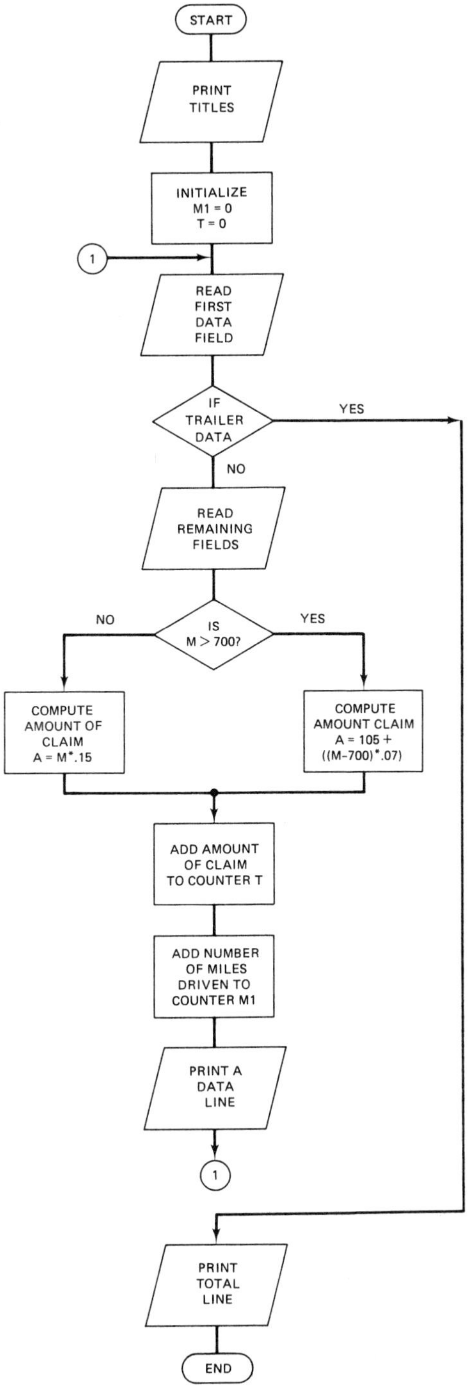

Then the READ statement and the IF test for the trailer data line were written, as shown below.

```
55  READ E$
60  IF E$ = "EXIT" GO TO 100
65  READ N$,M
```

The computer has now read the first data line and stored the data in E$, N$, and M. Before a line can be written, however, a decision must be made before determining the dollar amount of mileage that is being claimed. The computer must be programmed to decide whether to use 15 cents or 7 cents for figuring mileage. To do this, a logical IF is used, which sends the computer to one computation statement if the mileage is 700 miles or less, or directs it to another if it is more. Statement 70 is the statement used to solve this problem.

```
70  IF M > 700 GO TO 79
```

This statement tells the computer that if M (the field where the mileage is stored) is greater than 700, control should be transferred to Statement 79. At Statement 79 a computation will be made, but that will be discussed later. If the condition (the mileage is greater than 700) is not met, the computer drops to the next line and executes it. The next line would be the computation for mileage of 700 miles or less. The variable A will be the dollar amount of mileage claimed, M is the mileage driven, and .15 represents the 15 cents allowed for mileage up to and including 700 miles. Statement 75 handles the computation statement for the drivers with 700 or fewer miles.

```
75  A = M * .15
80  T = T + A
```

Statement 80 is necessary to add each employee's dollar claim to a total counter to find the total number of dollars in mileage claimed by all employees. The variable T is the total counter.

```
85  M1 = M1 + M
```

Statement 85 is used to total the mileage of all employees, as requested by the business manager. Then it is necessary to print a line and go back to the READ statement.

```
90  PRINT;TAB(9);E$;TAB(27);N$;TAB(44);
95  PRINT USING "####        ###.##",M,A
97  GO TO 55
```

These statements take care of the employee who has claimed 700 or fewer miles. What about those claiming more? Those cases will be handled by Statement 79. At Statement 79, the computation calculates the amount to be paid. The first 700 miles will be at 15 cents a mile, which is $105. All mileage over 700 is to be paid at 7 cents a mile.

```
79  A = 105 + ((M - 700) * .07)
```

Does Statement 79 do what it is supposed to do? The computer goes to the inside parentheses first and subtracts 700 from the total mileage. Then it performs the calculations inside the outer parentheses—it multiplies .07 (7 cents) times the mileage left after subtracting 700 from the original mileage. Then it adds that answer to 105 and stores it in A.

What would happen if the parentheses were omitted? The computer would do the multiplication first, which is 700 * .07. Then it would start from the left by adding 105 to the original mileage and from that answer subtract the sum of 700 * .07. Arithmetic statements should always be analyzed to be sure they are doing what they are supposed to do. After the arithmetic is calculated as a result of Statement 79, the computer drops to Statement 80.

```
80  T = T + A
```

The computer continues looping—reading data, branching to the correct computation statement, adding to totals, and then writing a line—until it finds the EXIT data. The computer now must be directed to write the total line. The 100 PRINT statement shown below ensures a blank line before the total line.

```
100 PRINT
102 PRINT;TAB(9);"TOTAL";TAB(44);
105 PRINT USING "####       !####.##",M1,"$",T
```

The "!" inside the 105 PRINT USING statement provides an alphanumeric field for the dollar sign.

Statement 105 could also be written with the dollar sign placed in front of the second formatted field, as shown below.

```
105  PRINT USING "####        $####.##",M1,T
```

As was stated previously, string characters in data lines need quotes around them if spacing is to be preserved. Therefore, the first string field in Statements 117 through 131 has the data in quotes. If the quotes were not placed around the data, there would be no spaces in the printout, and the name would appear B.DAWSON.

The computer listing and program printout of this program are shown in Figures 6-3 and 6-4.

Now the sample problem will be changed slightly to include three conditions. All mileage up to and including 700 miles will be reimbursed at the rate of 15 cents a mile. Mileage from 701 up to and including 1200 miles will be paid at 10 cents a mile, and all mileage above 1200 will be paid at 7 cents a mile. Two or three logical IF statements can handle the three conditions, depending on the programmer's wishes. The statements needed to handle the three conditions are shown below.

```
70  IF M > 700 AND M <= 1200 GO TO 79
72  IF M > 1200 GO TO 77
```

or

```
68  IF M <= 700 GO TO 75
70  IF M > 700 AND M <= 1200 GO TO  79
72  IF M > 1200 GO TO 77
```

In the first series of statements, when the computer cannot find the conditions it is looking for and M contains a number 700 or less, control drops down to the line following the IF statements. In the second series of statements, all conditions are stated in the statements.

Statement 79 in the original program must be changed. That statement, the other two arithmetic statements, and an added GO TO statement would appear as listed below.

```
75  A = M * .15
76  GO TO 80
77  A = 155+ ((M-1200) * .07)
78  GO TO 80
79  A = 105 + ((M-700) * .10)
```

The 155 figure in Statement 77 was obtained by adding the 105 (700 * .15) to 50 (500 * .10). The first 700 miles was at 15 cents a

FIGURE 6-3

Listing of Problem 6-1

```
PADUKA 08:59 AM         29-OCT-81
10  REM THIS PROGRAM PRINTS THE NAME OF THE EMPLOYEE, HIS
15  REM NUMBER, THE NUMBER OF MILES TRAVELED, AND THE AMOUNT
20  REM CLAIMED.  THE EMPLOYEE IS PAID 15 CENTS A MILE
25  REM FOR THE FIRST 700 MILES, 7 CENTS FOR ALL MILES IN
30  REM EXCESS OF 700.
35  REM E$=EMPLOYEE, N$=EMPLOYEE NO., M=MILES, A=AMOUNT, T=
37  REM TOTAL AMOUNT, M1=TOTAL MILES.
38  PRINT
40  PRINT;TAB(28);"CITY OF PADUKA"
42  PRINT
44  PRINT;TAB(23);"DEPARTMENT OF EDUCATION"
46  PRINT;TAB(28);"MILEAGE CLAIMS"
48  PRINT
50  PRINT
52  T = 0
53  M1 = 0
55  READ E$
60  IF E$ = "EXIT" GO TO 100
65  READ N$,M
70  IF M > 700 GO TO 79
75  A = M * .15
76  GO TO 80
79  A = 105 + ((M - 700) * .07)
80  T = T + A
85  M1 = M1 + M
90  PRINT;TAB(9);E$;TAB(27);N$;TAB(44);
95  PRINT USING "####        ###.##",M,A
97  GO TO 55
100 PRINT
102 PRINT;TAB(9);"TOTAL";TAB(44);
105 PRINT USING "####      !####.##",M1,"$",T
117 DATA "B. DAWSON","11-12-3596",1500
119 DATA "C. GROGAN","12-85-4121",800
121 DATA "D. HOWS","11-73-3763",650
123 DATA "A. HAMILTON","06-42-2195",1200
125 DATA "L. JACKSON","19-29-1183",500
127 DATA "E. KLIFT","21-75-2197",2100
129 DATA "G. MOORE","17-23-7250",480
131 DATA "H. SORENSON","15-56-6505",1070
133 DATA EXIT
135 END
```

mile, and the next 500 miles was at 10 cents a mile. Anything over 1200 miles (M–1200) is paid at the rate of 7 cents a mile.

FIGURE 6-4

Printout of Problem 6-1

```
RUN
PADUKA 08:59 AM        29-OCT-81

                        CITY OF PADUKA

                   DEPARTMENT OF EDUCATION
                        MILEAGE CLAIMS


         B. DAWSON      11-12-3596      1500      161.00
         C. GROGAN      12-85-4121       800      112.00
         D. HOWS        11-73-3763       650       97.50
         A. HAMILTON    06-42-2197      1200      140.00
         L. JACKSON     19-29-1183       500       75.00
         E. KLIFT       21-75-2197      2100      203.00
         G. MOORE       17-23-7250       480       72.00
         H. SORENSON    15-56-6505      1070      130.90

         TOTAL                          8300    $ 991.40
```

THE IF-THEN-ELSE STATEMENT[2]

The IF-THEN-ELSE statement is used when there are several conditions in a statement and each condition or combination of conditions commands the computer to branch to another statement.

```
90  IF Q1 < 0 THEN 75 ELSE IF Q1 = 0 THEN 95 ELSE IF Q1 > 0 THEN 110
```

The same test can and should be extended so that more than two conditions are applied to the same variable or variables. Statement 90 shown above may more efficiently be written in the following manner.

```
90  IF Q1<0 THEN 75 ELSE IF Q1 = 0 THEN 95 ELSE 110
```

If Q1 is not less than zero or does not equal zero, then it must be greater than zero. It is inefficient to cause the computer to render another decision when it is not necessary to do so.

The words AND and OR are used when all the conditions cause branching to the same statement. The words ELSE IF are used when

[2] The IF-THEN-ELSE statement is used on the RSTS/E operating system but not on all other systems.

FIGURE 6-5

Two Branching Statements

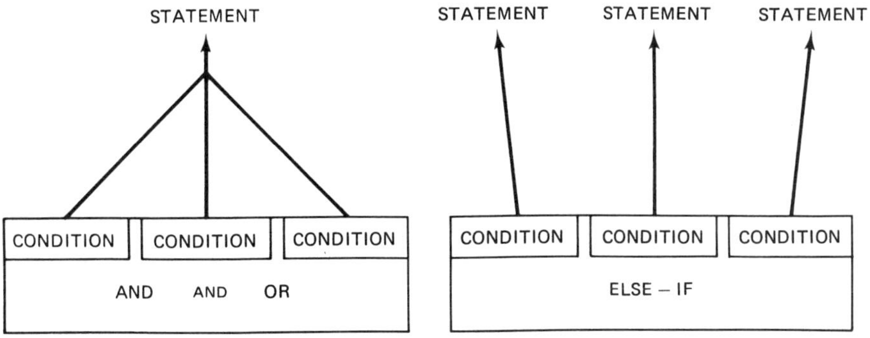

each of several conditions causes branching to different statements. The illustration of this branching principle is shown in Figure 6-5.

The difference between the IF-THEN-ELSE statement and the logical IF statement is that if the condition does not exist in the logical IF statement, the computer drops down and executes the following line.

```
50  IF A >= B OR C > D THEN 110
```

In Statement 50 if A is not greater than or equal to B, or if C is not greater than D, then the computer drops to the following line. In Statement 90, all of the conditions in that line send the computer to some particular statement. The only way the statement following Statement 90 can be executed is for another statement to branch to it.

There really is no limit to the number of branches that can exist in the IF-THEN-ELSE statement. If there are several branches in the statement, the programmer would be wise to use the LINE FEED and TAB keys instead of the RETURN key.[3] The computer treats all lines that are separated by the LINE FEED as one statement, so no statement number is used on succeeding lines.

```
30  IF A=B THEN 50
        ELSE IF A=D THEN 80
                ELSE IF A > B THEN 100
        ELSE IF A > D THEN 110
                ELSE IF A < B THEN 120
        ELSE IF A < D THEN 130
```

[3] The use of the LINE FEED to continue statements is not available on many systems.

The IF-THEN-ELSE statement can also be used to test relational conditions. If the condition is true, the THEN part of the statement is executed. If the condition is false, the ELSE part of the statement is executed.

```
50  IF A=B THEN 80 ELSE 90
```

This statement can also be used to cause the computer to apply any executable statement when certain conditions prevail, as shown in Statement 60.

```
60  IF A=B THEN PRINT "A=B" ELSE IF A > B THEN PRINT "A > B"
          ELSE IF A < B THEN PRINT "A < B"
```

Problem 6-2 in Figure 6-8 will be used to illustrate the use of this type of statement.

PROBLEM 6-2

The Fast Sell Realty has a contest for its salesmen once a year. Each salesman is given a quota based on the previous year's sales. Those who do not meet the quota receive no prize. Those who meet the quota or exceed it by less than $500 receive an expense-paid weekend in San Diego. Those who exceed their quota by $500 or more receive a three-day expense-paid vacation in Las Vegas. The flowchart is shown in Figure 6-6, and the computer listing and printout are shown in Figures 6-7 and 6-8.

Statement 50 demonstrates how the IF-THEN-ELSE statement would be applied.

```
50  IF S< Q THEN 75 ELSE IF S< Q+500 THEN 85
```

N$ is the salesman's name, Q is the quota, and S is the sales. Statements 75 and 77 print only the name, quota, and sales, as they print out data for those salesmen who did not meet their quotas.

Statements 85 and 87 print out the name, quota, and sales and place asterisks in the column labeled San Diego, since they print out data for those salesmen who exceeded their quotas but not by $500 or more. They are the salesmen who will receive a weekend in San Diego.

Statements 65, 67, and 68 print out the name, quota, and sales and place asterisks in the column labeled Las Vegas since those statements

FIGURE 6-6
Flowchart for Problem 6-2

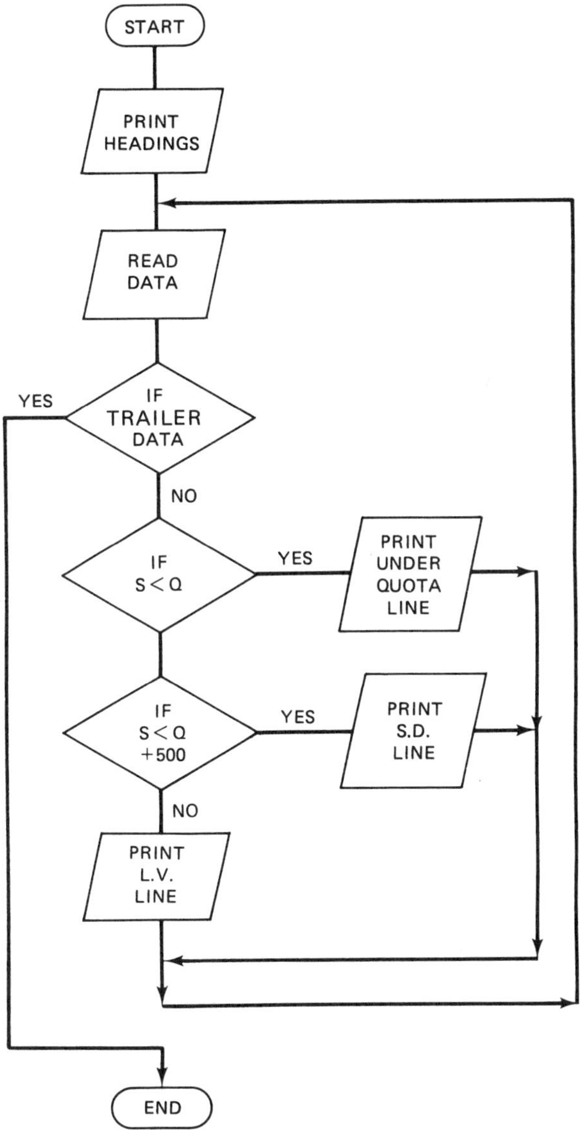

FIGURE 6-7

Listing for Problem 6-2

```
LIST
CH6P2                    03-JAN-81
10  PRINT
12  PRINT;TAB(27);"FAST SELL REALTY"
14  PRINT
16  PRINT;TAB(25);"YEARLY SALES CONTEST"
18  PRINT;TAB(29);"1981 RESULTS"
20  PRINT
22  PRINT
24  PRINT;TAB(22);"SALES     PERIOD"
30  PRINT;TAB(10);"NAME         QUOTA      SALES      "
"SAN DIEGO    LAS VEGAS"
35  PRINT
40  READ N$,Q,S
45  IF N$ = "EXIT" GO TO 111
50  IF S < Q THEN 75 ELSE IF S < Q+500 THEN 85
65  PRINT;TAB(7);N$;TAB(22);
67  PRINT USING "######    ######                         ",Q,S;
68  PRINT USING "!!!","*","*","*"
70  GO TO 90
75  PRINT;TAB(7);N$;TAB(22);
77  PRINT USING "######    ######",Q,S
80  GO TO 90
85  PRINT;TAB(7);N$;TAB(22);
87  PRINT USING "######    ######          !!!",Q,S,"*","*","*"
90  GO TO 40
95  DATA "B. ANDERSON",150000,150250
97  DATA "J. BARBER",125000,125750
99  DATA "L. COOPER",180000,200000
101 DATA "S. DAWSON",115000,110000
103 DATA "M. FRANKLIN",115000,115000
105 DATA "E. HARRISON",130000,128000
107 DATA "F. JACOBSON",140000,140450
109 DATA EXIT,0,0
111 END

READY

RUN
```

NOTE: Statement 30 employs the LINE FEED. The required use of quotes is demonstrated.

NOTE: In this listing there are GO TO statements branching to a GO TO statement. Excessive GO TO statements should be avoided, but in order to maintain the principles of top down and one-entry, one-exit programming, it is necessary to code the statements as illustrated.

FIGURE 6-8

Printout for Problem 6-2

```
                    FAST SELL REALTY

                 YEARLY SALES CONTEST
                     1981 RESULTS


               SALES     PERIOD
   NAME        QUOTA     SALES      SAN DIEGO    LAS VEGAS

B. ANDERSON    150000    150250        ***
J. BARBER      125000    125750                     ***
L. COOPER      180000    200000                     ***
S. DAWSON      115000    110000
M. FRANKLIN    115000    115000        ***
E. HARRISON    130000    128000
F. JACOBSON    140000    140450        ***
```

print out data for the salesmen who exceeded their quotas by $500 or more and will receive a three-day trip to Las Vegas.

SUMMARY

1. The logical IF statement may contain more than one comparison.
2. The characters used for comparison in the logical IF statement are the following.

>	greater than
>=	greater than or equal to
<	less than
<=	less than or equal to
<>	not equal to
=	equal to
==	approximately equal to

3. The IF-THEN-ELSE statement allows the transfer of control of the program to one other statement for each IF clause.
4. The IF-THEN-ELSE statement can specify only one condition to be executed in each IF clause.

```
10  IF A=B THEN PRINT "A=B" ELSE IF A=D THEN PRINT "A=D"
```

5. The IF-THEN-ELSE statement can be used for relational conditions. If the statement is true,the THEN part of the statement is executed; if the statement is false, the ELSE part is executed.

```
20  IF A=B THEN 100 ELSE 70
```

6. When a single variable is tested as less than, equal to, or greater than an entire range of possible values, only the first two conditions need be tested. The third will necessarily apply to any variable that did not satisfy the first two.
7. There can be many statements causing branching in the IF-THEN-ELSE statement, so for readability the programmer can use the LINE FEED and TAB keys instead of the RETURN key.

```
30  IF A=B THEN 50
         ELSE IF A=D THEN 80
                   ELSE IF A > B THEN 100
         ELSE IF A > D THEN 110
                   ELSE IF A < B THEN 120
         ELSE IF A < D THEN 130
```

SELF-TEST

1. What statements are needed to execute the following?
   a. If A is greater than B or less than C, go to Statement 30.
   b. If A is less than or equal to B, go to Statement 100.
   c. If A is approximately equal to D, then stop.
   d. If C is not equal to F, go to Statement 65.
   e. If C is equal to F and A is equal to B, then E equals H.
   f. If A is equal to B, go to Statement 10; if A is equal to D, go to Statement 50.
   g. If A is equal to B, go to Statement 10; if not, go to Statement 100.
   h. If A is less than B, go to Statement 50; if equal to B, go to Statement 80; if greater than B, go to Statement 80.
2. A Statement 50 should be prepared, telling the computer, "If A1

is less than or equal to 500, go to Statement 80." In Statement 55 the computer should be told, "If A1 is greater than 500 but less than 1000, go to Statement 105." In Statement 60 the computer should be told, "If A1 is equal to or greater than 1000, go to Statement 155." At Statement 80 the computer should multiply A1 times B and store the answer in T. At Statement 105 the computer is to add $5,000 to A1, then subtract 500 multiplied by C, and store the answer in T. At Statement 155 the computer is to add $15,000 to A1, then subtract 1000 multiplied by D, and store the answer in T.

3. What one statement would do what Statements 50, 55, and 60 do in Question 2?
4. What statement would command the computer to go to Statement 50 if C equals D or to Statement 100 if it does not?
5. What statement will cause the computer to print "equal" when A equals B and to print "unequal" when A does not equal B?
6. What statement using the LINE FEED and TAB keys would tell the computer that when A equals 100, it goes to Statement 60; when A is greater than 100 but less than or equal to 150, it goes to Statement 70; when A is greater than 150 but less than 200, it goes to Statement 80; and when A is equal to 200, the computer is to stop?

ASSIGNMENTS[4]

1. The Neighborhood Girls' Association consists of 13 clubs that are selling candy at $1.25 a box. The organization from which they buy their candy stipulates that each club that averages from 12 to 15 boxes per girl will receive 15 cents a box. Under 12 boxes they receive 10 cents a box, and over 15 boxes they will receive 20 cents a box. Below is a list of the 13 clubs, the number of members, and the total number of boxes sold. A program should be prepared to figure out the average number of boxes sold per girl per club and how much each club receives a box. There is to be a total of the number of boxes sold by all of the clubs and a total of the total amounts paid to all of the clubs. The flowchart,

[4] The rules for centering explained in Chapter 5 should be applied.

the computer listing, and the program printout should be prepared and handed in. An IF-THEN-ELSE statement must be used.

YUMMY CANDY COMPANY
Pittsburgh, Pennsylvania
Sales by Neighborhood Girls' Clubs

CLUB NO.	NO. OF MEMBERS	TOTAL BOXES SOLD PER CLUB	AVE. NO. OF BOXES PER GIRL	AMT. REC. PER BOX	TOT. REC. BY CLUB
1	25	330	XX	.XX	XX.XX
2	28	308	XX	.XX	XX.XX
3	32	412	XX	.XX	XX.XX
4	19	234	XX	.XX	XX.XX
5	27	285	XX	.XX	XX.XX
6	15	252	XX	.XX	XX.XX
7	24	298	XX	.XX	XX.XX
8	29	322	XX	.XX	XX.XX
9	28	360	XX	.XX	XX.XX
10	20	240	XX	.XX	XX.XX
11	19	210	XX	.XX	XX.XX
12	17	182	XX	.XX	XX.XX
13	19	215	XX	.XX	XX.XX
Total		XXXX			$XXX.XX

2. Space Airlines annually publishes a list of passengers who fly 900,000 miles or more on their airline. They are called Space Airlines VIP Passengers. The airline also issues Honorary Captain cards to those flying a million miles or more and Honorary Co-Captain cards to those flying 950,000 up to one million miles. There are too many passengers to list here, but a partial list is presented, showing how many miles certain passengers have flown. After the miles flown, those who flew a million or more miles are flagged with two asterisks. After the miles flown over 950,000, one asterisk appears. The asterisks must not appear in the data statements. The flowchart, the computer listing, and the program printout should be prepared and handed in. An IF-THEN-ELSE statement must be used.

SPACE AIRLINES
Space Airlines VIP Passengers

PASSENGER	MILES FLOWN
XXXXXXXXXXXXX	XXXXXXX
XXXXXXXXXXXXX	XXXXXXX *
XXXXXXXXXXXXX	XXXXXXX **

** Honorary Captain * Honorary Co-Captain

Raw data for Problem 2 is shown below.

PASSENGER	MILES FLOWN
A. Bendickson	920000
F. Carroll	935000
B. Cranston	980000
R. Donahue	915000
C. Evans	1003000
A. Fox	970000
I. Harold	920000
J. Imoto	910000
H. Nielson	1006000
K. Pickard	1000100
L. Richardson	940000
D. Smith	960000

3. Johnson and Sons is a wholesale furniture outlet. They offer discounts of 10% on all orders of $200,000 or over and 15% on all orders of $500,000 or over. They have thousands of customers, but only a few will be listed here. The sales manager feeds all orders into the computer so some of the customers listed here will not receive discounts. The manager wants a list of only those receiving discounts. However, all the customers' names and amounts ordered should be put into data statements. Discounts are to be rounded to whole dollars. The printout will show customer's name, amount ordered, amount of discount, and net amount paid for the order. The flowchart, the computer listing, and the program printout should be handed in. An IF-THEN-ELSE statement must be used.

JOHNSON AND SONS
Furniture Wholesalers
Customers Receiving Quantity Discounts

CUSTOMER	AMT. OF ORDER	AMT. OF DISCOUNT	NET AMT. OF ORDER
X. XXXXXXX	XXXXXX	XXXXX	XXXXXX

The data for this problem is shown below.

CUSTOMER	AMT. OF ORDER
D. Arnold	90000
F. Baker	220000
J. Bartell	400900
C. Benton	632765
P. Cope	332890
S. Daren	176000
T. Engels	210000
G. Farmer	165000
L. Franks	554095
V. Jackson	623427
L. Minor	117000
P. Norton	387760
H. Sipes	80000
M. Tustin	150000

7 THE ON–GO TO STATEMENT, THE PRINTING OF DATES, AND ADDITIONAL PROGRAMMING TECHNIQUES

The following topics are covered in this chapter.

A. Multiple statements
B. Additional PRINT USING techniques
C. Printing the date from the computer
D. The ON–GO TO statement

MULTIPLE STATEMENTS[1]

On the PDP-11 several statements may be written on a single line, provided each statement except the last is followed by a colon or a backslash. The following example demonstrates a way to code multiple statements.

[1] On some other computer systems, the only multiple statements that can be written are initialization, assignment, and arithmetic statements, as shown in Appendix B.

```
64  A = 0
66  T1 = 0
68  B1 = 0          or       64  A = 0:T1 = 0:B1 = 0:Q = 50:M = 5
70  Q = 50
72  M = 5           or       64  A = 0\T1 = 0\B1 = 0\Q = 50\M = 5
```

A single statement may be used to assign the same value to several variables. In Statements 64, 66, and 68, all the variables are assigned zero. Therefore, Statement 64 can be modified again, as shown below:

```
64  A,T1,B1 = 0:Q = 50:M = 5
```

There are inherent dangers in using multiple statements containing decisions. Any statements following the decision will not be executed if the condition in the decision is false. However, they will be executed if the condition is true. Therefore, it is best not to use decisions in multiple statements. A program demonstrating this rule is shown below.

```
LIST
MULTES  10:21 AM         22-Nov-81
10 READ X
15 IF X = -9 THEN 50
20 IF X = 2 THEN PRINT 'THE VALUE OF X IS ' ;  \PRINT X
30 GO TO 10
40 DATA 1,2,3,-9
50 END

Ready

RUN
MULTES 10:21 AM          22-Nov-81
THE VALUE OF X IS  2
```

Only when X equals 2 are the PRINT commands executed.

ADDITIONAL PRINT USING TECHNIQUES

The PRINT USING statement in previous chapters used the "#" symbol for formatting the numeric field and the exclamation point for an alphanumeric one-character field.

The following paragraphs will explain how to place dollar signs immediately before the first significant number on every line of data, and how to place lead asterisks instead of blanks in number fields.

PRINTING DOLLAR SIGNS IN OUTPUT

To print a dollar sign before each field, which is really incorrect form, the programmer should use the format consisting of two $ symbols to cause the dollar sign to float, as shown below.

```
20  PRINT USING "$$##.##",A
100 DATA 377.73,23.89,1.76
```

The output would appear as shown below.

```
RUN
SIGN        04:47:M            01-Feb-81
 $377.73
  $23.89
   $1.76
```

In Statement 20, the first "$" causes the dollar sign to be printed and the other one is used as if it were another "#". In other words, space has been allowed for a three-digit whole number in the PRINT USING statement at line 20. If the digit spaces fall anywhere within the designated field width (three digits), a dollar sign will be printed as the lead character in the field. This statement is used for specialized purposes, such as writing checks, and should not be used in printing out reports.

PRINTING ASTERISKS IN OUTPUT

If the programmer wishes to fill up number fields with asterisks preceding numbers that consist of fewer digits than the width of the field, the following PRINT USING statement in line 20 should be used. To cause the asterisks to float, two asterisks must be used. This statement is used for specialized purposes, such as writing checks.

```
20  PRINT USING "**##.##",A
100 DATA 2.75,1007.60,110.85
```

The output would appear as shown below.

```
***2.75
1007.60
*110.85
```

DATE LINES

The current date is contained within the computer, and the programmer may cause a date line to be printed in his program by using the following statement on the PDP-11 with a zero within the parentheses.[2]

```
10  PRINT DATE$(0)
```

In the sample problem for this chapter, Statement 30 is used to print out the date.

```
30  PRINT:PRINT;TAB(30);DATE$(0):PRINT:PRINT
```

THE ON–GO TO STATEMENT

The ON–GO TO statement always transfers control to another statement number.

```
100 ON K GO TO 130,160,200
```

One of the fields in the DATA statement is used as a code field, which has numbers beginning with 1. These numbers represent certain conditions–i.e., 1 = male and 2 = female; or 1 = .03, 2 = .07, and 3 = .10; or 1 = 5-dollar bonus, 2 = 10-dollar bonus, etc. In Statement 100, K is the code field, though any numeric variable name would be acceptable.

The numbers that can be stored in the code field must start with 1 for the first statement number in the ON–GO TO statement, 2 for the second number, and continue in consecutive order for as many numbers as can be placed on a line.

[2] Users of other computers are urged to refer to the systems manual for the method of printing the current date from the computer into a program output.

Statement 100 tells the computer that when there is a 1 in storage K, control should go to Statement 130. If 2 is stored in K, it should go to Statement 160; and if 3 is stored in K, it should go to Statement 200. The word "ON" is the key to this statement. Whenever the computer reads ON, it performs in the following manner.

```
40  ON Y GO TO 60,70,80,60,90,70,70,50
```

When Y = 1, the control would go to Statement 60.
When Y = 2, the control would go to Statement 70.
When Y = 3, the control would go to Statement 80.
When Y = 4, the control would go to Statement 60.
When Y = 5, the control would go to Statement 90.
When Y = 6, the control would go to Statement 70.
When Y = 7, the control would go to Statement 70.
When Y = 8, the control would go to Statement 50.

Another example with DATA statements is shown below.

```
10  READ A,M
15  IF A = -9 GO TO 80
20  ON A GO TO 25, 35, 45
25  Y = M * .03
30  GO TO 50
35  Y = M * .06
40  GO TO 50
45  Y = M * .10
50  PRINT A,M,Y
55  GO TO 10
60  DATA 3,76
65  DATA 1,59
70  DATA 2,33
75  DATA -9,0
80  END
```

The computer reads the first DATA statement and asks if A = -9. It does not, so control drops to the next line. The statement on the next line says if A = 1, go to Statement 25; if A = 2, go to Statement 35; and if A = 3, go to Statement 45. In the first DATA statement A = 3, so control goes to Statement 45, performs a computation, drops to the next line, and is told to print a line. The second time through, A = 1 so control is directed to Statement 25. When DATA Statement 70 is read, control branches to Statement 35 because A = 2.

FLOWCHARTING THE ON-GO TO STATEMENT

In Chapter 3 several examples of branching principles were illustrated. The ON—GO TO statement is another type of statement that causes branching. An example of this branching is shown in Figure 7-1.

FIGURE 7-1
Flowcharting the ON—GO TO Statement

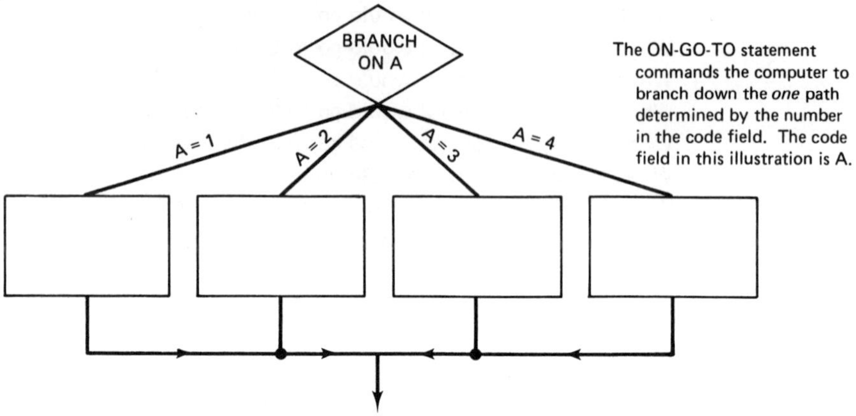

PROBLEM 7-1

The sample program for the chapter involves a Savings and Loan Association. This association has six different types of savings accounts that pay six different rates of interest compounded daily.

ACCOUNT	DAILY INTEREST	CODE
Regular account	.0001467	1
Ninety-day bonus account	.000146766	2
One-year plan	.000146819	3
Two and one-half year plan	.0001468888	4
Four-year certificate account	.000146988	5
Six-year certificate account	.000147	6

The problem is to list certain accounts in the association; their codes, signifying the type of account; the old balance; the daily interest paid, and the new balance.

The printout is to be like the example shown in Figure 7-3; the flowchart for this problem is shown in Figure 7-2.

FIGURE 7-2

Flowchart for Problem 7-1

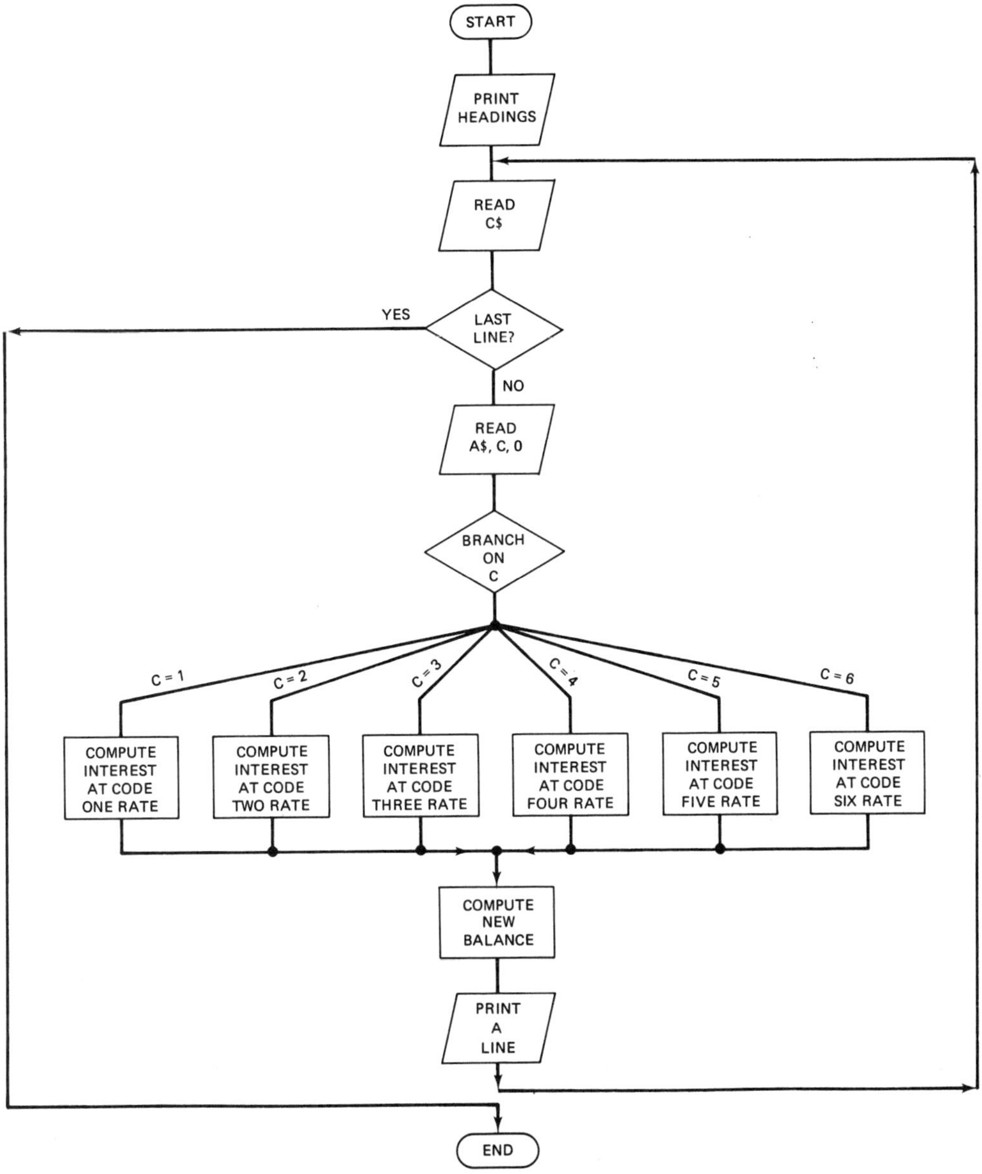

FIGURE 7-3

Printout of Program for Problem 7-1

```
KING SAVINGS AND LOAN

DAILY INTEREST

06-NOV-81
```

CUSTOMER NAME	ACCT. NUMBER	CODE	OLD BALANCE	INTEREST	NEW BALANCE
B. BLANKENSHIP	11-135-7	1	587.67	0.09	587.76
F. BROWN	05-476-7	6	1532.10	0.23	1532.33
C. CARTER	17-731-7	2	795.13	0.12	795.25
H. CROSBY	23-626-7	2	311.12	0.05	311.17
C. DEWEY	09-178-7	5	5763.27	0.85	5764.12
S. DORSEY	15-954-7	4	4176.85	0.61	4177.46
T. GARWIN	19-876-7	3	3215.76	0.47	3216.23
O. NEWMAN	06-313-7	1	212.86	0.03	212.89
O. PORTER	14-176-7	4	1211.00	0.18	1211.18
Y. SAUNDERS	06-813-7	1	176.11	0.03	176.14
G. SMITH	21-514-7	3	1580.00	0.23	1580.23

The following statements are REM statements. The lines following the first line go out to the margin, so the LINE-FEED key is used to continue the statement on consecutive lines. Although the LINE-FEED key does not result in a listing as neat looking as does that resulting from the use of the RETURN key and REM statement, it does save space and statement numbers.

```
10  REM THIS IS A PRINTOUT COMPUTING THE DAILY INTEREST
FOR A SPECIFIC GROUP OF ACCOUNTS.  REGULAR ACCOUNTS ARE
CODE 1;90-DAY BONUS, CODE 2;1-YEAR PLAN, CODE 3; 2 AND
ONE-HALF YEARS, CODE 4; 4-YEAR CERTIFICATE, CODE 5; AND
6-YEAR CERTIFICATE, CODE 6.
```

The next group of statements are for the purpose of printing the headings, date, and columnar headings. The use of the colon to allow for multiple statements and the use of the computer to print the current date in the heading are demonstrated.

```
20  PRINT:PRINT;TAB(24);"KING SAVINGS AND LOAN"
25  PRINT:PRINT;TAB(28);"DAILY INTEREST"
30  PRINT:PRINT;TAB(30);DATE$(0):PRINT:PRINT
35  PRINT;TAB(3);"CUSTOMER";TAB(31);"ACCT.";TAB(40);"OLD";TAB(65);"NEW"
40  PRINT;TAB(5);"NAME";TAB(20);"NUMBER     CODE    BALANCE      "
"INTEREST      BALANCE"
45  PRINT
```

Nothing new is involved in the next three statements—those used to read the DATA statements and check for the trailer DATA statement.

```
50  READ C$
55  IF C$ = "EXIT" GO TO 139
60  READ A$,C,B
```

The following statements are those involved with the ON—GO TO statement. The code numbers were placed in the "C" field. When the computer reads a DATA statement and that statement is not the trailer statement, it reads the ON—GO TO statement. At that line the computer is commanded to go to Statement 70 if code (C) is 1, 90 if code is 2, 96 if code is 3, 100 if code is 4, 104 if code is 5, and 106 if code is 6.

When the computer goes to the statement to which it is directed, it computes the daily interest—B (old balance) times rate is placed in I (interest). The computer is then directed to Statement 108 where the old balance is added to interest and stored in new balance (N). The computer then prints a line and goes back and reads another DATA statement.

The second field in the DATA statements is placed in quotes for two reasons: (1) because the punctuation requires the field be treated as string, and (2) because string fields beginning with other than letters require quotes. As was explained in Chapter 3, if spacing is desired in the printout of a field, the data must be placed in quotes.

```
65  ON C GO TO 70,90,96,100,104,106
70  I = B * .0001467
75  GO TO 108
90  I = B * .000146766
95  GO TO 108
96  I = B * .000146819
98  GO TO 108
100 I = B * .0001468888
```

```
102 GO TO 108
104 I = B * .000146988
105 GO TO 108
106 I = B * .000147
108 N = B + I
110 PRINT;C$;TAB(19);A$;TAB(32);C;TAB(38);
111 PRINT USING "####.##        #.##         ####.##",B,I,N
112 GO TO 50
114 DATA "B. BLANKENSHIP","11-135-7".1,587.67
116 DATA "F. BROWN","05-476-7",6,1532.10
118 DATA "C. CARTER","17-731-7",2,795.13
120 DATA "H. CROSBY","23-626-7",2,311.12
122 DATA "C. DEWEY","09-178-7",5,5763.27
124 DATA "S. DORSEY","15-954-7",4,4176.85
126 DATA "T.. GARWIN","19-876-7",3,3215.76
128 DATA "O. NEWMAN","06-313-7",1,212.86
130 DATA "O. PORTER","14-176-7",4,1211.00
132 DATA "Y. SAUNDERS","06-813-7",1,176.11
134 DATA "G. SMITH","21-514-7",3,1580.00
136 DATA EXIT
139 END
```

The printout is shown in Figure 7-3, and the complete program is shown in Figure 7-5.

There is always a possibility that the operator might mistype a code in a DATA statement. There would be no way the computer could tell that the programmer typed a 4 instead of a 5, or a 2 instead of a 3. It can tell, however, when a code number is outside of the series of numbers that are designated for a program. If there were three statement numbers in an ON—GO TO statement, for example, the numbers one to three are the only legitimate code numbers. If any other numbers appear, the computer will quit printing the data and print OUT OF RANGE AT 65. The number in the OUT OF RANGE statement would be the number of the ON—GO TO statement (Statement 65 in Problem 7-1).

The operator then must go through the DATA statements and look for the error or errors. One thing is certain: The first line that did not print contains an error. That is the reason the computer stopped.

The computer can be programmed to continue printing the data with correct code numbers and to list the ones that are incorrect. For example purposes, the DATA statements in the sample problem will be altered somewhat. DATA Statement 118 will be changed, and DATA Statements 136 and 137 will be added. The trailer data statement will then have a new statement number—138.

```
118 DATA "C. CARTER","17-731-7",0,795.13
136 DATA "L. STINSON","11-312-7",7,3334.54
137 DATA "R. TOPPER","23-551-7",8,4532.44
138 DATA EXIT
```

When these statements are changed in the program for Problem 7-1 and the word RUN is typed, the computer will print the heading, subheadings, columnar headings, and the lines for B. Blankenship and F. Brown, and then it will type OUT OF RANGE AT 65. The operator should then check the DATA statement and, while he is about it, the remaining data statements. If the code numbers are changed to the proper numbers, the program will then run perfectly. The word REPLACE, typed after all the new statements are added, will cause the copy of the program in auxiliary storage to be changed. The word REPLACE is not necessary if the program has not previously been saved.

A technique that will allow the program to print, even though there are some incorrect codes in the DATA statements, is shown below. Assuming that the three statements with the incorrect codes are left in the program, a few more statements will be added.

```
55  IF C$ = "EXIT" GO TO 143
62  IF C < 1 OR C > 6 GO TO 139
139 PRINT C$;TAB(19);A$;TAB(32);C;TAB(38);
141 PRINT USING   "####.##                                   !!",0,"*","*"
142 GO TO 50
143 PRINT
144 PRINT  "**THESE CUSTOMERS HAD CODE PUNCHED INCORRECTLY"
145 END
```

Statement 55 had to be changed because more lines were added and Statement 139 is no longer the END statement. Statement 62 is a logical IF statement used to take care of mistyped codes. If anything less than 1 or greater than 6 is typed in the code field, the computer goes to Statement 139 and prints a line different from the correctly coded ones—the interest and new balance are not computed, and a space and two asterisks appear at the end of the line. The computer then goes back and reads a DATA statement.

At the end of the printout in Figure 7-4 is a footnote explaining the reasons for the blank interest and new balance fields. The footnote is referenced by the asterisks.

```
** THESE CUSTOMERS HAD CODE PUNCHED INCORRECTLY
```

Instead of flagging a line containing an error with asterisks and footnotes, the programmer may cause an error message to be printed on the same line on which the incorrect code occurs. In Figure 7-4, the error lines would appear as follows, if this method were used.

```
C. CARTER      17-731-7    0     795.13          INCORRECT CODE
L. STINSON     11-213-7    7    3334.54          INCORRECT CODE
R. TOPPER      23-551-7    8    4532.44          INCORRECT CODE
```

To get this printout, Statement 141 would be changed as follows.

```
141 PRINT USING "####.##",B;:PRINT;TAB(52);"INCORRECT CODE"
```

It is the programmer's discretion as to which method to use. They are both correct. The amended program is in Figure 7-6.

The programmer should use a statement to catch incorrect codes in every program utilizing an ON–GO TO statement.

FIGURE 7-4

Printout for the Amended Program for Problem 7-1

```
                    KING SAVINGS AND LOAN

                       DAILY INTEREST

                         07-NOV-81


   CUSTOMER          ACCT.            OLD                     NEW
     NAME           NUMBER   CODE   BALANCE    INTEREST     BALANCE

B. BLANKENSHIP     11-135-7    1     587.67      0.09        587.76
F. BROWN           05-476-7    6    1532.10      0.23       1532.33
C. CARTER          17-731-7    0     795.13                          **
H. CROSBY          23-626-7    2     311.12      0.05        311.17
C. DEWEY           09-178-7    5    5763.27      0.85       5764.12
S. DORSEY          15-954-7    4    4176.85      0.61       4177.46
T. GARWIN          19-876-7    3    3215.76      0.47       3216.23
O. NEWMAN          06-313-7    1     212.86      0.03        212.89
O. PORTER          14-176-7    4    1211.00      0.18       1211.18
Y. SAUNDERS        06-813-7    1     176.11      0.03        176.14
G. SMITH           21-514-7    2    1580.00      0.23       1580.23
L. STINSON         11-213-7    7    3334.54                          **
R. TOPPER          23-551-7    8    4532.44                          **

** THESE CUSTOMERS HAD CODE PUNCHED INCORRECTLY
```

FIGURE 7-5

Listing of Problem 7-1

```
10  REM THIS IS A PRINTOUT COMPUTING THE DAILY INTEREST
FOR A SPECIFIC GROUP OF ACCOUNTS.  REGULAR ACCOUNTS ARE
CODE 1; 90-DAY BONUS, CODE 2; 1-YEAR PLAN, CODE 3; 2 AND
ONE-HALF YEARS, CODE 4; 4-YEAR CERTIFICATE, CODE 5; AND
6-YEAR CERTIFICATE, CODE 6.
20  PRINT:PRINT;TAB(24);"KING SAVINGS AND LOAN"
25  PRINT:PRINT;TAB(28);"DAILY INTEREST"
30  PRINT:PRINT;TAB(30);DATE$(0):PRINT:PRINT
35  PRINT;TAB(3);"CUSTOMER";TAB(21);"ACCT.";TAB(40);"OLD";TAB(65);"NEW"
40  PRINT;TAB(5);"NAME";TAB(20);"NUMBER     CODE   BALANCE      "
"INTEREST      BALANCE"
45  PRINT
50  READ C$
55  IF C$ = "EXIT" GO TO 139
60  READ A$,C,B
65  ON C GO TO 70,90,96,100,104,106
70  I = B * .0001467
75  GO TO 108
90  I = B * .000146766
95  GO TO 108
96  I = B * .000146819
98  GO TO 108
100 I = B * .0001468888
102  GO TO 108
104  I = B * .000146988
105 GO TO 108
106 I = B * .000147
108 N = B + I
110 PRINT;C$;TAB(19);A$;TAB(32);C;TAB(38);
111 PRINT USING "####.##        #.##        ####.##",B,I,N
112 GO TO 50
114 DATA "B. BLANKENSHIP","11-135-7",1,587.67
116 DATA "F. BROWN","05-476-7",6,1532.10
118 DATA "C. CARTER","17-731-7",2,795.13
120 DATA "H. CROSBY","23-626-7",2,311.12
122 DATA "C. DEWEY","09-178-7",5,5763.27
124 DATA "S. DORSEY","15-954-7",4,44176.85
126 DATA "T. GARWIN","19-876-7",3,3215.76
128 DATA "O. NEWMAN","06-313-7",1,212.86
130 DATA "O. PORTER","14-176-7",4,1211.00
132 DATA "Y. SAUNDERS","06-813-7",1,176.11
134 DATA "G. SMITH","21-514-7",3,1580.00
136 DATA EXIT
139 END
```

FIGURE 7-6

Program for Amended Program for Problem 7-1

```
10  REM THIS IS A PRINTOUT COMPUTING THE DAILY INTEREST
FOR A SPECIFIC GROUP OF ACCOUNTS.  REGULAR ACCOUNTS ARE
CODE 1;90-DAY BONUS, CODE 2;1-YEAR PLAN, CODE 3; 2 AND
ONE-HALF YEARS, CODE 4; 4-YEAR CERTIFICATE, CODE 5; AND
6-YEAR CERTIFICATE, CODE 6.
20  PRINT:PRINT;TAB(24);"KING SAVINGS AND LOAN"
25  PRINT:PRINT;TAB(28);"DAILY INTEREST"
30  PRINT:PRINT;TAB(30);DATE$(0):PRINT:PRINT
35  PRINT;TAB(3);"CUSTOMER";TAB(21);"ACCT.";TAB(40); OLD";TAB(65);"NEW"
40  PRINT;TAB(5);"NAME";TAB(20);"NUMBER     CODE   BALANCE      "
"INTEREST     BALANCE"
45  PRINT
50  READ C$
55  IF C$ = "EXIT" GO TO 143
60  READ A$,C,B
62  IF C < 1 OR C > 6 GO TO 139
65  ON C GO TO 70,90,96,100,104,106
70  I = B * .0001467
75  GO TO 108
90  I = B * .000146766
95  GO TO 108
96  I = B * .000146819
98  GO TO 108
100 I = B * .0001468888
102 GO TO 108
104 I = B * .000146988
105 GO TO 108
106 I = B * .000147
108 N = B + I
110 PRINT;C$;TAB(19);A$;TAB(32);C;TAB(38);
111 PRINT USING "####.##         #.##         ####.##",B,I,N
112 GO TO 50
114 DATA "B. BLANKENSHIP","11-135-7",1,587.67
116 DATA "F. BROWN","05-476-7",6,1532.10
118 DATA "C. CARTER","17-731-7",0,795.13
120 DATA "H. CROSBY","23-626-7",2,311.12
122 DATA "C. DEWEY","09-178-7",5,5763.27
124 DATA "S. DORSEY","15-954-7",4,4176.85
126 DATA "T. GARWIN","19-876-7",3,3215.76
128 DATA "O. NEWMAN","06-313-7",1,212,86
130 DATA "O. PORTER","14-176-7",4,1211.00
132 DATA "Y. SAUNDERS","06-813-7",1,176.11
134 DATA "G. SMITH","21-514-7",3,1580.00
136 DATA "L. STINSON","11-312-7",7,3334.54
137 DATA "R. TOPPER","23-551-7",8,4532.44
138 DATA EXIT
139 PRINT C$;TAB(19);A$;TAB(32);C;TAB(38);
141 PRINT USING   "####.##                                !!",B,"*","*"
142 GO TO 50
143 PRINT
144 PRINT  "**THESE CUSTOMERS HAD CODE PUNCHED INCORRECTLY"
145 END
```

SUMMARY

1. It is possible to write more than one statement on a line on the PDP-11. This is done by following each statement except the last with a colon or backslash.

```
55  A = 5:B = 12:C = 19      or     55  A =5\B = 12\C=19
```

2. More than one variable can be assigned the same value in a single statement on the PDP-11.

```
70  A,B,C = .07
```

3. If the PRINT USING statement formats for only two decimal places, the computer will round all numbers with three or more decimal places if the third decimal position is five or greater. It will truncate all positions to the right of the second decimal position if the third position is less than five.

```
20  A = 114.725:B = 317.632
25  PRINT USING "###.##    ###.##",A,B
```

The printout would be: 114.73 317.63

4. If a dollar sign is desired immediately preceding the first digit in the output on the PDP-11, the following format for a floating dollar sign is used.

```
30  PRINT USING "$$##.##",A
```

The output would look like this:

```
  $1.23
 $24.35
$568.94
```

5. If the number fields are to be filled with asterisks preceding numbers that consist of fewer digits than the width of the field, the following PRINT USING statement is used on the PDP-11.

```
10  PRINT USING "**##.##",A
```

The output would look like this:

```
***1.27
*125.30
7654.50
```

6. On the PDP-11 the current date can be printed by calling out the one stored in the computer by using the following statement.

```
30  PRINT DATE$(0)
```

7. In the ON–GO TO statement, control is transferred to other statements depending on the value in a code field. The code is given a numeric variable name, which is referenced in the ON–GO TO statement. If the code number is 1, the computer branches to the first statement number after the GO TO; if the code is 2, the computer branches to the second statement number, etc., for as many statement numbers as are listed.

```
85  ON Y GO TO 110,130,150
```

Control is transferred to 110 if Y = 1, to 130 if Y = 2, and to 150 if Y = 3.

8. To protect against a mistyped code, Logical IF statements can be used to take care of numbers less than one and greater than the highest code desired. For example, if there are four codes (and Y is designated as the code field), the following Logical IF could be used:

```
20  IF Y < 1 OR Y > 4 GO TO 120
25  ON Y GO TO 45, 60, 75, 90
```

SELF-TEST

1. Using D as the code field, what statement would be necessary to do the following parts of a program?
   a. Code 1 represents a 4% rate.
   b. Code 2 represents a 4.5% rate.
   c. Code 3 represents a 5% rate.
   d. Code 4 represents a 5.5% rate.
   e. Code 5 represents a 6% rate.

f. The code statement is 65 and the computer is to be sent to Statements 75 for 1, 85 for 2, 95 for 3, 105 for 4, and 115 for 5.

2. What happens when the computer reads a 7 in the code field when the ON–GO TO statement reads as follows?

```
50  ON X GO TO 75, 90, 105, 120, 135, 150
```

3. What kind of a statement would keep the computer from defaulting when 7 was read in Question 2?

4. What multiple statement would replace the following statements?

a.
```
10  PRINT
14  PRINT
18  PRINT;TAB(25);"THE MCNAUGHTON CORPORATION"
```

b.
```
20  A = .05
25  B = .07
30  C = .09
```

5. What single statement would replace the following statements?

```
20  A = .12
30  B = .12
35  C = .12
```

6. The largest number in field A will be 9999.99. What PRINT USING statement would print A?

7. The following printout is desired. What statements would print it? The fields are A, B, and C.

```
Col.              Col.            Col.
 28                40              53
 ↓                 ↓               ↓
 $37.95            $7350.90        $951.80
```

8. The following output is desired for C. What statement would print C?

```
1763.97
***1.83
**11.76
*305.58
```

9. The following output is desired for B. What statement would print B?

```
 $372.56
$5812.75
   $3.32
```

10. What statement would be necessary to print out the current date?

ASSIGNMENTS[3]

1. The Wholesalers of America give different rates of discounts to different purchasers. Each purchaser has a code in field C. Code 1 is a 10 percent discount; Code 2, a 12 percent discount; Code 3, a 15 percent discount; and Code 4, a 20 percent discount. The printout, which follows, should contain the customer's name, code number, amount of the order before discount, amount of discount, and net amount of order. Also, a total of the original orders, the total of discounts, and total of the net amounts are to be prepared and handed in.

   If the code is incorrect, an error line should be printed which will show the customer name, code, amount of order before discount, and, beginning in the fourth column, the words INCORRECT CODE.

WHOLESALERS OF AMERICA
PURCHASES FOR THE WEEK OF XX-XXX-XX

CUSTOMER'S NAME	CODE	AMOUNT OF ORIGINAL ORDER	AMT. OF DISCOUNT	NET AMOUNT OF ORDER
B. Baker	3	3176.83	XXXX.XX	XXXX.XX
F. Caldwell	1	285.97		
S. Dickens	4	8729.76		
T. Everett	3	5481.32		
C. Harold	2	763.50		
G. Isaac	5	942.27		
D. Kurtz	1	337.61		
E. Langley	0	7395.45		
P. Manning	4	8621.98		
I. Pavoloski	1	395.06		
TOTAL		$XXXXXX.XX	$XXXXX.XX	$XXXXXX.XX

[3] The rules for centering explained in Chapter 5 should be applied.

2. The Western World uses a code for markup on its merchandise. Code 1 is a 20 percent markup; Code 2, a 25 percent markup; Code 3, a 30 percent markup; Code 4, a 40 percent markup; and Code 5, a 45 percent markup. The company marks up on selling price. To take markup on selling price, the complement of the markup (the markup subtracted from 100) must be found. Then the complement is divided into the cost price. When the cost is $90 and the markup on selling price is 20 percent, 20 percent should be subtracted from 100 percent to find the complement (80 percent). When 90 (cost) is divided by .80 (complement), the resulting selling price will be $112.50.

   If the code is incorrect, an error line should be printed which will show the name of the merchandise, code, cost, and, beginning in the fourth column, the words INCORRECT CODE.

WESTERN WORLD
Price List
(Current Date Here)

ITEM	CODE	COST	SELLING PRICE
Girls Jeans–G18	1	16.75	XXX.XX
Girls Deluxe Shirts–G25	3	22.15	
Mens Jeans–M32	1	14.30	
Mens Western Shirts–M17	3	11.76	
Halter–H18	0	10.25	
Western Saddle–S13	5	289.00	
English Saddle–S27	5	225.90	
Bridle–I26	7	25.90	
Saddle Tree–T95	4	175.80	
Reins–R20	6	15.82	
Girls Boots–B17	2	21.75	
Mens Boots–B22	2	25.33	

The flowchart, computer listing, and printout should be prepared and handed in.

3. The Gillis Credit Union has five classes of loans. The interest on these loans is computed on the number of days between payments. The loan rates are based on collateral consisting of the savings account as collateral, which is the cheapest, to the signature loan which is the most expensive. Banks and other institutions use a formula to have the computer figure the number of days between payments. At the Gillis Credit Union every day of

the year has a number, starting with January 1 as number 1. The number of the day when the last payment was made is input by the operator. The number of the day paid is also input by the operator. The codes are as follows: Code 1 = .0001351 a day, Code 2 = .0001426 a day, Code 3 = .0001501 a day, Code 4 = .0001576 a day, and Code 5 = .0001801 a day. The data and example of the printout are shown below. To find the amount of interest, the computer is to compute the number of days between payment days and multiply the resulting number of days times daily interest rate and then times old balance. Interest is to be added to the old balance, and the payment subtracted from the old balance to secure the new balance. The flowchart, computer listing, and printout should be prepared and handed in.

If the code is incorrect, an error line should be printed which will show the customer name, account number, code, and, beginning in the fifth column, the words ERROR—INCORRECT CODE.

GILLIS CREDIT UNION

ACCOUNT RECORDS FOR THE WEEK OF XX-XXX-XX

CUSTOMER NAME	ACCT. NUMBER	CODE	DATE PAID	OLD BALANCE	PAYMENT	NEW BALANCE
X. XXXXXXXXX	XX-XXX-X	X	XX-XX	XXXX.XX	XX.XX	XXXX.XX

The data for this problem is shown below. Column 1 contains the customer name; Column 2, the account number; Column 3, the code (class of loan); Column 4, the day of the year of the last payment; Column 5, the date paid; Column 6, the number of the day of the year of the current payment; Column 7, the old balance; and Column 8, the amount of the payment.

B. Anderson	05-312-5	5	59	03-31	90	1256.32	63.00
A. Burke	13-327-4	1	61	04-02	92	1575.89	50.00
D. Caldwell	21-212-4	6	62	04-03	93	1798.40	51.20
L. Evans	13-127-1	5	60	03-30	89	526.15	61.75
H. Goldsmith	12-897-5	3	59	03-31	90	978.46	38.23
C. Ingverson	04-432-4	4	64	04-02	92	1183.95	57.49
G. Jenkins	09-695-5	2	63	04-04	94	1576.76	62.12
I. Lloyd	14-731-6	0	59	04-01	91	343.97	63.19
P. Manning	27-815-3	1	60	03-30	89	676.31	95.11

Y. Oldhan	18-471-2	4	62	04-03	93	895.43	78.23
E. Parker	12-213-1	3	64	04-04	94	1069.11	85.17
H. Stevenson	05-555-8	3	59	03-31	90	327.85	63.12
I. Taylor	03-913-1	5	61	04-02	92	1978.35	92.19

8

A PROGRAM WITH MULTIPLE TOTALS

The following topics are covered in this chapter.

A. The comment at the end of a statement
B. The switch
C. An additional method of comparison
D. The date printed in the heading
E. Multiple totals

THE COMMENT AT THE END OF A STATEMENT[1]

In previous chapters, the REM statement was used to make comments within the program. The same thing can be accomplished with an exclamation mark. The computer ignores everything following the exclamation mark, even though the comment will be shown on the listing.

[1] Many systems use an apostrophe in place of an exclamation point in this statement

```
10  X = B! THIS PLACED THE BONUS IN X
15  ! THE FOLLOWING STATEMENTS ARE USED TO FIGURE COMPOUND INTEREST
```

In Statement 10, the computer will store the value of B at the address X. Then the comment following the exclamation mark will be listed but otherwise treated as nonexecutable.

THE SWITCH

The switch used in programming performs exactly like the switch on a railroad line. As long as the switch on the main line is open, the train continues on the main track. When the switch is thrown, or closed, the train cannot continue on the main track but is forced to go off on a side track. Why would the switch be closed? To force the train off on the side track for some special reason such as to make a delivery, to pick up empty cars, or to free the main track for an express train. The same principle holds true in programming.

Why a programmed switch? To go off the main track of the program to do something special.

PROBLEM 8-1

A short problem that uses a switch will be shown below. Whenever numbers representing dollars and cents are listed, only the first line of the figures should have a dollar sign. Another dollar sign should be placed before the total, as shown in Figure 8-1. This problem will be analyzed from the point of view of a programmer.

FIGURE 8-1

Problem 8-1

```
        $ 71.32    $ 52.05    $ 33.17
          22.09      15.06      33.05
          27.05      19.05      76.32

TOTAL   $120.46    $ 86.16    $142.54
```

Because the first line requires a dollar sign, a special process is required to get that line printed. A switch is needed. The programmer constructs a flowchart using the following steps.

1. Because a switch is to be used, it must be initialized. The programmer has designated the variable name of the switch to be S. S = 0 means the switch is closed, and S = 1 means the switch is open. On the other hand, the programmer could use D$ for the switch and initialize the closed condition as "Closed" and the open condition as "Open". Any number represented by a numeric variable, or any word or words represented by a string variable, can be used for the open or closed condition of the switch.

   The programmer also notes that total counters are required. He initialized the counters as T1, T2, T3 = 0.

2. The next step would be to have the computer read a data line.
3. The next step would be to test for the trailer data. The programmer ignores the "yes" branch from the decision for the present and continues down the main flow, which is the "no" branch (no, it is not the trailer data).
4. The programmer checks to see what is to be done once the data is read and stored. In this particular problem, a line of data is to be printed and the amount of sales must be added to the total counters.

   However, a decision must be made as to whether to print a line with a dollar sign or one without. The first line is to be printed with a dollar sign. How can the programmer write a statement that will write a line with a dollar sign one time and without a dollar sign another time?

   a. The decision statement to determine if a dollar sign is to be printed would be "Is $ Switch closed?"
   b. As the dollar sign switch was initialized as closed, the answer to the question would be yes.
   c. The programmer has determined that if the switch is closed, the computer must do the following steps.
      1. Print a line using a dollar sign.
      2. Open the switch so the computer will not branch to print a line with a dollar sign again.
      3. Add to the total counters.
      4. Go back to read data.
   d. The programmer then follows the flow from the "no" part of the decision "Is $ Switch Closed?" The computer would do the following steps.
      1. Print a line without a dollar sign.
      2. Join the "yes" branch and add to total.
      3. Go back and read data.

5. The loop of read data, print a line, add to totals continues until the trailer data has been read. When this happens, the computer is commanded to branch, print a blank line, and then a total line. The output symbol, to print the total line, is added to the flowchart.
6. Once the total line is printed, the program is completed, so the "End" symbol is added to the flowchart.
7. Now that the flowchart is written, the programmer codes from it.

The flowchart appears in Figure 8-2 and the coded program appears in Figure 8-3.

A METHOD OF COMPARISON

In business, reports requiring minor totals and grand totals are common, much like the one shown in Figure 8-4.

How can a computer be programmed to branch to print a total for one company and to start totalling sales for the next company? Comparison statements are used for this purpose.

For example, in Problem 8-2 the company number is placed in a storage location addressed N. Then that same company number will be placed in another storage location called N1. Each time through the read-print cycle, a statement, testing to see if N and N1 are equivalent, will be read by the computer. As long as the two numbers are equal, the computer prints a line, adds to the total counter, and reads another line.

However, when a new company number is read and stored in N and the question is asked "IS N1 = N?", the answer will be "no" as the old company number is still stored in N1. Because the answer is "no", the computer will branch, print a total line, and do other details which will be explained as the program for Problem 8-2 is analyzed in the next section.

PROBLEM 8-2

Following is a step-by-step analysis of the problem shown in Figure 8-4 and preparation of the flowchart for Problem 8-2, shown in Figures 8-5 and 8-6.

The programmer begins by placing a legend at the top of the flowchart designating the variables, something that probably most programmers should do.

FIGURE 8-2

Flowchart of Problem 8-1

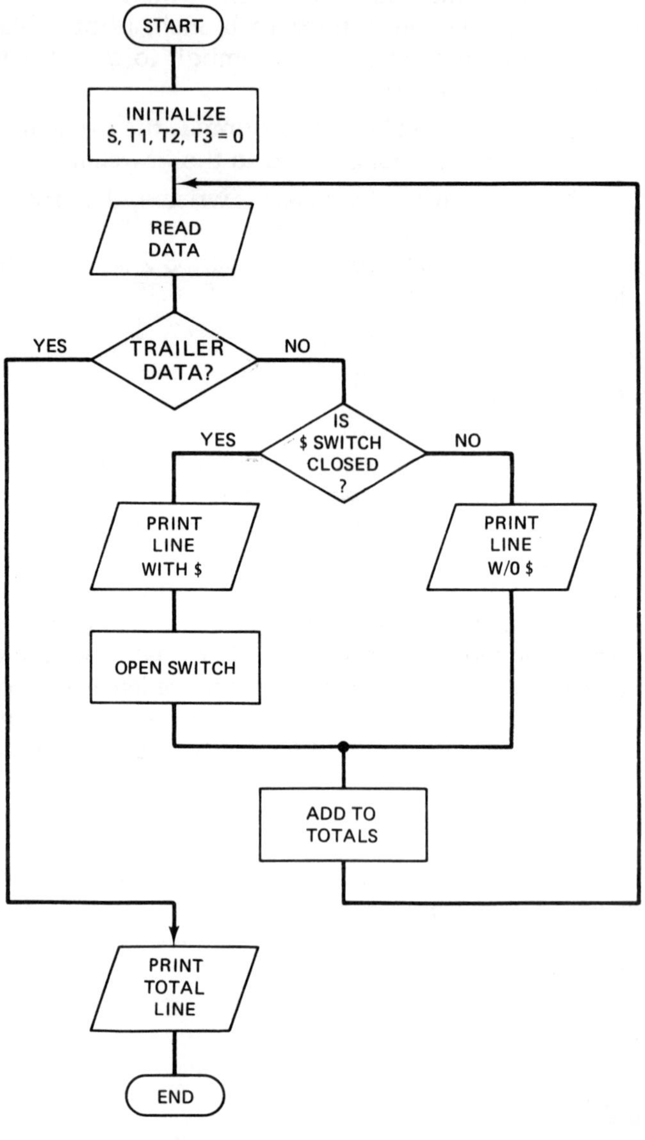

FIGURE 8-3

Listing of Problem 8-1

```
5   S,T1,T2,T3 = 0
10  READ A,B,C
12  IF A = -9 GO TO 55
18  IF S = 0 GO TO 34
22  PRINT;TAB(15);
26  PRINT USING "  ##.##      ##.##      ##.##",A,B,C
30  GO TO 46
34  PRINT;TAB(15);
38  PRINT USING "$ ##.##    $ ##.##    $ ##.##",A,B,C
42  S = 1
46  T1 = T1 + A:T2 = T2 + B:T3 = T3 + C
50  GO TO 10
55  PRINT:PRINT;TAB(8);"TOTAL   ";
60  PRINT USING "$###.##    $###.##    $###.##",T1,T2,T3
65  DATA 71.32,52.05,33.17
68  DATA 22.09,15.06,33.05
71  DATA 27.05,19.05,76.32
73  DATA -9,0,0
75  END
```

The programmer notes that a heading is to be printed and that one line of the heading should show the current date. So after the START symbol, he places PRINT HEADING W/CURRENT DATE on the flowchart.

Because there will be two switches used, one to branch to print the line with a dollar sign (M) and one to cause the computer to branch to place the company number in a storage location (S), they are initialized. Also, there are two total counters, T for total sales by company and T1 for total sales. The next item entered on the flowchart is INITIALIZE S,M,T,T1=0.

In this problem, the programmer decides to break up the reading of the data and to read the company number in one statement, check if it is the last data, and then read the remaining data. Thus, the three following symbols and labels are included on the flowchart: READ N, IF N = -999, and READ C$,I,I$,S1.

In the explanation of comparison statements, it was stated that the company number would be placed in a storage location for comparison purposes. This step must be outside the main flow of the program, so a switch is used to cause the computer to branch to the statement that will cause the company number to be placed in a storage location. Therefore it is necessary to test if the S switch is open. It is not because it was initialized to zero (closed). The programmer follows the "no" branch and puts in a symbol opening the switch (S=1). Then he

FIGURE 8-4

Printout for Problem 8-2[2]

```
RUN
DYKES    03:41 PM        03-MAY-81

                              BOB DYKES

                      MACHINE PARTS WHOLESALER

                          DAILY SALES REPORT
                              03-MAY-81

   COMPANY          COMPANY              NO. OF    ITEM
   NUMBER            NAME                 ITEMS    NUMBER      SALES

    1213    ADAMS MACHINE SHOP              24      13A2    $  437.20
    1213    ADAMS MACHINE SHOP               2      14B3       532.17
    1213    ADAMS MACHINE SHOP               1      12C5       392.19

                           TOTAL SALES BY COMPANY           $ 1361.56

    4718    RICKLES MACHINE SHOP             6      17A4    $  954.17
    4718    RICKLES MACHINE SHOP             3      13C3       816.25
    4718    RICKLES MACHINE SHOP            12      13B5       532.98
    4718    RICKLES MACHINE SHOP             4      11D5       444.32

                           TOTAL SALES BY COMPANY           $ 2747.72

                           TOTAL SALES                      $ 4109.28
```

adds a symbol showing N1=N (placing the company number in a comparison location). Going back to the "yes" branch, the programmer joins the "no" branch at the decision "IS N1=N?"

The programmer follows the "no" branch and puts into a symbol PRINT TOT. SALES BY CO. The next symbol reads T1=T1+T, which places the total sales into the final total. The next symbol reads T=0, which will zero out the total. The programmer then places M=0 into a symbol (to close the $ switch because the first line for the next company must print a line with a dollar sign), and finally, N1=N, to place the new company number into the comparison location. The flow line joins the "yes" branch at the decision "IS $ SWITCH CLOSED?"

[2] In this problem the columnar titles of Columns 3 and 4 were used in computing the spacing.

The flow from the "yes" branch of the decision "IS N1=N?" drops directly to join the "no" branch at "IS $ SWITCH CLOSED?" The "no" branch of the $ switch goes to "PRINT LINE W/O $", joins the "yes" branch, and adds to the total sales by company, T=T+S1.

The "yes" branch of "IS $ SWITCH CLOSED?" goes to a symbol stating PRINT LINE WITH $, followed by M=1 (which opens the switch) and then the flow joins the "no" branch to add to the total sales by company, T=T+S1.

After adding to the total sales by company, the flow branches back to read the first item of a line of data, READ N.

Going back to the decision symbol "IF N = -999", the programmer follows the "yes" branch to the end of the flowchart where he writes PRINT TOT. SALES BY CO., T1=T1+T, PRINT TOTAL SALES, and then END. The flowchart is illustrated in Figures 8-5 and 8-6.

After Problem 8-2 has been flowcharted, it must be coded.

Bob Dykes is a wholesaler of machine parts. Every morning a report, part of which is presented in Figure 8-4, is prepared of the previous day's sales.

Several principles are illustrated in this problem.

1. Using the day's date from the computer, a principle described in Chapter 7.
2. Using the Line Feed key.
3. Using a switch to have the computer branch to print a dollar sign on the first line but not on the following lines.
4. Using comparison statements to determine when a subtotal is to be printed.

The REM statements and those printing out the headings and current data are Statements 5, 10, 15, 20, 25, 27, and 28. They are shown in the listing in Figure 8-7.

The programmer not only used the Line Feed on Statements 5 and 28, but he also indented these lines to facilitate reading.

THE FIRST DATA SWITCH

Statement 35 is the first use of a switch in this problem. The programmer used the variable S for the switch, and used zero for closed and one for open.

```
35  IF S = 1 GO TO 55
45  S = 1:N1 = N
```

FIGURE 8-5
Flowchart for Problem 8-2

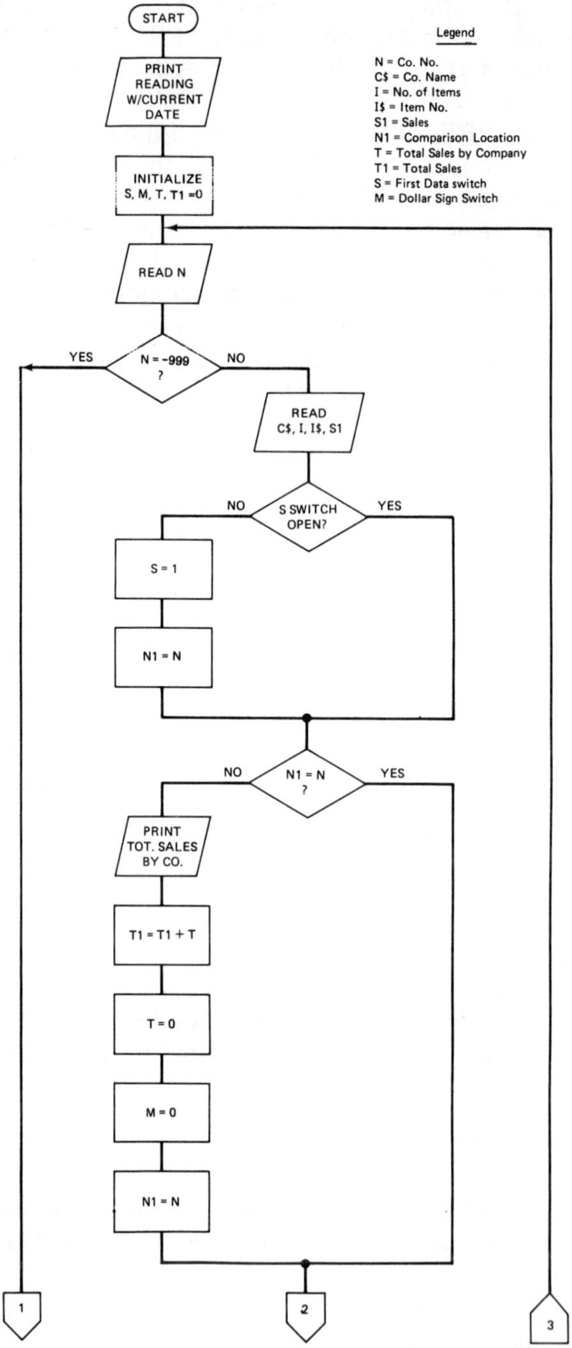

FIGURE 8-6
Flowchart for Problem 8-2 Continued

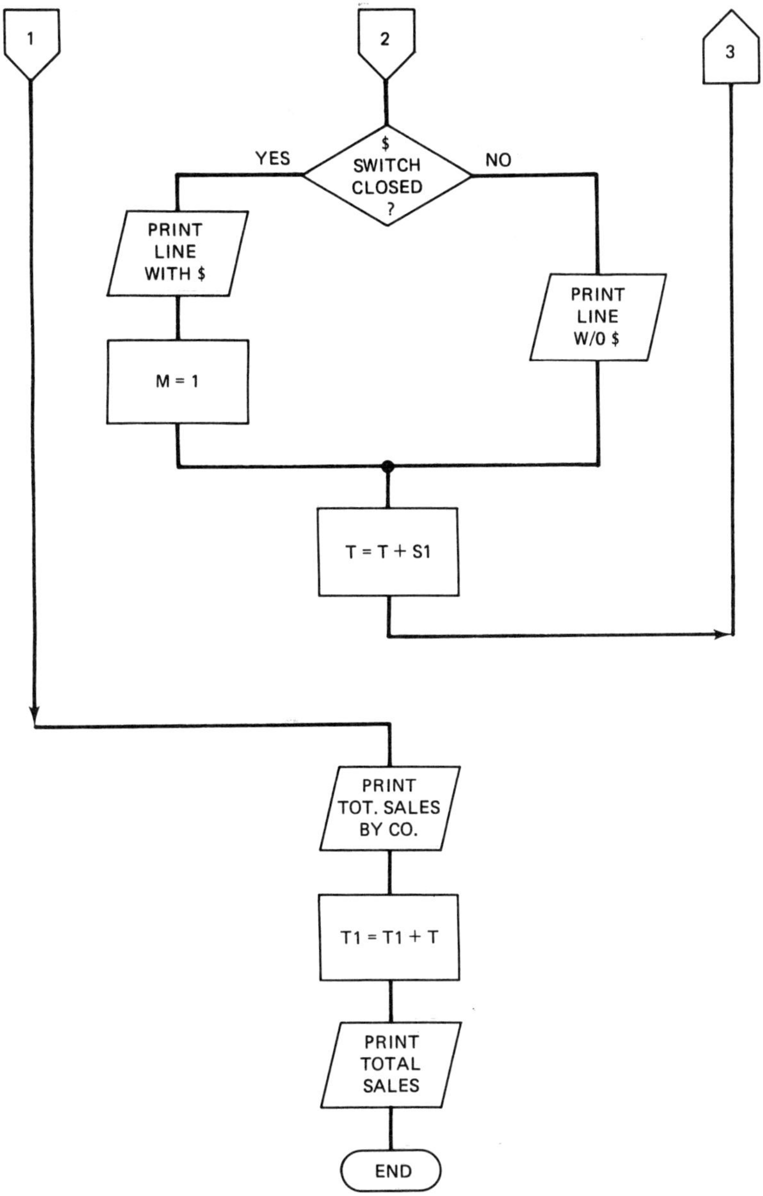

FIGURE 8-7

Computer Listing for Problem 8-2

```
LIST
DYKES   06:05 PM        07-MAY-81

5   REM N=COMPANY NUMBER, C$=COMPANY NAME, I=NUMBER OF ITEMS
    I$=ITEM NUMBER, S1=SALES, N1=COMPARISON LOCATION, T=TOTAL
    COUNTER, T1=FINAL TOTAL COUNTER, S=FIRST COMPARISON SWITCH,
    M=SWITCH FOR DOLLAR SIGN.
10  PRINT:PRINT;TAB(30);"BOB DYKES"
15  PRINT:PRINT;TAB(23);"MACHINE PARTS WHOLESALER"
20  PRINT:PRINT;TAB(26);"DAILY SALES REPORT"
25  PRINT;TAB(30);DATE$(0):PRINT:PRINT
27  PRINT;TAB(5);"COMPANY        COMPANY              NO. OF    ITEM"
28  PRINT;TAB(5);"NUMBER           NAME               ITEMS    NUMBER"
    "     SALES":PRINT
29  S,M,T,T1 = 0
30  READ N
32  IF N = -999 GO TO 115
34  READ C$,I,I$,S1
35  IF S = 1 GO TO 55
45  S = 1:N1 = N
55  IF N1 = N GO TO 80
60  PRINT:PRINT;TAB(31);"TOTAL SALES BY COMPANY   ";
65  PRINT USING "$#####.##",T:PRINT
70  T1 = T1 + T:T = 0:M = 0:N1 = N
80  IF M = 0 GO TO 95
82  PRINT;TAB(6);
84  PRINT USING "####",N;
86  PRINT;TAB(14);C$;TAB(40);
88  PRINT USING "##",I;
90  PRINT;TAB(49);I$;TAB(57);
92  PRINT USING "####.##",S1
94  GO TO 105
95  PRINT;TAB(6);
96  PRINT USING "####",N;
97  PRINT;TAB(14);C$;TAB(40);
98  PRINT USING "##",I;
99  PRINT;TAB(49);I$;TAB(55);
100 PRINT USING "$ ####.##",S1
102 M = 1
105 T = T + S1
110 GO TO 30
115 PRINT:PRINT;TAB(31);"TOTAL SALES BY COMPANY   ";
117 PRINT USING "$#####.##",T
120 T1 = T1 + T : PRINT
125 PRINT;TAB(31);"TOTAL SALES               ";
127 PRINT USING "$#####.##",T1
129 DATA 1213, "ADAMS MACHINE SHOP",24,"13A2",437.20
131 DATA 1213, "ADAMS MACHINE SHOP",2,"14B3",532.17
133 DATA 1213, "ADAMS MACHINE SHOP",1,"12C5",392.19
135 DATA 4718, "RICKLES MACHINE SHOP",6,"17A4",954.17
137 DATA 4718, "RICKLES MACHINE SHOP",3,"13C3",816.25
139 DATA 4718, "RICKLES MACHINE SHOP",12, "13B5",532.98
141 DATA 4718, "RICKLES MACHINE SHOP",4,"11D5",444.32
143 DATA -999
145 END
```

Statement 35 is shown out of order so that the purpose of the switch can be demonstrated. Why was it necessary to use the switch in the first place? The reason for the switch in this problem is to duplicate the company number in another storage area for comparison purposes (N1 = N). Every day the operator could look at the first company number and assign it to the comparison storage location. However, a program in business is usually set up to be used for a long period of time and to eliminate human participation as much as possible. The computer is far less likely to make an error than is a human. By inserting a switch in this program, the computer can be used to put in the first company number with lightning speed and dependable accuracy. Time is money in business; therefore, the switch saves time and money. Also, the switch is subsequently opened so that control will not come back to Statement 45 and will be allowed to continue the normal loop.

THE USE OF THE COMPARISON STATEMENT

In Statement 55 the use of a comparison statement is demonstrated. The command at this statement says that if N1 (the comparison location) is equal to N (the customer number), control must go to Statement 80.

```
55  IF N1 = N GO TO 80
```

Statement 80 checks to see whether the dollar sign switch (M) is closed. If it is closed, control branches to Statement 95 where Statements 95 through 100 will cause the computer to print a line with a dollar sign. If the switch is open, control falls through to Statements 82 through 92, which cause the computer to print out a line without the dollar sign.

```
80  IF M = 0 GO TO 95
82  PRINT;TAB(6);
84  PRINT USING "####",N;
86  PRINT;TAB(14);C$;TAB(40);
88  PRINT USING "##",I;
90  PRINT;TAB(49);I$;TAB(57);
92  PRINT USING "####.##",S1
```

The program is set up so the flow is always from the top down. If N1 is not equal to N, the computer drops to the next statement and causes the computer to print out the total sales of the company.

CLOSING THE SWITCH

After the computer executes Statements 60 and 65, which print out the total sales by company, several things must happen. They are accomplished by Statement 70.

1. The total sales by company must be deposited into the total sales counter and the total sales by company counter turned back to zero so that it may be used again.
2. The dollar sign switch must be closed so that control will branch and print the first line of the company's sales with a dollar sign.
3. The new company number must be placed in a comparison location.

```
70  T1 = T1 + T:T = 0:M = 0:N1 = N
```

GO TO STATEMENTS

A number of GO TO statements are used in this program. They should be avoided whenever possible, but to maintain the top-down principle and the one-entry, one-exit concept, the GO TO's are necessary. The flow is always down and goes up only at the end of the loop to read another line of data.

LAST DATA TEST

When the computer finally picks up the trailer constant in Field N, it is sent to Statement 115. Statements 115, 117, and 120 command the computer to print out the total sales by company and add that total into the total sales counter.

```
115 PRINT:PRINT;TAB(31);"TOTAL SALES BY COMPANY  ";
117 PRINT USING "$#####.##",T
120 T1 = T1 + T :PRINT
```

Statements 125 and 127 cause the computer to print out the final total.

```
125 PRINT;TAB(31);"TOTAL SALES                ";
127 PRINT USING "$#####.##",T1
```

The complete listing of the program is shown in Figure 8-7.

PROBLEM 8-3

Problem 8-3 is similar to the first two problems except that in this problem the computer will be asked to print minor totals, intermediate totals, and a final total. The final total is printed when the trailer constant is read, so no new principle is introduced.

MULTIPLE TOTALS

In Problem 8-3 whenever the employee number changes, a total is taken of his units produced. When the section number changes, a total of the units produced for the last employee in the section and then a total for all of the employees in the section are printed. Whenever a new plant number appears, three totals have to be taken: the total of the last employee's units produced, the total of all of the units produced in the section, and a total of all of the units produced in all of the sections in the plant.

The computer printout of Problem 8-3 is shown in Figure 8-8, the flowchart in Figures 8-9 and 8-10, and the computer listing in Figure 8-11.

The explanations of this problem will begin with the READ statement. The first two statements should need no explanation.

```
52  READ W,E,S,P,U
55  IF W = -9 GO TO 140
```

USE OF COMPARISON STATEMENTS

Statement 60 is the switch statement that, when closed, falls through to the next statement, Statement 70. At Statement 70 the computer opens the switch (H=1), places the employee number (E) into the employee comparison location (E2), places the section number (S) into the section comparison location (S2), places the plant number into the plant comparison location (P2 = P), and then falls through to Statement 75.

FIGURE 8-8

Printout of Problem 8-3

```
                    NELSON'S IRON WORKS

                   REPORT FOR APRIL, 1981

         NUMBER OF UNITS PRODUCED BY WESTERN PLANTS


         EMPLOYEE                  PLANT      UNITS
WEEK      NUMBER      SECTION     NUMBER    PRODUCED

 1         157          12          1          37
 2         157          12          1          40

              TOTAL UNITS BY EMPLOYEE  77

 1         158          12          1          44
 2         158          12          1          48

              TOTAL UNITS BY EMPLOYEE  92
              TOTAL UNITS BY SECTION  169

 1         162          14          1          42
 2         162          14          1          43.

              TOTAL UNITS BY EMPLOYEE  85
              TOTAL UNITS BY SECTION   85
              TOTAL UNITS BY PLANT    254

 1         172          18          2          48
 2         172          18          2          45

              TOTAL UNITS BY EMPLOYEE  93
              TOTAL UNITS BY SECTION   93
              TOTAL UNITS BY PLANT     93
              TOTAL UNITS             347
```

```
60  IF H = 1 GO TO 75
70  H = 1:E2 = E:S2 = S:P2 = P
```

Comparison locations must be used in this problem. The key is to list the statements testing the equality of numbers to those in the comparison locations in *reverse* of the order in which they are printed out.

FIGURE 8-9
Flowchart for Problem 8-3

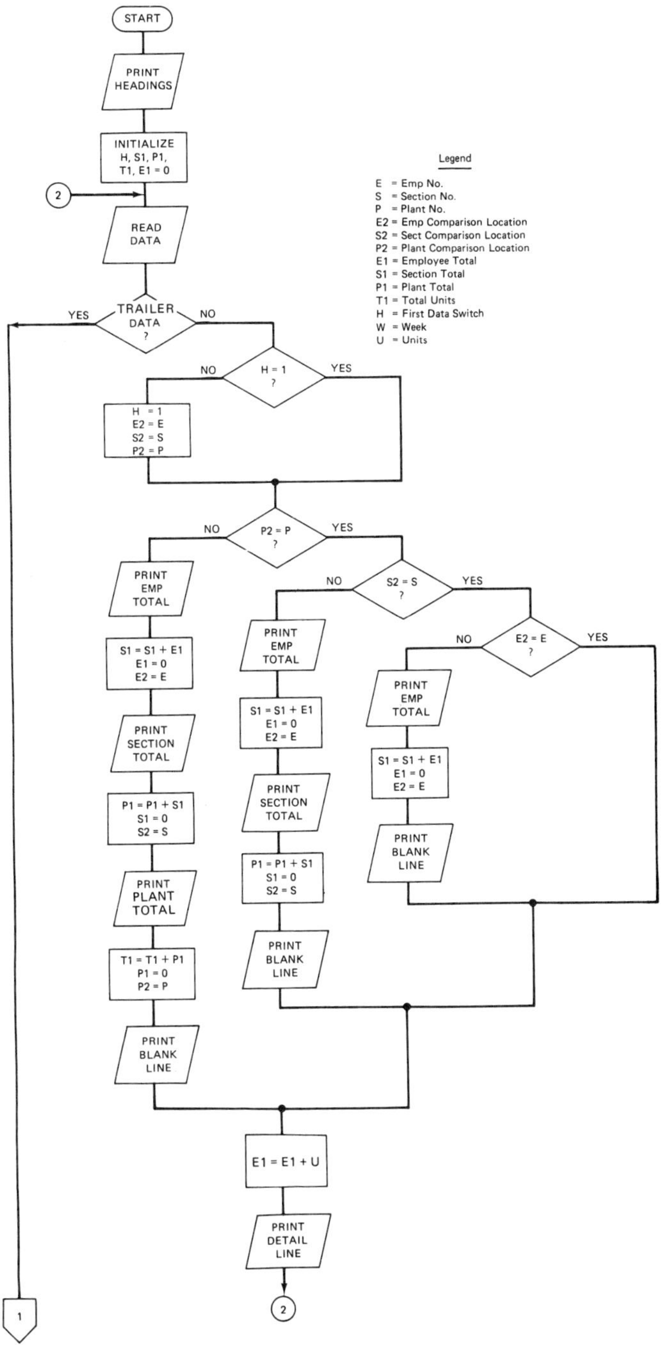

FIGURE 8-10

Flowchart for Problem 8-3 Continued

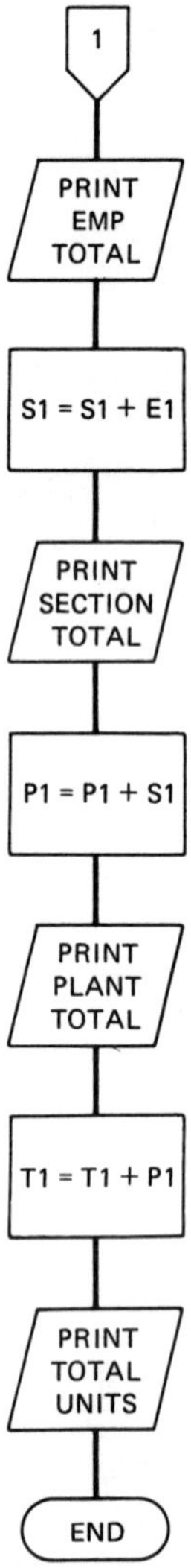

FIGURE 8-11

Listing of Problem 8-3

```
LIST
COMPAR   06:05 PM          07-MAY-81
10  REM WEEK=W,EMP.NO.=E,SECT.=S,PLANT=P,UNITS PRODUCED=U
15  REM EMP.TOT=E1,SECT.TOT.=S1,PLANTTOT=P1,AND GRANDTOT=T1
20  REM SWITCH=H,OPEN=1,CLOSED=0,COMPARISON LOCATIONS ARE:
    EMP.NO.=E2,SECT.=S2,PLANT=P2.
30  PRINT:PRINT;TAB(25);"NELSON'S IRON WORKS"
35  PRINT:PRINT;TAB(24);"REPORT FOR APRIL,1981"
40  PRINT:PRINT;TAB(14);"NUMBER OF UNITS PRODUCED BY WESTERN PLANTS"
45  PRINT:PRINT:PRINT;TAB(20);"EMPLOYEE";TAB(45);"PLANT       "UNITS"
47  PRINT;TAB(10);"WEEK          NUMBER       SECTION      NUMBER    PRODUCED"
48  PRINT
50  H,S1,P1,T1,E1 = 0
52  READ W,E,S,P,U
55  IF W = -9 GO TO 140
60  IF H = 1 GO TO 75
70  H = 1:E2 = E:S2 = S:P2 = P
75  IF P2 = P GO TO 105
80  PRINT:PRINT;TAB(33);"TOTAL UNITS BY EMPLOYEE";
82  PRINT USING "   ##",E1
84  S1 = S1 + E1:E1 = 0:E2 = E
86  PRINT;TAB(33); "TOTAL UNITS BY SECTION";
88  PRINT USING "   ###",S1
90  P1 = P1 + S1:S1 = 0:S2 = S
92  PRINT;TAB(33); "TOTAL UNITS BY PLANT";
94  PRINT USING "    ####",P1
96  T1 = T1 + P1:P1 = 0:P2 = P:PRINT
102 GO TO 133
105 IF S2 = S GO TO 125
107 PRINT:PRINT;TAB(33); "TOTAL UNITS BY EMPLOYEE";
109 PRINT USING "   ##",E1
111 S1 = S1 + E1:E1 = 0:E2 = E
113 PRINT;TAB(33); "TOTAL UNITS BY SECTION";
115 PRINT USING "   ###",S1
117 P1 = P1 + S1:S1 = 0:S2 = S:PRINT
119 GO TO 133
125 IF E2 = E GO TO 133
127 PRINT:PRINT;TAB(33);"TOTAL UNITS BY EMPLOYEE";
129 PRINT USING "   ##",E1
131 S1 = S1 + E1:E1 = 0:E2 = E:PRINT
133 E1 = E1 + U
134 PRINT;TAB(11);
135 PRINT USING "#            ###          ##           #",W,E,S,P;
136 PRINT USING "           ##",U
137 GO TO 52
140 PRINT:PRINT;TAB(33);"TOTAL UNITS BY EMPLOYEE";
142 PRINT USING "   ##",E1
144 S1 = S1 + E1
146 PRINT;TAB(33);"TOTAL UNITS BY SECTION";
148 PRINT USING "   ###",S1
150 P1 = P1 + S1
152 PRINT;TAB(33);"TOTAL UNITS BY PLANT";
154 PRINT USING "    ####",P1
156 T1 = T1 + P1
158 PRINT;TAB(33);"TOTAL UNITS               ";
159 PRINT USING "####",T1
160 DATA 1,157,12,1,37
162 DATA 2,157,12,1,40
164 DATA 1,158,12,1,44
166 DATA 2,158,12,1,48
168 DATA 1,162,14,1,42
170 DATA 2,162,14,1,43
172 DATA 1,172,18,3,48
174 DATA 2,172,18,2,45
176 DATA -9,0,0,0,0
178 END
```

The logic of this is that there can be many changes of employees without changing the section. However, when the section changes, so do the employees. There can be many section changes without plant changes, but when the plant changes, so do the sections and employees.

The order of printing out is employee total, section total, and plant total. However, the comparison IF statements are in the reverse of the order in which the totals are printed.

In a problem of this nature the programmer would be wise to follow the "no" branch from the comparison statement to its conclusion. The first of these comparison statements is Statement 75.

If P2 does not equal P, the computer will fall through to the next statements in the "no" branch and Statements 80, 82, 86, 88, 92, and 94 will cause the computer to print out all three totals: TOTAL UNITS BY EMPLOYEE, TOTAL UNITS BY SECTION, and TOTAL UNITS BY PLANT.

```
75  IF P2 = P GO TO 105
80  PRINT:PRINT;TAB(33):"TOTAL UNITS BY EMPLOYEE";
82  PRINT USING "    ##",E1
84  S1 = S1 + E1:E1 = 0:E2 = E
86  PRINT;TAB(33);"TOTAL UNITS BY SECTION";
88  PRINT USING "    ###",S1
90  P1 = P1 + S1:S1 = 0:S2 = S
92  PRINT;TAB(33);"TOTAL UNITS BY PLANT";
94  PRINT USING "     ####",P1
96  T1 = T1 + P1:P1 = 0:P2 = P:PRINT
```

Statement 84 deposits the employee total into the section total counter, zeroes out the employee total so it can be used for the next employee's total, and places the new employee number into the comparison location.

Statement 90 deposits the section total into the plant total counter, zeroes out the section total so it can be used again, and places the new section number into the comparison location.

Statement 96 deposits the plant total into the grand total counter, zeroes out the plant total so it can be used again, and places the new plant number into the comparison location.

At Statement 75 (IF P2 = P GO TO 105), the "yes" branch causes the following part of the program to be executed. If P2 is equal to P, the computer is sent to the next comparison statement, Statement 105.

```
105  IF S2 = S GO TO 125
```

If S2 is not equal to S, the "no" branch from Statement 105 is executed. The computer falls through to Statements 107 through 117. Statements 107, 109, 113, and 115 cause the computer to print out TOTAL UNITS BY EMPLOYEE and TOTAL UNITS BY SECTION.

```
107 PRINT:PRINT:TAB(33);"TOTAL UNITS BY EMPLOYEE";
109 PRINT USING "   ##",E1
111 S1 = S1 + E1:E1 = 0:E2 = E
113 PRINT;TAB(33);"TOTAL UNITS BY SECTION";
115 PRINT USING "   ###",S1
117 P1 = P1 + S1:S1 = 0: S2 = S:PRINT
```

Statement 111 adds the employee total to the section total counter, zeroes out the employee total, and places the new employee number into the comparison location.

Statement 117 adds the section total to the plant total counter, zeroes out the section total, and places the new section number into the comparison location.

At Statement 105, if S2 is equal to S, the "yes" branch causes the computer to go to the last comparison statement, Statement 125.

```
125 IF E2 = E GO TO 133
```

If E2 is not equal to E, the "no" branch from Statement 125 is executed. The computer falls through to Statements 127 through 136, which will print out TOTAL UNITS BY EMPLOYEE.

```
127 PRINT:PRINT;TAB(33);"TOTAL UNITS BY EMPLOYEE";
129 PRINT USING "   ##",E1
131 S1 = S1 + E1:E1 = 0:E2 = E:PRINT
```

Statement 131 deposits the employee total in the section total counter, zeroes out the employee total, and places the new employee number into the comparison location.

To follow the top down and one-entry, one-exit principles, Statements 102 and 119 send the computer to Statement 133. When the computer has finished executing Statement 131, it falls through to Statement 133.

At Statement 125, if E2 is equal to E, the "yes" branch causes the computer to go to Statement 133.

```
133 E1 = E1 + U
134 PRINT;TAB(11);
135 PRINT USING "#            ###            ##              #",W,E,S,P;
136 PRINT USING "            ###",U
```

Statement 133 deposits the number of units per employee into the employee total, and then goes on to Statements 134, 135, and 136, which print a line of data. Then Statement 137 sends the computer back to read a line of data.

When the answer to Statement 55, which asks if the line of data being read is the trailer, is "yes" the computer is sent to Statement 140.

Statements 140 and 142 print out TOTAL UNITS BY EMPLOYEE, Statement 144 deposits the employee total into the section total counter, Statements 146 and 148 print out TOTAL UNITS BY SECTION, and Statement 150 deposits the section total into the plant total counter. Statements 152 and 154 print out TOTAL UNITS BY PLANT, and Statement 156 deposits the plant total into the grand total counter. Statement 158 prints out TOTAL UNITS, and control then falls through the nonexecutable DATA statements to Statement 178, the END statement.

```
140 PRINT:PRINT;TAB(33);"TOTAL UNITS BY EMPLOYEE";
142 PRINT USING "    ##",E1
144 S1 = S1 + E1
146 PRINT;TAB(33);"TOTAL UNITS BY SECTION"'
148 PRINT USING "    ###",S1
150 P1 = P1 + S1
152 PRINT;TAB(33);"TOTAL UNITS BY PLANT";
154 PRINT USING "     ####",P1
156 T1 = T1 + P1
158 PRINT;TAB(33);"TOTAL UNITS                ";
159 PRINT USING "####",T1
178 END
```

The computer listing for this problem is shown in Figure 8-11, and the computer printout is shown in Figure 8-8.

SUMMARY

1. An exclamation mark can be used to make comments within the program. The computer ignores everything beyond the exclamation mark.

```
10  X = B! THIS PLACES THE BONUS IN X.
```

2. The switch is like a railway switch; it is either open or closed. It is not a mechanical switch. The programmer uses one number in a storage area to close the switch, another to open it. In this book "0" (zero) is closed, "1" is open. In the statement below, the computer is commanded to go to Statement 40 if the switch (S) is closed (0).

```
22  IF S = 0 GO TO 40
```

   If the switch is equal to 1, it is open. Therefore, control drops to the next statement.

3. When the computer finds the switch closed at Statement 22, it is sent to Statement 40, which caused the switch to be opened.

```
40  S = 1
```

4. Comparison statements are used to command the computer to branch whenever a certain number changes. In this chapter the comparison statements are used to branch to PRINT statements whenever an employee number, section number, or plant number changes. The comparison location is a storage area into which a number is placed, i.e., E2=E. The storage area E2 is the comparison location. The storage area E contains the employee number. E2=E places the employee number in the comparison location.
5. The following statement shows how, using a comparison, the computer is directed to go to another statement.

```
IF E2 <> E GO TO 70
```

   This statement commands that if what is located in storage E2 (the comparison location) is not equal to the value stored in E, control is transferred to Statement 70. These two storage locations will be equal until a new employee number is picked up by the computer and stored in E. Then the two values will be unequal.

6. One of the tasks to be done after the computer reaches Statement 70 is to place the new employee number in the comparison location so that the computer will go back to the normal routine.

```
70  E2 = E
```

7. When comparison statements are used to branch to print minor, intermediate, and final totals, the IF statements used to compare comparison locations should be in the reverse order to that in which the totals are printed. In Problem 8-3 the totals were printed in the following order: employee, section, plant, and final. The IF statements should be listed in the reverse order.

```
IF P2<>P GO TO 100
IF S2<>S GO TO 120
IF E2<>E GO TO 132
```

SELF-TEST

1. What statements, other than heading and data statements, will cause the computer to execute the following problem?

ITEM	COST
117	$35.76
126	15.25
185	7.03
132	27.65
TOTAL	$85.69

2. What statement will place employee number (E) into a comparison location (E1)?
3. This problem has multiple totals. The first total is by item number (A2). The second total is by salesman number (N2). The third total is by department number (D2), and the fourth total is by the store number (S2). Item number is A, salesman number is N, department number is D, and store number is S. Comparison locations are A1 for item, N1 for salesman, D1 for department, and S1 for store.
   a. What is the correct order of the IF statements that send the computer to the statements to write the totals—150 for item total; 140 for item and salesman total; 130 for item, salesman, and department total; and 115 for item, salesman, department, and store total?
   b. What statement or statements originally place the numbers into the comparison locations?
4. What is the primary reason for a switch?

5. In this problem the switch is S.
   a. How do the authors suggest that a statement be written to use a switch at the beginning of the program to go to Statement 75, to open the switch, and to place numbers in comparison locations?
   b. What statement should be used to close the switch?

ASSIGNMENTS[3]

1. The following program should employ switch and comparison statements. A minor total is taken every time the department number changes. There is a total of all department sales. The computer should print out the current date as the report date. A flowchart and the computer listing and the printing of the report should be prepared. The output format is shown below.

```
                BENGAL'S SPORTS STORE

                 WEEK'S SALES REPORT
                   (Current Date)

Qty     Item    Department      Sales

 8      37          12         $117.85
10      22          12          105.13
 4      19          12           15.72

        DEPARTMENT TOTALS      $XXX.XX

 3      11          14         $ 55.93
11      25          14          127.62
 6       7          14           37.53

        DEPARTMENT TOTALS      $XXX.XX

        TOTAL WEEKLY SALES               $XXX.XX
```

[3] The rules for centering explained in Chapter 5 should be applied.

2. The following report should take the current date from the computer for the report date. Minor totals are taken every time a department number changes. An intermediate total is taken when the section changes, and a final total is taken of all units produced at the report's end. A flowchart and the computer listing and the printing of the report should be prepared. The program format is shown below.

```
                RANDALL ELECTRONICS

                   WEEKLY REPORT
                   (Current Date)

Emp.       Dept.                      Units
 No.        No.         Sect.       Produced

 22          1            7             50
 24          1            7             47

Total Units Produced by Dept.          XXX

 28          2            7             52
 43          2            7             48

Total Units Produced by Dept.          XXX
Total Units Produced by Sect.         XXXX

 52          3           12             51
 48          3           12             49

Total Units Produced by Dept.          XXX
Total Units Produced by Sect.         XXXX
Total Units Produced by Store        XXXXX
```

3. The following program should employ switch and comparison statements. A minor total is taken every time there is a change in department number, an intermediate total is taken every time there is a change in store number, a final total is taken every time there is a change in district number, and a grand total is taken of all of the totals. A flowchart and the computer listing and the printing of the report should be prepared. The output format is shown below.

HARLEY'S SUPERMARKETS

WEEKLY SALES REPORT

In Thousands of Dollars

Week of XX-XXX-XX

Employee Number	Department	Store	District	Total Sales
17	8	1	2	100
22	8	1	2	87
		DEPT. TOTAL		XXX
5	10	1	2	70
14	10	1	2	99
		DEPT. TOTAL		XXX
		STORE TOTAL		XXXX
38	8	2	2	100
27	8	2	2	98
		DEPT. TOTAL		XXX
		STORE TOTAL		XXXX
		DISTRICT TOTAL		XXXXX
43	10	2	5	89
35	10	2	5	92
		DEPT. TOTAL		XXX
		STORE TOTAL		XXXX
		DISTRICT TOTAL		XXXXX
		GRAND TOTAL		XXXXXX

9

BACKSLASHES, FOR/NEXT STATEMENTS, AND OVERFORMATTING

This chapter covers the rules for the use of backslashes and FOR/NEXT statements. Nested loops and overformatting are also discussed.

USE OF BACKSLASHES[1]

String variables may be printed as the result of a PRINT USING statement by using pairs of backslashes (\). Each backslash stands for a character, and each space between pairs of backslashes stands for a character. For instance, a backslash, two spaces, and a backslash stand for four characters. The backslashes will print anything that is in the field that is formatted by the backslashes.

```
20  READ A$,B,C
30  DATA "JOHNSON, BILL",70,100
40  PRINT USING "         \           \ ##     ####",A$,B,C
50  END
```

[1] Backslashes are not used on all systems. The TRS-80 uses percent signs.

The preceding statements would cause the following printout.

```
JOHNSON, BILL  70      100
```

The first letter in the string variable A$ is printed in the space filled by the first backslash, and the following letters are printed up to and including the space filled by the second backslash. String fields formatted with backslashes are left justified. If the string field is longer than the space formatted, the characters beyond the formatted area are omitted. No diagnostic is generated.

FOR/NEXT STATEMENTS

One often hears the word "loop" used by programmers. This text has demonstrated statements in past programs that perform a loop. An example follows.

```
10  READ A$,B,N
20  If A$ = "EXIT" GO TO 70
30  C = B * N
40  PRINT USING "          \             \  ##      ####",A$,B,C
50  GO TO 10
```

This example is only part of the program, but it does illustrate a program loop. The computer reads a DATA statement storing values in A$, B, and N. Then it checks whether it has read the trailer DATA statement; and if it has not, it performs a calculation. Then it prints out a line of data and is told to go back to Statement 10. It continues this loop until the trailer DATA statement is read.

Another method of commanding the computer to perform operations in a loop is done with FOR/NEXT statements. One of the basic rules about the FOR/NEXT statements is that both a FOR and a NEXT statement *must* be used if either of these statements are incorporated in the program.

An example of a FOR statement would be as follows.

```
10  FOR N=1 TO 10 STEP 2
```

The word FOR is the descriptive word in the statement that tells the computer it is beginning a loop. The letter N is a variable that actually acts as a counter in the loop. Any numeric variable name can be used for this counter. In the example shown above, the number 1 is the number at which the counter is initialized. The counter may be initialized to a positive or negative number, or even to a zero. The word TO must be in the statement and the 10 is the terminal value of the counter. The word STEP is used to mean "increment." In this instance, STEP tells the computer to advance the counter by increments, or steps, of 2. The counter will read 1 the first time through the loop, 3 the second time, 5 the next time, etc.

As stated previously, a statement ending the loop must be supplied for the loop to operate properly. This statement is called the NEXT statement: 50 NEXT N. The NEXT statement must have in it the same variable name as is used for the counter in the FOR statement. As soon as the computer reads the NEXT statement, it advances the counter the number of steps or increments stated after STEP and then compares the counter value with the terminal value. If the counter value is beyond the terminal value, then the computer proceeds to the statement following the NEXT statement.

If the programmer wishes to increment by +1, he does not need the STEP part of the FOR statement: 10 FOR N=1 TO 10. The computer assumes a value of +1 if no STEP figure is given.

There may be minus values in FOR/NEXT loops. Assignment 1 at the end of this chapter, for instance, decreases the counter from 8 to 1. The FOR statement would read as follows.

```
50  FOR N = 8 TO 1 STEP -1
```

Statement 50 initializes N to eight, and the STEP commands the computer to reduce the counter by one every time through the loop.

PROBLEM 9-1

Every year the Gurney Mortgage Company issues to its borrowers a 12-payment table showing how much monthly interest is paid on the mortgage, what the monthly payment is on the balance, and what the new balance is. The program coded here is for those 12 payments. There is a $31,000 principal, an interest rate of 8-1/2 percent a year on the balance, a 30-year mortgage, and a payment of $350 a month, of which $111 is impounded for taxes and insurance. Although the chart shows a payment of $350, only $239 is used in the computations, as that is the amount that is applied to the principal and interest.

The flowchart for this problem is shown in Figure 9-1, and the complete computer listing and program printout appear in Figures 9-2 and 9-3. Statements 10 through 18 are REM statements. Statements 25

FIGURE 9-1
Flowchart for Problem 9-1

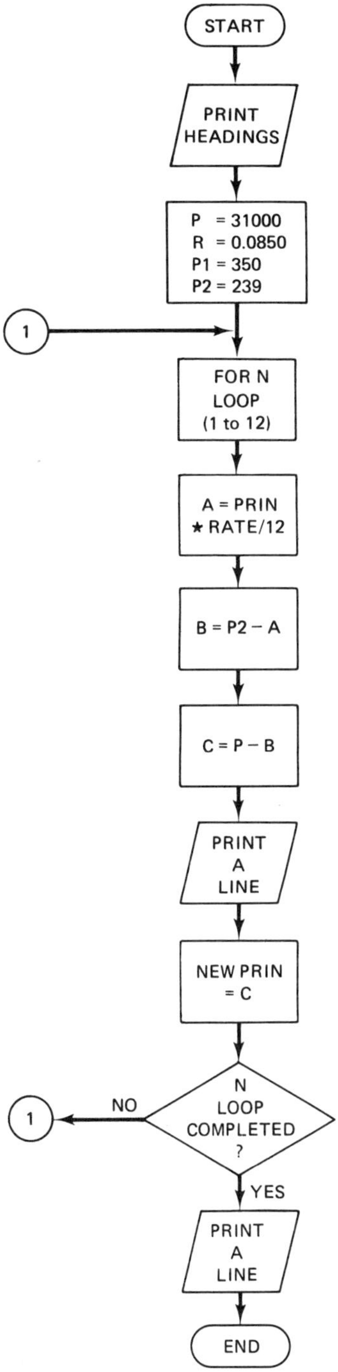

FIGURE 9-2

Listing for Problem 9-1

```
DO       12:45 PM           18-Jan-81
10  REM THIS PROGRAM FIGURES THE AMOUNT OF INTEREST AT THE RATE
12  REM OF .085 ON AN ORIGINAL PRINCIPAL OF $31,000 FOR A
14  REM ONE-YEAR PERIOD.  P=PRIN, R=.085, P1=PAYMENT,P2=AMT
15  REM PD. ON PRINCIPAL AND INTEREST.
16  REM A=INTEREST PER MONTH, B=AMOUNT APPLIED TO PRINCIPAL
18  REM EACH MONTH, C=NET PRINCIPAL AFTER MONTHLY PAYMENT.
25  PRINT:PRINT;TAB(23);"GURNEY MORTGAGE COMPANY"
27  PRINT:PRINT;TAB(27);"PAYMENT RECORD *"
29  PRINT;TAB(28);"1-YEAR PERIOD"
31  PRINT:PRINT;TAB(21);"ORIGINAL PRINCIPAL--$31,000"
33  PRINT;TAB(25);"INTEREST RATE--.085"
35  PRINT;TAB(22);"MORTGAGE PERIOD--30 YEARS"
37  PRINT:PRINT:PRINT;TAB(3);"NO. OF";TAB(22);"AMT. OF"
"   INT.   AMT. PD.      NEW"
39  PRINT;TAB(2);"PAYMENT  PRINCIPAL  PAYMENT   PAID   ON"
" PRIN.  PRINCIPAL"
41  PRINT
45  P = 31000
50  R = .085
55  P1 = 350
60  P2 = 239
65  FOR N = 1 TO 12
70  A = P*R/12
75  B = P2-A
80  C = P-B
85  PRINT USING "    ##       #####.##    ###.##      ###.##",N,P,P1,A;
87  PRINT USING "    ###.##    #####.##",B,C
90  P = C
95  NEXT N
96  PRINT:PRINT;TAB(2);"*  IMPOUND OF $111 A MONTH NOT INCLUDED"
98  END
```

through 41 are the PRINT statements to print the headings. The remaining part of the program is explained on this page and the following pages.

```
45  P = 31000
50  R = .085
55  P1 = 350
60  P2 = 239
```

Statement 45 initializes P (principal) at 31000. R (rate) is initialized at .085 in Statement 50. The monthly payment (P1) is initialized at 350 in Statement 55, and the amount actually paid on the principal and interest (P2) is initialized at 239 in Statement 60.

FIGURE 9-3

Printout for Problem 9-1

```
RUN
DO       12:45 PM            18-Jan-81

                         GURNEY MORTGAGE COMPANY

                              PAYMENT RECORD *
                               1-YEAR PERIOD

                       ORIGINAL PRINCIPAL--$31,000
                           INTEREST RATE--.085
                        MORTGAGE PERIOD--30 YEARS
```

NO. OF PAYMENT	PRINCIPAL	AMT. OF PAYMENT	INT. PAID	AMT. PD. ON PRIN.	NEW PRINCIPAL
1	31000.00	350.00	219.58	19.42	30980.60
2	30980.60	350.00	219.45	19.55	30961.00
3	30961.00	350.00	219.31	19.69	30941.30
4	30941.30	350.00	219.17	19.83	30921.50
5	30921.50	350.00	219.03	19.97	30901.50
6	30901.50	350.00	218.89	20.11	30881.40
7	30881.40	350.00	218.74	20.26	30861.20
8	30861.20	350.00	218.60	20.40	30840.80
9	30840.80	350.00	218.46	20.54	30820.20
10	30820.20	350.00	218.31	20.69	30799.50
11	30799.50	350.00	218.16	20.84	30778.70
12	30778.70	350.00	218.02	20.98	30757.70

* IMPOUND OF $111 A MONTH NOT INCLUDED

```
65  FOR N = 1 TO 12
```

The FOR statement, Statement 65, uses N as the counter, initializes the counter to 1, and places the maximum limit for the counter at 12. Because there is no STEP given in the FOR statement, the computer will assume an increment of +1.

```
70  A = P*R/12
75  B = P2-A
80  C = P-B
85  PRINT USING "   ##       #####.##    ###.##      ###.##",N,P,P1,A;
87  PRINT USING "   ###.##    #####.##",B,C
```

```
90 P = C
95 NEXT N
96 PRINT:PRINT;TAB(2);"*  IMPOUND OF $111 A MONTH NOT INCLUDED"
98 END
```

Statement 70 commands the computer to multiply the principal times the rate, divide that answer by 12, and store the answer in A. The rate is .085 a year and the interest is figured monthly, so the amount of interest computed must be divided by the number of months in a year. Statement 75 subtracts the value stored in A from the amount stored in P2—the amount of the monthly payment that is applied to the principal and interest (239)—and stores the answer in B. As C is the new principal, Statement 80 finds that figure by subtracting B from P and storing it in C.

Statements 85 and 87 are used to print out the payment number (N), principal (P), amount of payment (P1), interest paid (A), amount paid on principal (B), and the new principal (C).

In Statement 90, the new principal located in C is stored in P so that the next time through the loop, interest will be figured on the adjusted principal.

Statement 95 is the last statement in the loop. It adds the increment to the counter; compares the counter value with the top limit of the counter; and if the counter value exceeds the top limit value, the computer is directed to read the next statement—Statement 96. If the counter value is less than or equal to the top limit, control is sent back to Statement 65.

Statement 96 prints out a line notifying the customer of the fact that his impounds are not included in the computations. Statement 98 is the last statement of the program.

NESTED LOOPS

When a loop is placed inside another loop, it is called a *nested loop*. The nested loop is completed within another loop; the loops cannot overlap.

PROPER NESTING

```
10 FOR N = 1 TO 10
15 FOR J = 5 TO 9
20 NEXT J
25 NEXT N
```

IMPROPER NESTING

```
10 FOR N = 1 TO 10
15 FOR J = 5 TO 9
20 NEXT N
25 NEXT J
```

A problem most beginning programmers experience is determining which of two loops is the outer and which is the inner. If the programmer carefully analyzes the sequence of computer activity using each of the loops as the outer one, he can imagine what the output would be like.

To find the amount of interest paid on principals of $1,000, $2,000, and $3,000 at rates of interest of 8%, 9%, and 10%, two loops would be used. The output for this problem will vary depending on which data is put in the inner loop and which is put in the outer loop.

```
10  FOR P = 1000 TO 3000 STEP 1000
15  FOR N = 8 TO 10
20  R=N * .01:A=P*R
25  PRINT P,R,A
30  NEXT N
40  NEXT P
45  END
```

The output for this loop arrangement would be the following:

```
1000        .08        80
1000        .09        90
1000        .1         100
2000        .08        160
2000        .09        180
2000        .1         200
3000        .08        240
3000        .09        270
3000        .1         300
```

The next program is made up of the same statements rearranged so that the inner and outer loops have been interchanged.

```
10  FOR N = 8 TO 10
15  FOR P = 1000 TO 3000 STEP 1000
20  R=N*.01:A=P*R
25  PRINT P,R,A
30  NEXT P
40  NEXT N
45  END
```

The output for this loop arrangement would be the following.

```
1000        .08        80
2000        .08        160
3000        .08        240
1000        .09        90
```

```
2000          .09          180
3000          .09          270
1000          .1           100
2000          .1           200
3000          .1           300
```

An example of a complete program using a nested loop is given in Problem 9-2.

PROBLEM 9-2

Most banking and savings and loan institutions are now paying interest compounded daily on their customer's savings accounts. This problem will have the computer set up a table of daily compound interest for 30 days at interest rates of 5.5%, 6%, 6.5%, 7%, 7.5%, 8%, and 8.5%. The interest will be figured on a deposit of $100.

The flowchart for the problem is in Figure 9-4, and the computer listing is in Figure 9-5. Statements 10 to 53 are REM and PRINT statements and can be found on the computer listing. The complete printout of the program is shown in Figure 9-6.

```
55  P=100
60  FOR D = 1 TO 30
63  PRINT USING " ## ",D;
```

Statement 55 initializes the deposit to 100. Whenever a value is constant, it should be initialized outside of the loop. Whenever the value changes with each set of data, so that it is not a constant, it must be treated inside of the loop. Statement 60 is the beginning statement of the outer loop. The counter, variable D, is initialized at 1 and has a top limit of 30. Because there is no STEP designated in the statement, the counter will assume a step, or increment, of +1. Then the PRINT USING statement is used to print out the value stored in D. The semicolon is placed after D so the printer will not move until told to do so in the next statement causing printing.

```
70  FOR R = 55 TO 85 STEP 5
72  R1 = R/1000
74  R2 = R1/360
76  A = P*(1.+R2)**D
80  PRINT USING "######.##",A;
85  NEXT R
90  PRINT
```

FIGURE 9-4
Flowchart for Problem 9-2

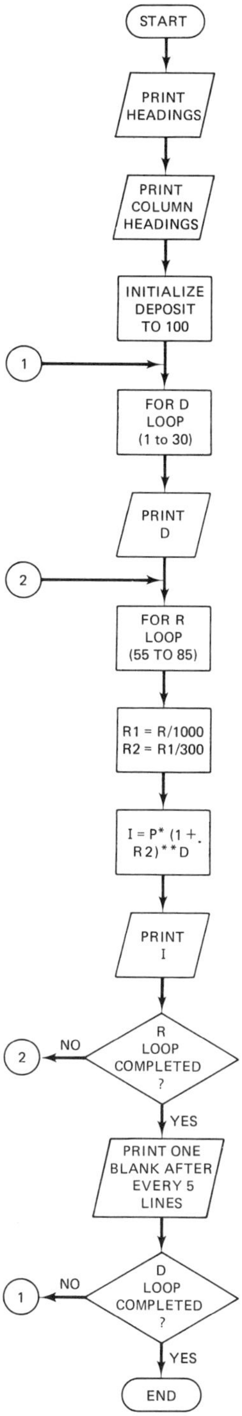

FIGURE 9-5

Listing for Problem 9-2

```
INT      08:20 PM         22-Jan-81
10  REM THIS TABLE LISTS THE INTEREST COMPOUNDED DAILY ON A
15  REM DEPOSIT OF $100 AT RATES OF 5.5%, 6%, 6.5%, 7%,
20  REM 7.5%, 8%, AND 8.5%.
25  PRINT:PRINT;TAB(21);"TABLE OF COMPOUND INTEREST"
30  PRINT:PRINT;TAB(24);"AMOUNT DEPOSITED--$100"
35  PRINT;TAB(22);"INTEREST COMPOUNDED DAILY"
40  PRINT;TAB(23);"RATES--.055 THROUGH .085"
45  PRINT;TAB(27);"PERIOD--30 DAYS"
50  PRINT:PRINT
52  PRINT"DAY   5.5%       6%       6.5%       7%       7.5%"
"      8%       8.5%"
53  PRINT
55  P=100
60  FOR D = 1 TO 30
63  PRINT USING "##",D;
70  FOR R = 55 TO 85 STEP 5
72  R1 = R/1000
74  R2 = R1/360
76  A = P*(1.+R2)**D
80  PRINT USING "######.##",A;
85  NEXT R
90  PRINT
95  IF D=5 THEN PRINT
96  IF D=10 THEN PRINT
97  IF D=15 THEN PRINT
98  IF D=20 THEN PRINT
99  IF D=25 THEN PRINT
100 NEXT D
103 PRINT
105 END
```

Statement 70 is the first statement of the inner, or nested loop. Statement 72 changes the integer value in R to a real value by dividing by 1000. In BASIC, Statement 70 could read 70 FOR R = .055 TO .085 STEP .005. There can be, however, a problem using decimal values instead of integer values in the counter and as increments. This problem occurs because data is stored in binary numbers. Not all decimal fractions can be changed to exact binary fractions, just as not all mixed fractions can be written exactly in decimals, i.e., one third. One third will never be resolved; it is an infinite number. The same thing occurs when the computer changes decimals to binary numbers. Some numbers are not exact equivalents.

As explained earlier, the computer adds the increment to the counter when it reaches the NEXT statement. It then compares the value in the counter with the top limit. If the counter value is greater than the

FIGURE 9-6

Printout for Problem 9-2

```
RUN
INT      08:21 PM          22-Jan-81
```

TABLE OF COMPOUND INTEREST

AMOUNT DEPOSITED--$100
INTEREST COMPOUNDED DAILY
RATES--.055 THROUGH .085
PERIOD--30 DAYS

DAY	5.5%	6%	6.5%	7%	7.5%	8%	8.5%
1	100.02	100.02	100.02	100.02	100.02	100.02	100.02
2	100.03	100.03	100.04	100.04	100.04	100.04	100.05
3	100.05	100.05	100.05	100.06	100.06	100.07	100.07
4	100.06	100.07	100.07	100.08	100.08	100.09	100.09
5	100.08	100.08	100.09	100.10	100.10	100.11	100.12
6	100.09	100.10	100.11	100.12	100.13	100.13	100.14
7	100.11	100.12	100.13	100.14	100.15	100.16	100.17
8	100.12	100.13	100.15	100.16	100.17	100.18	100.19
9	100.14	100.15	100.16	100.18	100.19	100.20	100.21
10	100.15	100.17	100.18	100.20	100.21	100.22	100.24
11	100.17	100.18	100.20	100.21	100.23	100.25	100.26
12	100.18	100.20	100.22	100.23	100.25	100.27	100.28
13	100.20	100.22	100.24	100.25	100.27	100.29	100.31
14	100.21	100.23	100.25	100.27	100.29	100.31	100.33
15	100.23	100.25	100.27	100.29	100.31	100.33	100.36
16	100.25	100.27	100.29	100.31	100.33	100.36	100.38
17	100.26	100.28	100.31	100.33	100.36	100.38	100.40
18	100.28	100.30	100.33	100.35	100.38	100.40	100.42
19	100.29	100.32	100.34	100.37	100.40	100.42	100.45
20	100.31	100.33	100.36	100.39	100.42	100.45	100.47
21	100.32	100.35	100.38	100.41	100.44	100.47	100.50
22	100.34	100.37	100.40	100.43	100.46	100.49	100.52
23	100.35	100.38	100.42	100.45	100.48	100.51	100.55
24	100.37	100.40	100.43	100.47	100.50	100.54	100.57
25	100.38	100.42	100.45	100.49	100.52	100.56	100.59
26	100.40	100.43	100.47	100.51	100.54	100.58	100.62
27	100.41	100.45	100.49	100.53	100.56	100.60	100.64
28	100.43	100.47	100.51	100.55	100.59	100.62	100.65
29	100.44	100.48	100.53	100.57	100.61	100.65	100.69
30	100.46	100.50	100.54	100.59	100.63	100.67	100.71

terminal value, control goes to the statement following the NEXT statement.

Apparently when adding the value .005 to .08 in binary, the answer is greater than .085 because the computer does not go through the loop using the value .085, but drops through the loop when the counter reaches that value. That is why Statement 70 has integer values instead of decimal values. The programmer should always use whole numbers in the FOR statement to avoid the problem of encountering infinite real numbers.

In Statement 74 the yearly interest rate is changed to a daily interest rate by dividing by 360. Statement 76 consists of the formula for computing compound interest.

OVERFORMATTING

Statement 80 is written to print out a five-digit number, pointing off two places from the right, and placing three spaces between the columns. This printout was achieved by a process called *overformatting.* Because the computer prints numbers from the right, the number that is to be printed actually would be formatted thusly: ###.##. By overformatting, allowing more spaces than necessary, the computer leaves more spaces than are necessary for the number. Each time the computer goes through the loop, it prints out a five-digit number in an eight-digit field, automatically spacing three spaces between columns since the numbers are printed from the right.

The semi-colon at the end of the statement directs the computer not to move after printing the value until it receives another command. As long as there is a semi-colon at the end of Statement 80, the computer will keep printing items on the same line. How is the computer told to stop printing on the same line? Statement 90 takes care of that problem. It commands the printer to print nothing on the rest of that line and then to return to the left margin on the next line.

Statements 95 through 99 were placed in the program to cause the computer to leave a blank line after every five printed lines to make the table easier to read.

```
95  IF D=5 THEN PRINT
96  IF D=10 THEN PRINT
97  IF D=15 THEN PRINT
98  IF D=20 THEN PRINT
99  IF D=25 THEN PRINT
100 NEXT D
103 PRINT
105 END
```

Statement 100 is the last statement of the D loop. Statement 103 commands the computer to print a blank line after the table. The blank line is for readability. Statement 105 is the last statement of the program.

SUMMARY

1. Backslashes (\) can be used in PRINT USING statements to format string data. The computer prints anything in the field designated by the pairs of backslashes and the space between them.

```
40  PRINT USING "\           \",A$
```

2. The FOR statement is the beginning statement of the FOR/NEXT loop.
3. The following is an example of a FOR statement.

```
40  FOR N = 1 TO 30 STEP 2
```

   a. The word FOR initiates the loop.
   b. The variable N is a counter. The counter name can be any numeric variable.
   c. The first number is the value at which the counter is initialized. Although the value can be either real or integer, the programmer should use only integers to be assured the computer will loop the proper number of times. Also, the counter can be initialized to a positive number, a negative number, or a zero.
   d. The TO is a necessary part of the FOR statement.
   e. The 30 is the terminal value the counter is allowed to reach.
   f. The STEP 2 is the amount added to the counter each time the computer completes a loop. If the STEP phrase is left out of the FOR statement, the computer assumes an increment of +1.
4. Every FOR statement must have a NEXT statement ending the loop. The NEXT statement must contain the same variable name as does the FOR statement.

```
50  NEXT N
```

5. When the computer executes the NEXT statement, it adds the in-

crement to the counter; it compares the counter value to the terminal value; and if the counter value is equal to or less than the terminal value, it is sent back through the loop. If the counter value is beyond the terminal value, then the computer proceeds to the statement following the NEXT statement.

6. There can be a loop placed within a loop. The inner loop is called a *nested loop.*

```
30  FOR A = 1 TO 10
35  FOR B = 5 TO 8
40  NEXT B
45  NEXT A
```

SELF-TEST

1. What statement would print out a string variable (S$) 14 characters wide starting at Column 7, a numeric variable (N) consisting of three whole numbers and two decimal places starting at Column 35, and a numeric variable (A) consisting of 3 whole numbers starting at Column 48?
2. What are each of the parts called in the following statement?

```
10  FOR N = 1 TO 50 STEP 3
```

   a. The FOR is ?
   b. The N is ?
   c. The number 1 is ?
   d. The number 50 is ?
   e. The STEP 3 is ?

3. Is this a valid statement?

```
10  FOR N = 1 TO 10
```

4. If Statement 10 above is valid, what does the computer have to assume?
5. Is this a valid nesting of loops?

```
10  FOR N = 1 TO 10
15  FOR B = 5 TO 8
20  NEXT N
25  NEXT B
```

6. Is this a valid loop?

```
10  FOR N = 1 TO 10
15  NEXT M
```

ASSIGNMENTS

1. The Bancroft Mfg. Company is depreciating a $12,500 lathe over an eight-year period. The lathe is expected to have a scrap value of $500 at the end of the eighth year. The Bancroft Mfg. Company uses the Sum-of-the-Years' Digits method of depreciation. When depreciating an item using this method, the depreciation expense for each year is figured by multiplying the purchase price less scrap value by a fraction that becomes smaller each year. To find the denominator of this fraction, the years are added together (Year 1 + Year 2 + . . . + Year 8 = 36). The numerator of the Sum-of-the-Years' Digits fraction begins with the number of years the item is to be depreciated (eight in this problem) for the first year and decreases by one until it reaches one, the last year of depreciation. The computer should be instructed to do all of these computations, but an example of how this formula will work in this problem will be given here. The programmer may wish to use a FOR/NEXT loop employing a minus increment.

   Denominator = (1+2+3+4+5+6+7+8)
   Denominator = 36
   Year 1 depreciation = 12000 * (8/36)
   Year 2 depreciation = 12000 * (7/36)
   Year 3 depreciation = 12000 * (6/36)

   Book value of an item is the original price of the item less the total amount of depreciation up to the point when book value is figured. Book value at the end of the first year is 12500 minus the first year's depreciation. Book value at the end of the second year is 12500 minus the sum of the depreciation for year one and year two. The manager of Bancroft wants to know the yearly depreciation and the yearly book value of the lathe at the end of every year of the eight years. A flowchart and a computer listing of the problem and the running of the program should be prepared. The printout should have the original price of $12,500 and dollar signs appearing in only the first detail line.

```
                    BANCROFT MFG. COMPANY

                   Depreciation Schedule
                        Item--Lathe
                      No. of Years--8
             Original Purchase Price--$12,500
              Sum-of-the-Years' Digits Method

   Original                  Amt. of             Book
    Price        Year      Depreciation          Value

   $12,500        1          $XXXX.XX          $XXXXX.XX
```

2. Bill went to the Acme Finance Company and borrowed $1,000. He is to pay yearly interest of 8½% on the outstanding balance each month. His payment is $50 a month, which includes interest and the amount paid on principal. Interest is found by multiplying the outstanding principal times monthly interest rate. The new principal is found by adding the monthly interest to the principal and subtracting the monthly payment. Using a FOR/NEXT loop, make a table showing the principal each month, amount of interest, payment number, amount of payment, and the new balance. The terminal value of the counter in the FOR/NEXT loop must be set high enough to allow the computer to run until the New Balance Column finally contains zeros. Dollar signs should appear on only the first detail line. *Hint*: An IF statement may be used to exit the loop. A flowchart, a computer listing of the problem, and the printing of the report should be prepared.

```
                         ACME FINANCE COMPANY

                       Amount Borrowed--$1000
                   Yearly Rate of Interest--8.5%

Payment        Amount        Monthly       Amt. of        New
  No.           Owed         Interest      Payment      Balance

  XX          $XXXX.XX        $X.XX        $50.00       $XXX.XX
```

3. A person might want to know how many dollars he needs to invest today to have X number of dollars 10 years from now at an interest rate compounded yearly. This is called the present value

of a dollar. The formula for the present value of a dollar is: P = 1/((1 + A)**N). N is the number of periods and A is the interest rate. The problem that is to be done is to use FOR/NEXT loops to figure the present value of a dollar for 10 periods at interest rates of 7% to 8½% compounded yearly. A flowchart, a computer listing of the problem, and printing of the report should be prepared.

```
                THE PRESENT VALUE OF $1.00

                   No. of Periods--10
       Interest Rates--7% to 8.5% Compounded Yearly


Period          7%          7.5%          8%          8.5%

  1           .XXXX        .XXXX        .XXXX        .XXXX
```

10

TABLES, ARRAYS, MATRICES, RESTORE STATEMENTS, DIM STATEMENTS, SUBSCRIPTS, AND INPUT STATEMENTS

This chapter covers the following topics.

A. Tables, arrays, or matrices
B. The RESTORE statement
C. DIM statements
D. Single-subscripted variables
E. Double-subscripted variables
F. INPUT statements

TABLES, ARRAYS, OR MATRICES

The terms *tables, arrays*, and *matrices* are synonymous in computer terminology and refer to a method of storage of retrievable data. The singular for *matrices* is *matrix*. The individual units of data stored in arrays are called *elements*. Subscripts are the means of storing and retrieving data in arrays. This chapter consists of writing programs using subscripts.

THE RESTORE STATEMENT

To cause the computer to read the same data over again, a RESTORE statement may be used. This statement commands the computer to begin reading data starting from the first DATA item. This statement enables the programmer to reuse the same DATA statements as many times as he desires, eliminating the necessity of typing the same DATA statements more than once.

```
50  RESTORE
```

Statement 50 tells the computer that at the next READ statement encountered, all the data starting with the first DATA statement is to be read, despite the fact the data may have previously been used.

SUBSCRIPTED VARIABLES AND DIM STATEMENTS

SINGLE-SUBSCRIPTED VARIABLES

Any variable can be subscripted—A(1),B1(1), S$(1). The subscript is the number in parentheses following the variable and is referred to as "A sub-1," "B1 sub-1," and "S$ sub-1." The subscript is used to refer to the location of the element in storage. If the storage is referenced as A, there is only one value or element stored in A. If the storage is referenced as A(10), that value is stored as the tenth element in a table under the family name of A. A table referenced as A(6) would appear in memory with one column of six rows.

```
10  FOR N = 1 TO 6
25  A(N) = 2 * N
30  NEXT N
35  END
```

The array above would appear schematically in storage as shown in Figure 10-1.[1]

The first time through the loop, N equals 1; so the computer stores the product of two times N (1) in storage A(1) in the first row. The

[1] The array has a zero location, which means that a programmer would have one more location than subscripted. In the variable A(7) there would be eight locations available if the programmer used A(0) as a subscripted variable. This text ignores the zero subscript, and any subscript listed will be the actual number of locations. Thus, in A(8) only eight locations in A will be used.

FIGURE 10-1

Storage A

2	A(1)
4	A(2)
6	A(3)
8	A(4)
10	A(5)
12	A(6)

second time through the loop N equals 2, so the product of 2 times N (2) is stored in A(2) in the second row. This process continues until all six elements of A are stored in the Table A.

Subscripts may also be variables. If X has a value of 10, A(X) means the tenth element or row in A.

DIM STATEMENTS

DIM is short for DIMENSION and the DIM statement defines the maximum number of elements to be stored in a table or array referenced by the subscripted variable. Actually, the DIM statement orders the computer to *reserve* storage for a certain number of elements. If there is no DIM statement, the computer assumes a maximum of 10 elements in an array. If the programmer desires more storage, it has to be reserved by the use of a DIM statement. Good programming consists of using DIM statements every time subscripts are used even if there will be fewer than 10 elements. If the programmer needs storage for 15 elements each for variables A, B, S$, he would write the following DIM statement.

```
10  DIM A(15),B(15),S$(15)
```

If the programmer does not use a DIM statement but subscripts for more than 10 elements or if he uses a DIM statement and programs for more elements than are defined in the DIM statement, the computer will print an error message when it reaches the maximum storage spaces allowed but more elements are subscripted. For example, in the following program, the computer would have processed 10 lines of data and then printed the following error message: SUBSCRIPT OUT OF RANGE AT LINE 15.

```
10  FOR N = 1 TO 12
15  A(N) = 2 * N
20  PRINT USING "     ####",A(N)
25  NEXT N
30  END
```

DIM statements can be placed anywhere in the program and do not necessarily appear prior to the first subscripted reference, although they usually appear near the beginning of a program to allow for corrections if they are found to be necessary. Also, a programmer could allow more subscripts than he currently needs in case future program changes will require more. By reserving extra storage, he does not have to rewrite DIM statements.

PROBLEM 10-1

The following program will be used to demonstrate the input and output of a single-subscripted table using a DIM statement. The computer will compute and print the amount of interest on $100 compounded daily at 8.5% interest at each of twelve 30-day periods. The printout will consist of the period number and the $100 plus interest.

The flowchart is shown in Figure 10-2; the computer listing and printout are shown in Figure 10-3.

PROBLEM 10-2

DOUBLE-SUBSCRIPTED VARIABLES

The DIM statement is necessary to dimension double-subscripted variables.

```
10  DIM A(3,3),D(3,4),E(3,5)
```

Schematically, the tables would appear in storage as shown in Figure 10-4.

FIGURE 10-2
Flowchart for Problem 10-1

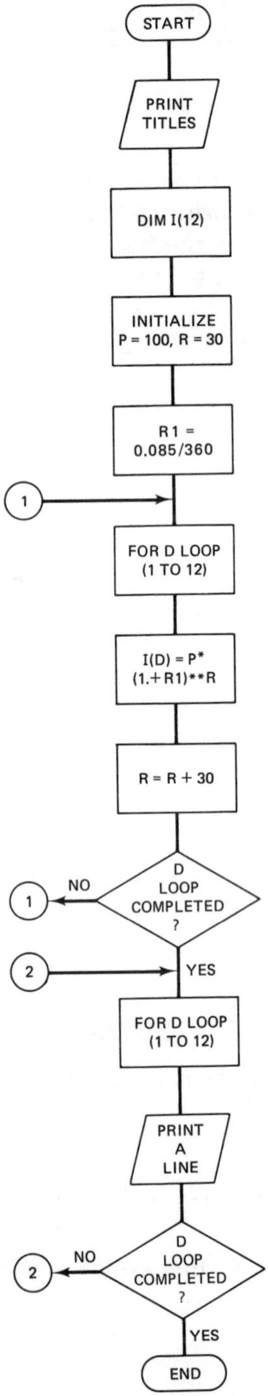

FIGURE 10-3

Listing and Printout for Problem 10-1

```
10  REM THIS TABLE LISTS THE INTEREST COMPOUNDED DAILY ON A
15  REM DEPOSIT OF $100 AT 8.5% AT THE END OF 30-DAY PERIODS FOR
20  REM 360 DAYS.
25  PRINT:PRINT;TAB(21);"TABLE OF COMPOUND INTEREST"
30  PRINT:PRINT;TAB(24);"AMOUNT DEPOSITED--$100"
35  PRINT;TAB(22);"INTEREST COMPOUNDED DAILY"
40  PRINT;TAB(30);"RATE--.085"
45  PRINT;TAB(20);"PERIOD--12 THIRTY-DAY PERIODS"
50  PRINT:PRINT:PRINT;TAB(24);"PERIOD       INTEREST"
53  PRINT
54  DIM I(12)
55  P=100
56  R=30
60  R1=.085/360
65  FOR D = 1 TO 12
75  I(D)=P*(1+R1)**R
80  R=R+30
85  NEXT D
90  FOR D=1 TO 12
95  PRINT USING "                            ##           ###.##",D,I(D)
100 NEXT D
105 END

RUN
COMP   01:35 PM          16-MAY-81

                     TABLE OF COMPOUND INTEREST

                        AMOUNT DEPOSITED--$100
                      INTEREST COMPOUNDED DAILY
                              RATE--.085
                    PERIOD--12 THIRTY-DAY PERIODS


                        PERIOD       INTEREST

                          1          100.71
                          2          101.43
                          3          102.15
                          4          102.87
                          5          103.61
                          6          104.34
                          7          105.08
                          8          105.83
                          9          106.58
                         10          107.34
                         11          108.10
                         12          108.87
```

FIGURE 10-4

Schematic of Storage for Double-Subscripted Variables

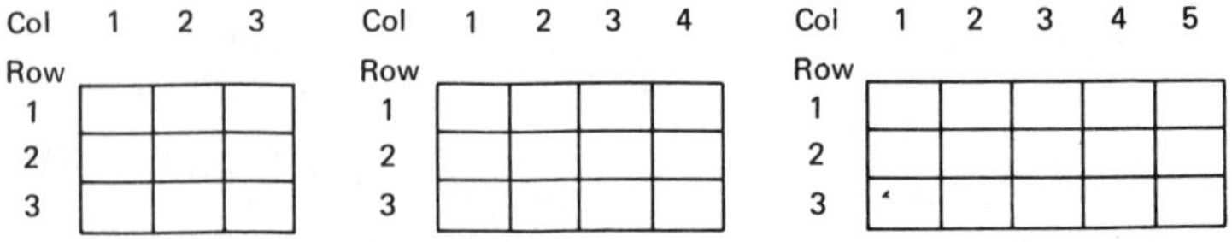

The first subscript in double subscripts always refers to the row, the second subscript to the column. When the computer goes through the loops (a nested loop is necessary when doing double subscripts), it fills out row 1 all the way across, then row 2, etc.

An unsubscripted variable may have the same name as a subscripted one, but the same variable name cannot be single-subscripted and double-subscripted in the same program. The variables A and A(1) or A and A(1,1) would be valid if used in the same program. The variable A, A(1), and A(1,1) would not be valid nor would the variables A(1) and A(1,1) be valid if used in the same program.

Problem 9-2 will be done again to show how that same table can be entered into main storage and be printed out by the use of double subscripts. The flowchart for this problem is shown in Figure 10-5; the listing and printout are shown in Figures 10-6 and 10-7.

Statement 5 defines the table. Variable A is dimensioned for 30 rows and 7 columns.

```
5   DIM A(30,7)
```

Statements 60 and 65 are the loop statements. The computer sets the counter D to one, drops to Statement 65, sets the counter R to one, and then reads the first item of data (.055) and stores it in N.

```
60  FOR D=1TO30
65  FOR R=1TO7
70  READ N
```

In Statement 75 the computer divides N by 360 (the number of days) and stores the result in B. In Statement 80 the computer computes compound interest at 5.5% for one day (D) and stores it in A, row 1, column 1.

FIGURE 10-5

Flowchart for Problem 10-2

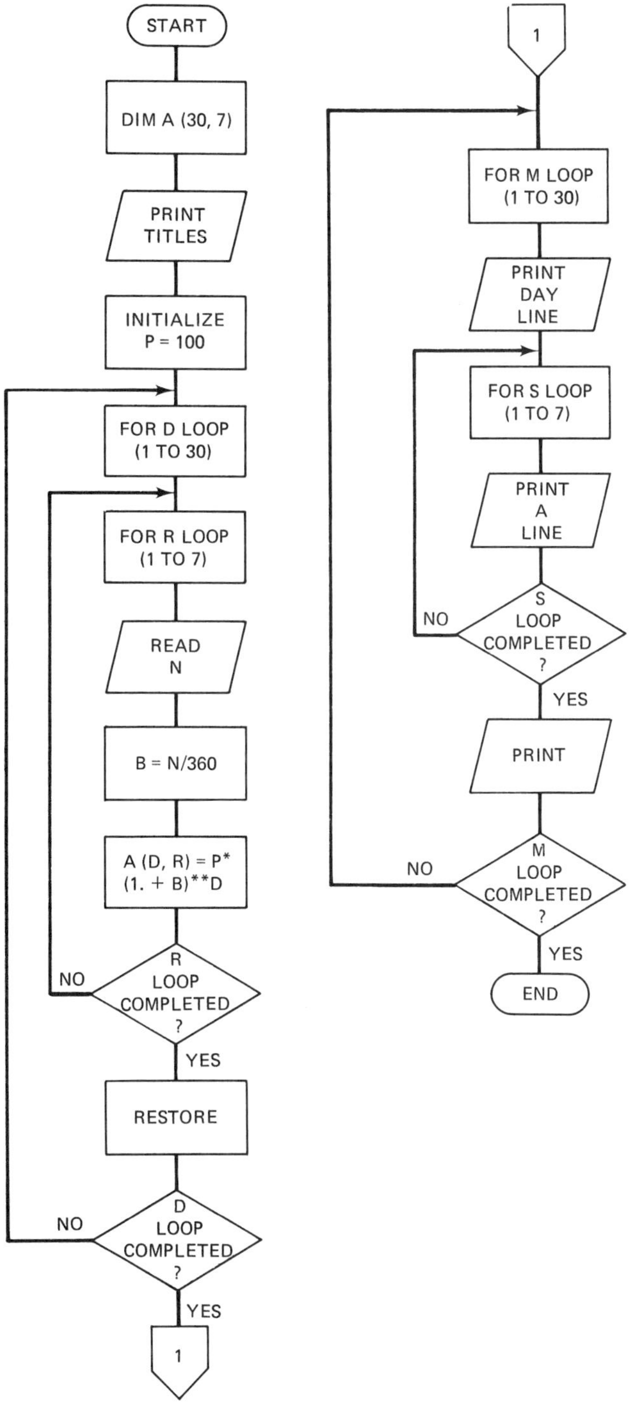

FIGURE 10-6

Listing for Problem 10-2

```
LIST
SUB2    11:43 AM        28-Jan-81
5   DIM A(30,7)
10  REM THIS TABLE LISTS THE INTEREST COMPOUNDED DAILY ON A
15  REM DEPOSIT OF $100 AT RATES OF 5.5%, 6%, 6.5%, 7%
20  REM 7.5%, 8%, 8.5%.
25  PRINT:PRINT;TAB(25);"TABLE OF COMPOUND INTEREST"
30  PRINT:PRINT;TAB(27);"AMOUNT DEPOSITED--$100"
35  PRINT;TAB(25);"INTEREST COMPOUNDED DAILY"
40  PRINT;TAB(26);"RATES--.055 THROUGH .085"
45  PRINT;TAB(30);"PERIOD--30 DAYS"
50  PRINT:PRINT
52  PRINT"DAY     5.5%       6%       6.5%       7%      7.5%"
"     8%       8.5%"
53  PRINT
55  P=100
60  FOR D=1TO30
65  FOR R=1TO7
70  READ N
75  B=N/360
80  A(D,R)=P*(1.+B)**D
85  NEXT R
90  RESTORE
95  NEXT D
100 FOR M=1TO30
105 PRINT USING " ##",M;
110 FOR S=1TO7
115 PRINT USING "#####.##",A(M,S);
120 NEXT S
125 PRINT
130 IF M=5 THEN PRINT
131 IF M=10 THEN PRINT
132 IF M=15 THEN PRINT
133 IF M=20 THEN PRINT
135 IF M=25 THEN PRINT
140 NEXT M
145 PRINT
150 DATA .055,.06,.065,.07,.075,,08,.085
155 END
```

FIGURE 10-7

Printout for Problem 10-2

TABLE OF COMPOUND INTEREST

AMOUNT DEPOSITED--$100
INTEREST COMPOUNDED DAILY
RATES--.055 THROUGH .085
PERIOD--30 DAYS

DAY	5.5%	6%	6.5%	7%	7.5%	8%	8.5%
1	100.02	100.02	100.02	100.02	100.02	100.02	100.02
2	100.03	100.03	100.04	100.04	100.04	100.04	100.05
3	100.05	100.05	100.05	100.06	100.06	100.07	100.07
4	100.06	100.07	100.07	100.08	100.08	100.09	100.09
5	100.08	100.08	100.09	100.10	100.10	100.11	100.12
6	100.09	100.10	100.11	100.12	100.13	100.13	100.14
7	100.11	100.12	100.13	100.14	100.15	100.16	100.17
8	100.12	100.13	100.15	100.16	100.17	100.18	100.19
9	100.15	100.15	100.16	100.18	100.19	100.20	100.21
10	100.15	100.17	100.18	100.20	100.21	100.22	100.24
11	100.17	100.18	100.20	100.21	100.23	100.25	100.26
12	100.18	100.20	100.22	100.23	100.25	100.27	100.28
13	100.20	100.22	100.24	100.25	100.27	100.29	100.31
14	100.21	100.23	100.25	100.27	100.29	100.31	100.33
15	100.23	100.25	100.27	100.29	100.31	100.33	100.36
16	100.25	100.27	100.29	100.31	100.33	100.36	100.38
17	100.26	100.28	100.31	100.33	100.36	100.38	100.40
18	100.28	100.30	100.33	100.35	100.38	100.40	100.43
19	100.29	100.32	100.34	100.37	100.40	100.42	100.45
20	100.31	100.33	100.36	100.39	100.42	100.45	100.47
21	100.32	100.35	100.38	100.41	100.44	100.47	100.50
22	100.34	100.37	100.40	100.43	100.46	100.49	100.52
23	100.35	100.38	100.42	100.45	100.48	100.51	100.55
24	100.37	100.40	100.43	100.47	100.50	100.54	100.57
25	100.38	100.42	100.45	100.49	100.52	100.56	100.59
26	100.40	100.43	100.47	100.51	100.54	100.58	100.62
27	100.41	100.45	100.49	100.53	100.56	100.60	100.64
28	100.43	100.47	100.51	100.55	100.59	100.62	100.66
29	100.44	100.48	100.53	100.57	100.61	100.65	100.69
30	100.46	100.50	100.54	100.59	100.63	100.67	100.71

```
75  B=N/360
80  A(D,R)=P*(1.+B)**D
```

When the computer reaches Statement 85, it has completed one time through the inner loop, so it adds one to the R counter. When it goes back through the loop, D (the row) is still 1; but the column R is now 2. Therefore, the interest is stored in row 1, column 2 of A. The computer continues looping for seven times, establishing row 1, columns 1 through 7, then it drops down out of the R loop. Statement 90 restores the data so that the same DATA statement need not be written 30 times. Then Statement 95 sets the counter D to 2 and the computer goes through another cycle with the row set at 2 and the columns at 1 through 7. This process continues until the D counter reaches 31, filling all 30 rows and 7 columns with data. Then the computer moves to Statement 100.

```
85  NEXT R
90  RESTORE
95  NEXT D
```

At Statement 100 the counter M is set at 1. The computer moves to Statement 105 and prints out the counter value in M, which is 1. Then control drops to Statement 110 where the counter S is set at 1. The computer goes to Statement 115 where it is told to go to storage A row 1, column 1, (M,S), and print out the element found there. The computer continues through the S loop seven times, printing all seven columns of the elements found in row 1 of A on the same line. The semi-colon at the end of Statement 115 holds the printer on the same line. Statement 125 is necessary to move the printer to the next line. Then control drops to Statements 130 through 135. These are conditional IF statements that will cause the computer to print one blank line after every five lines. Then control goes back to Statement 100 where the counter is set to 2, the row number. Then loop S is repeated seven more times, picking up the data in the seven columns of row 2 and printing them out in the table. This process is continued until the computer has gone through the M loop 30 times.

One of the valuable uses of subscripted tables is that any element in the table can be referenced and used. If a programmer wished to use the element in row 15, column 5 of the sample table, multiply it by 8 and store that result in C, he can easily do it by using the following statement.

```
10  C=A(15,5)*8
```

INPUT STATEMENTS

In most of the previous chapters, the data were input into the computer through READ and DATA statements. Another method of inputting data, and one used a great deal in business, is through the use of INPUT statements. When using INPUT statements, the READ, IF trailer constant, and DATA statements are not used.

To show how INPUT statements operate, Problem 4-2 will be used. The computer listing of that problem can be found in Figure 4-6; the complete computer listing of that problem using INPUT statements is listed in Figure 10-9, and the corresponding flowchart is shown in Figure 10-8.

Statements 10, 15, 20, and 25 remain the same. Since arrays are used in this version of the program, Statement 27 is added.

```
27  DIM S$(20),A(20),S(20),R(20)
```

When using INPUT statements, the program is written to be used over and over again, so it is designed to be flexible. The operator at the terminal receives some instructions to guide him. The first instruction is a result of Statement 30, which asks him how many salesmen are included in this run. Statement 35 allows the data to be entered by the operator from the keyboard.

```
30  PRINT "HOW MANY SALESMEN ARE THERE?"
35  INPUT N1
```

When the program is being run and the computer comes to Statements 30 and 35, the following appears on the screen.

```
HOW MANY SALESMEN ARE THERE?
?
```

When the question mark appears, the operator then keys in the number of salesmen that are included in this program. The operator will type in 6. The following will now be on the screen.

```
HOW MANY SALESMEN ARE THERE?
?6
```

FIGURE 10-8

Flowchart of Problem 4-2 Utilizing INPUT Statements

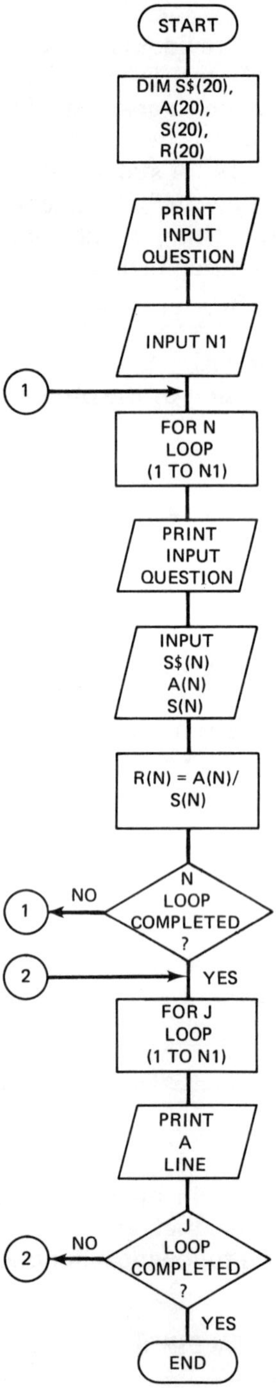

FIGURE 10-9

Listing of Problem 4-2 Utilizing INPUT Statements

```
10  REM THE PURPOSE OF THIS PROGRAM IS TO CALCULATE THE
15  REM RATE OF COMMISSION OF LONG BEACH AREA'S SALESMEN.
20  REM S$=SALESMAN, A=AMT OF COMMISSION, S=SALES, R=RATE
25  REM OF COMMISSION.
27  DIM S$(20),A(20),S(20), R(20)
30  PRINT "HOW MANY SALESMEN ARE THERE?"
35  INPUT N1
40  FOR N = 1 TO N1
45  PRINT "SALESMAN=S$,AMT OF COMMISSION=A,SALES=S"
50  INPUT S$(N),A(N),S(N)
52  R(N)=A(N)/S(N)
55  NEXT N
60  PRINT:PRINT:PRINT
65  FOR J=1 TO N1
70  PRINT;TAB(8);S$(J);TAB(29);
72  PRINT USING "###",A(J);
74  PRINT;TAB(40);
75  PRINT USING "#####",S(J);
80  PRINT;TAB(55);
85  PRINT USING ".##",R(J)
90  NEXT J
95  END
```

The data are input by the use of a FOR/NEXT loop and are printed out with a second FOR/NEXT loop. The two loops result in a readable report, printed after and separate from the input operation, as shown below.

```
SALESMAN=S$,AMT OF COMMISSION=A,SALES=S
?"A. JOHNSON",495,9900
SALESMAN=S$,AMT OF COMMISSION=A,SALES=S
?"B. NELSON",480,8000
SALESMAN=S$,AMT OF COMMISSION=A,SALES=S
?"C. SMITH",624,7800
SALESMAN=S$,AMT OF COMMISSION=A,SALES=S
?"D. HANSON",580,11680
SALESMAN=S$,AMT OF COMMISSION=A,SALES=S
?"E. FOUNTAIN",533,8200
SALESMAN=S$,AMT OF COMMISSION=A,SALES=S
?"F. SHERIDAN",616,8800
```

The report will be printed out as shown below.

```
A. JOHNSON          495        9900        .05
B. NELSON           480        8000        .06
C. SMITH            624        7800        .08
D. HANSON           580       11680        .05
```

E. FOUNTAIN	533	8200	.07
F. SHERIDAN	616	8800	.07

When the computer executed Statements 30 and 35 in Figure 10-9, it prompted the operator to enter the number of salesmen involved in the program. The operator entered 6. The number 6 is now stored in Variable N1. When the computer processes Statement 40, the FOR statement, it will take the value stored in N1 (6) as the terminal value of the counter.

```
40  FOR N = 1 TO N1
45  PRINT "SALESMAN=S$,AMT OF COMMISSION=A,SALES=S"
50  INPUT S$(N),A(N),S(N)
```

When the computer processes Statement 45, it prints the following line at the margin.

```
SALESMAN=S$,AMT OF COMMISSION=A,SALES=S
```

When the computer executes Statement 50, it places a question mark at the margin under SALESMAN.

```
SALESMAN=S$,AMT OF COMMISSION=A,SALES=S
?
```

When the question mark appears, the operator enters the first record and hits the return, and the computer prints "SALESMAN=S$, AMT OF COMMISSION=A,SALES=S," goes back to the margin, and enters a question mark. The operator enters the second record. This process continues until the counter goes beyond the terminal value, at which time the computer exits the loop.

The variables in Statement 50 have subscripts after them—S$(N), A(N), S(N). The computer is being told to store more than one element in each storage location. The first time through the loop, the variable N equals one, so the value input the first time through the loop is stored in the first slot in each variable. The second time through the loop, the variable N equals two, so the input value becomes the second element stored in the variables S$, A, and S. If there were no subscripts, the new value would replace the old one each time through the loop; and when the program is run, there would be but one element in each storage location, the last one input.

The first time the computer goes through the FOR/NEXT loop N, the variable N equals one; so when Statement 52 is executed the computer goes to storage locations A and S, takes out the first element in each location and divides A by S, and stores the quotient as the first element in Storage R. It continues looping until all of the commissions are computed and stored.

The computer then drops into the FOR/NEXT loop J where it prints out the first element in storage locations S$, A, S, and R. It continues looping until all six elements in these locations are printed.

The question might be asked why input and output cannot be accomplished within the same FOR/NEXT loop. It could be, resulting in the printout shown in Figure 10-10.

The result for the problem previously discussed starts with Statement 30 and contains the prompter and data entry commands within the FOR/NEXT loop. Most businessmen would not find the resulting printout very readable, so inputting and outputting is usually not done in the same loop. To obtain a more readable printout, the programmer uses two loops—one to input data with INPUT statements and another to print out the report, as previously demonstrated.

A PRINT statement need not always precede the INPUT statement. The question asked and the field for the answer can both be included in the INPUT statement. This procedure allows the answer to appear right after the questions, as is shown below. The question of whether to use PRINT and INPUT statements or only an INPUT statement revolves around the programmer's preference.

```
40  INPUT "AMOUNT OF LOAN";A
45  INPUT "NUMBER OF YEARS";Y
50  INPUT "PERCENT OF INTEREST";X
55  INPUT "NUMBER OF PAYMENTS A YEAR";P
```

The computer output would appear as follows after the operator has keyed in the answers to the questions.

```
AMOUNT OF LOAN ? 5000
NUMBER OF YEARS ? 10
PERCENT OF INTEREST ? 10
NUMBER OF PAYMENTS A YEAR ? 12
```

Placing a semi-colon before the variable field in the statements above causes the data to be entered on the same line immediately following the question. A comma would cause the answer to be entered in the next print zone on the same line.

```
30  INPUT "AMOUNT OF LOAN",A

AMOUNT OF LOAN                ? 5000
```

FIGURE 10-10

Listing and Printout Using INPUT Statements and One Loop To Input and Output Data—Problem 4-2 (Modified)

```
30  PRINT "HOW MANY SALESMEN ARE THERE?"
35  INPUT N1
40  FOR N = 1 TO N1
45  PRINT "SALESMAN=S$,AMT OF COMMISSION=A,SALES=S"
50  INPUT S$(N),A(N),S(N)
65  R(N)=A(N)/S(N)
70  PRINT;TAB(8);S$(N);TAB(29);
72  PRINT USING "###",A(N);
74  PRINT ;TAB(40);
75  PRINT USING "#####",S(N);
80  PRINT ;TAB(55);
85  PRINT USING ".##",R(N)
90  NEXT N
95  END
```

```
RUN
SUB      09:57 AM          29-SEP-81
HOW MANY SALESMEN ARE THERE?
?6
SALESMAN=S$,AMT OF COMMISSION=A,SALES=S
? "A. JOHNSON",495,9900
       A. JOHNSON           495         9900          .05
SALESMAN=S$,AMT OF COMMISSION=A,SALES=S
? "B. NELSON",480,8000
       B. NELSON            480         8000          .06
SALESMAN=S$,AMT OF COMMISSSSION=A,SALES=S
? "C. SMITH",624,7800
       C. SMITH             624         7800          .08
SALESMAN=S$,AMT OF COMMISSION=A,SALES=S
? "D. HANSON",580,11680
       D. HANSON            580        11680          .05
SALESMAN=S$,AMT OF COMMISSION=A,SALES=S
? "E. FOUNTAIN",533,8200
       E. FOUNTAIN          533         8200          .07
SALESMAN=S$,AMT OF COMMISSION=A,SALES=S
? "F. SHERIDAN",616,8800
       F. SHERIDAN          616         8800          .07
```

If no punctuation is used, the data is entered on the following line.

```
30  INPUT "AMOUNT OF LOAN" A
AMOUNT OF LOAN
? 5000
```

However, on a print line like Statement 45 in Figure 10-10, the input data would require more space than is available. Therefore, a

PRINT statement with the fields requested and the INPUT statement with the fields for the answer are used.

SUMMARY

1. The words *tables, arrays*, and *matrices* are synonymous in computer language. *Matrix* is the singular of *matrices*. An *element* is one single unit of data stored in an array.
2. The same data may be used over again by employing a RESTORE statement. The RESTORE statement tells the computer that in the READ statement following the RESTORE statement, it is to start over again with the first DATA item.
3. A subscript is used to reference a location of an element in storage. The variable A(4) means the fourth element stored in Array A.
4. Any variable can be subscripted: S$(1), A1(5), B(1,5).
5. Subscripts can be either numbers or variables: A(1), B(N).
6. A variable can be unsubscripted and subscripted in the same program: A and A(1), or A and A(1,1).
7. A variable cannot be single-subscripted and double-subscripted in the same program. A(1) and A(1,1) cannot operate in the same program.
8. Subscripts permit any element in a subscripted table to be retrieved and used, for example: A=B(7)*C(6). The computer retrieves the seventh element of B, multiplies it times the sixth element of C and stores the result in A.
9. A single-subscripted variable stores a vertical one-column table.
10. Double-subscripted variables store two-dimensional tables. Columns are vertical; rows are horizontal. There are four rows and six columns in the table below.

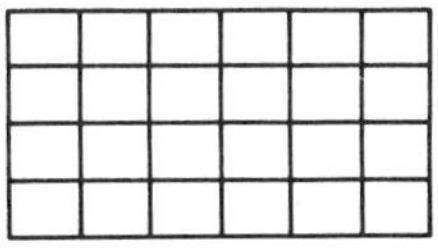

11. The computer stores double-subscripted tables by rows—row 1, column 1; row 1, column 2; row 1, column 3; etc.
12. The DIM statement is used to reserve storage for a table. The following DIM statement will reserve 12 elements for A, 17 elements for B, and 15 elements for D.

```
10  DIM A(12), B(17), D(15)
```

13. A zero subscript is available in arrays. This subscript gives the programmer one more element than dimensioned if he uses the subscript zero. The authors of this text have ignored the zero subscript.
14. If a DIM statement is not used, the computer assumes a maximum of 10 elements. However, good programming dictates the use of DIM statements for all subscripting, even for those under 10.
15. If the programmer tries to input more elements than subscripted, the computer will print out the following error message: SUBSCRIPT OUT OF RANGE AT LINE XX.
16. DIM statements can be placed anywhere in the program, but they are usually placed at the beginning of the program in case any changes must be made.
17. Dimensioning for more elements than are currently being used in a program will allow for later expansion of the program.
18. A DIM statement is necessary for double-subscripted tables.
19. The first number in a double-subscripted variable refers to the row, the second number to the column.
20. Data can be input by an operator through the use of INPUT statements.

```
30  INPUT S$,A,S
```

21. INPUT statements are often preceded by PRINT statements that tell the operator what information is to be input and in what order.

```
40  PRINT "SALESMEN=S$,AMT OF COMMISSION=A,SALES=S"
45  INPUT S$,A,S
```

22. As a result of Statements 40 and 45, the following printout will appear when they are processed by the computer. The operator enters the data when the question mark appears.

```
SALESMEN=S$,AMT OF COMMISSION=A,SALES=S
?
```

23. When the programmer wishes a statement and then an answer following the statement, he uses the following type of INPUT statement.

```
40  INPUT "HOW OLD ARE YOU";A
```

The printout would appear as follows when A is 15.

```
HOW OLD ARE YOU? 15
```

24. If the programmer wishes the answer to be entered on the same line but in the next print zone, he inserts a comma before the variable name.

```
40  INPUT "HOW OLD ARE YOU",A
```

The printout would appear as follows when A is 15.

```
HOW OLD ARE YOU              ? 15
```

25. If the programmer wishes the answer on the next line, he leaves out punctuation before the variable.

```
30  INPUT "AMOUNT OF LOAN" A
```

The printout would appear as follows when A is 5000.

```
AMOUNT OF LOAN
? 5000
```

SELF-TEST

1. Is the following a valid statement?

```
10 A(1) = B(2,1) * C(3)
```

2. Are the terms *tables, matrices*, and *arrays* synonymous?
3. Which of the following subscripts refers to the row; which one to the column–A(4,3)?

4. Write a dimension statement that defines Table A as having 14 rows and 20 columns.
5. What does the statement in Question 4 do?
6. Why would the computer print the following: SUBSCRIPT OUT OF RANGE AT LINE 70?
7. What is the individual value stored in an array called?
8. When using an INPUT statement, when does the operator type in data?
9. What statement would print out the following question?

```
HOW OLD ARE YOU?
```

10. What statement would define the following subscripted variables: A, B, and C? Variable A consists of 12 elements, variable B consists of 16 elements, and variable C consists of 18 elements.
11. The computer has read all of the data in the program. What should be written at Statement 80 that will enable the computer to read the same data again?

ASSIGNMENTS

1. A flowchart, computer listing, and printout of the report should be prepared for a program using FOR/NEXT loops and double-subscripted variables. A times table for 4, 5, 6, and 7 multiplied by 1 through 12 should be printed out in the following format. The ARRAY should be stored before it is printed.

TIMES TABLES
Numbers 4 Through 7
Times 1 Through 12

No. of Times	Number 4	Number 5	Number 6	Number 7
XX	XX	XX	XX	XX

2. The Beckley Mfg. Company is depreciating a $15,000 lathe over a 10-year period using the Double-Declining Balance Method. The formula for this method is the number of years to be depre-

ciated divided into 1, and that answer is doubled and multiplied times book value to find the amount of depreciation. Book value is the total depreciation to date subtracted from the original value. A depreciation table should be plotted with the use of subscripts. The report will have original price and dollar signs on only the first line. A flowchart, computer listing, and printout should be prepared.

BECKLEY MFG. COMPANY

Depreciation Schedule
Item–Lathe
Cost of Item–$15,000
Years to be Depreciated–10
Method of Depreciation–Double-Declining Balance

Year	Original Price	Amt. of Depreciation	Book Value
XX	$15000	$XXXX.XX	$XXXXX.XX

3. Bill Barnes borrowed $1,000 from the Ace Finance Company at 10% a year interest. He pays on the outstanding balance each month. His pay period is 2 years, and his monthly payment is $46.14. Ace Finance Company sent him a payment schedule showing the payment number, balance at the beginning of the month, amount of payment, amount of interest paid, and balance after payment. This table should be set up like the one below and should show the amount of the last payment, which might not be exactly $46.14. Dollar signs should appear on only the first line. Subscripts should be used, and a flowchart, computer listing, and printout should be prepared.

ACE FINANCE COMPANY

Amount Loaned–$1,000
Number of Payments–24
Yearly Interest Rate–10%
Amount of Monthly Payment–$46.14

Payment No.	Balance	Amt. of Interest	Amt. of Payment	New Balance
XX	$XXXX.XX	$X.XX	$XX.XX	$XXX.XX

4. Assignment 2 at the end of Chapter 5 is to be done using INPUT statements instead of DATA statements. The total 7611 must be accumulated by the program. A flowchart, computer listing, and printout should be prepared.

11 FUNCTIONS, SUBROUTINES, AND RANDOM NUMBERS

This chapter covers the following topics.

A. Library functions
B. User-defined functions
C. Subroutines
D. Random numbers

LIBRARY FUNCTIONS

Library functions are subroutines or "canned" programs that have been stored in the library of the computer memory. These functions can be called by a user through his own programs whenever certain mathematical operations are to be performed.

The square root of the variable Y is derived by the command B = SQR(Y). B is assigned the square root value of Y. The expression in the parentheses is called the *argument* of the function and represents a predetermined value for Y. The argument can be a single variable, a constant, or any mathematical expression, such as (A - B**3/C).

Some of the most commonly used functions are listed below.

FUNCTION	RESULT
SQR(X)	The square root of the argument X is calculated.
LOG(X)	The natural logarithm of the argument X is calculated.
ABS(X)	The absolute value of the argument X is calculated. (This function always makes X positive; it determines how far X is from zero.)
EXP(X)	The value of E, which is 2.718282, is raised to the power represented by the argument X.
RND(0)	The same sequence of random numbers is generated each time a program is run.
ATN(X)	The arctangent of X is calculated; the arctangent is given in radians.
SGN(X)	The sign of argument X is printed as +1 if the argument is positive, -1 if the argument is negative, and zero if the argument is equal to zero.
SIN(X)	The sine of X is calculated; X must be expressed in radians.
INT(X)	The decimal part of the argument X is truncated, resulting in the largest integer that does not exceed X. (5.7 would become 5, and -5.7 would become -6.)
TAN(X)	The tangent of X is calculated; the tangent is expressed in radians.
COS(X)	The cosine of X is calculated; the cosine is expressed in radians.

USER-DEFINED FUNCTIONS

The programmer is not limited to library functions, except on some small computer systems. Whenever a formula is used in several different places in a program, he may wish to create his own function to simplify coding. He defines his own functions by the use of a DEF statement. The form of the DEF statement is as follows: DEF FNA = (expression). DEF and FN are required. Any numeric variable name may be substituted for A. The function definition cannot be executed, so it may appear anywhere in the program. However, it is usually placed at the beginning of the program. Example 1 is a computer listing and printout of a sample user-defined function.

Example 1

```
10  DEF FNA = X**2 * 3**2/4**2
20  X = 2
30  Y = FNA * X
40  PRINT Y
50  END

RUN
 4.5
```

In Example 1, the function FNA is assigned the value of the expression to the right of the equal sign. When X is assigned a value of 2, FNA in Statement 10 will equal 2.25. In Statement 30, Y = FNA * X will assign a value of 4.5 to Y.

User-defined functions can also be used with arguments. Below is a computer listing and printout of a user-defined function with arguments.

Example 2

```
10  DEF FNB(X) = 4 * X**2
20  Y = FNB(5)
30  PRINT Y
40  R = 6
50  PRINT FNB(R)
60  END

RUN
 100
 144
```

In Statement 10, the argument X in the function FNB(X) is a dummy argument. It has no value unless or until it is assigned a value to be used in the expression. In Statement 20, FNB(5) causes X to equal 5 and substitutes for the argument in FNB(X), as well as in the expression to the right of the equal sign in Statement 10. When Y in Statement 30 is printed, it will equal 4 * 5**2. In Statement 50, FNB(R) substitutes R for X in the function and in the expression in Statement 10. When FNB(R) is printed, it will equal 4 * 6**2.

A user-defined function may have up to five dummy arguments. Even though there may be a number of variables in the argument, the expression on the right of the assignment (=) symbol does not have to contain all of the arguments.

A formula will be demonstrated here as an example of multiple arguments.

```
10  DEF FNA(P,R1,N) =  P*(1+R1) **N
```

A short program will be presented that will demonstrate how, somewhere in the program, values will be given to P, R1, and N. Then the formula may be used many times throughout the program by merely using a statement similar to the following.

```
45  X = FNA(P,R1,N)
```

FIGURE 11-1

Computer Listing and Printout Demonstrating Dummy Arguments

```
10  PRINT;TAB(10);"PRINCIPAL    RATE       DAY      BALANCE"
15  PRINT
20  R=.085
21  R1=R/360
22  DEF FNA(P,R1,N)=P*(1+R1)**N
25  FOR P=1000 TO 3000 STEP 1000
30  PRINT;TAB(12);
35  PRINT USING "####        .###",P,R;
40  FOR N=1 TO 5
45  X=FNA(P,R1,N)
50  PRINT;TAB(32);
51  PRINT USING "#      ####.##",N,X
55  NEXT N
60  PRINT
65  NEXT P
70  END
RUN
          PRINCIPAL    RATE       DAY     BALANCE

            1000       .085        1      1000.24
                                   2      1000.47
                                   3      1000.71
                                   4      1000.94
                                   5      1001.18

            2000       .085        1      2000.47
                                   2      2000.94
                                   3      2001.42
                                   4      2001.89
                                   5      2002.36

            3000       .085        1      3000.71
                                   2      3001.42
                                   3      3002.13
                                   4      3002.83
                                   5      3003.54
```

Another computer listing and printout of a user-defined function is shown below.

Example 3

```
10  REM THE PERIMETER (P) OF A RECTANGLE EQUALS 2 TIMES THE
20  REM LENGTH (L) PLUS 2 TIMES THE WIDTH (W).
30  DEF FNC    = 2 * L + 2 * W
40  READ L,W
50  P = FNC
60  PRINT "THE PERIMETER OF A RECTANGLE WITH A LENGTH OF"
65  PRINT "10 FEET AND A WIDTH OF 8 FEET IS ";P
70  DATA 10,8
80  END

RUN
THE PERIMETER OF A RECTANGLE WITH A LENGTH OF
10 FEET AND A WIDTH OF 8 FEET IS 36
```

An example of a user-defined function using a library function INT(X) is shown in the computer listing and printout below.

Example 4

```
10  DEF FNE(A) = A * B + C
20  C = 6
30  B = INT(C * 2 * .9)
40  X = FNE(2 * C)
50  PRINT X
60  END

RUN
 126
```

Statement 20 in Example 4 assigns a value of 6 to storage location C. In Statement 30, the INT function truncates .8 from 10.8, assigning a value of 10 to B. Statement 40 substitutes (2 * C), or 12, for A in the argument and in the expression in Statement 10. The expression in Statement 10 will be 12 * 10 + 6.

SUBROUTINES

A program may have a series of statements that are to be used several times in the program. Rather than rewrite the statements every time they are used in the program, the series of statements can be written only once and then referred to when needed by means of the GOSUB statement. The GOSUB statement is similar to the GO TO statement, except program control is transferred to a series of statements called a *subroutine*, rather than to a single statement. The series of statements at the new location is executed sequentially until a RETURN statement is encountered at the end of the subroutine. Control is then transferred to the statement following the GOSUB statement. A RETURN statement must be the last statement in the subroutine. A subroutine need not begin with any special statement. A REM statement may be the first statement of the subroutine to remind the programmer of the purpose of the subroutine. When the GOSUB statement transfers control to the first statement of the subroutine, the computer remembers the number of the statement following the GOSUB statement so it can return to that statement when it encounters the RETURN statement at the end of the subroutine.

A computer listing and a printout of an example of a subroutine are shown below and the flowchart is shown in Figure 11-2.

Example 5

```
100 K = 2
110 GOSUB 400
120 PRINT A,B,C
200 K = 4
210 GOSUB 400
215 PRINT A,B,C
220 M = A + 2 + B + 3 + C
230 PRINT M
240 GO TO 440
400 A = K * K**2
410 B = K * K * K**2
420 C = K * K * K/K**2
430 RETURN
440 END

RUN
 8              16              2
 64             256             4
 329
```

In Example 5, Statement 110 transfers control to Statement 400 where calculations are performed through Statement 420; Statement 430 returns program control to Statement 120. The subroutine is entered again from Statement 210, after which control returns to Statement 215.

FIGURE 11-2
Flowchart of Example 5

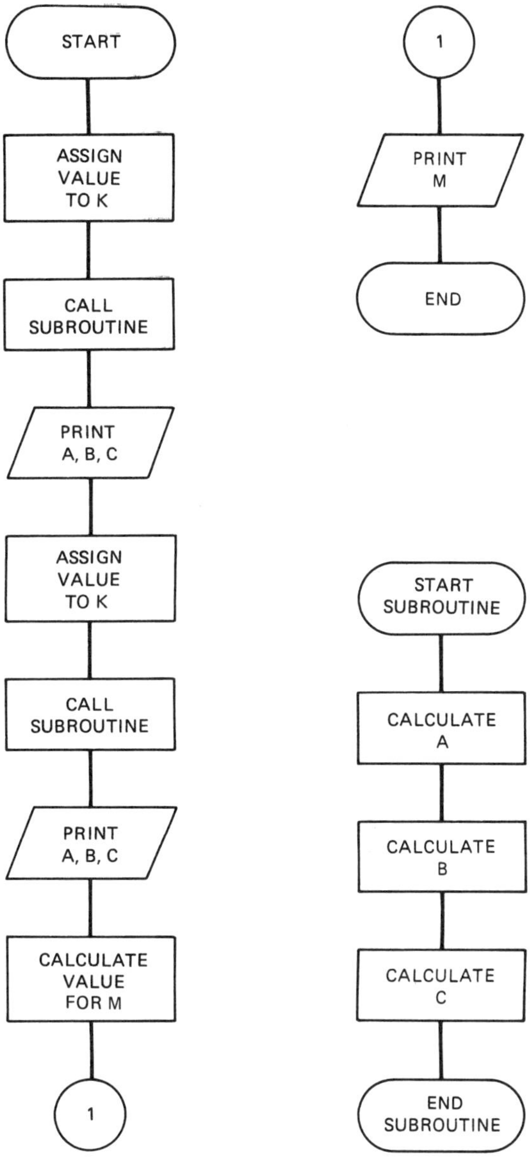

A subroutine may contain one or more GOSUB statements, as illustrated in the computer listing and printout below.

Example 6

```
10  REM P=PRINCIPAL. A=INTEREST, B=PRINCIPAL + INTEREST, R=RATE
20  READ P,R
30  IF P = 0 THEN 545
40  GOSUB 400
50  GO TO 20
400 A = P * R
410 B = P + A
420 GOSUB 500
430 T = T + P
440 RETURN
500 PRINT P,A,B
510 T1 = T1 + A
520 T2 = T2 + B
530 RETURN
545 PRINT T,T1,T2
550 DATA 100,.05,100,.06,100,.07,0,0
560 END

RUN
 100          5          105
 100          6          106
 100          7          107
 300          18         318
```

When the computer reaches Statement 40, it transfers to Statement 400. When it reaches Statement 420, it is sent to Statement 500. The computer encounters a RETURN at Statement 530 and it returns to Statement 430, the statement following the one from which it last departed. When it encounters another RETURN at Statement 440, it returns to Statement 50, the statement following the one from which it had departed earlier. Statement 50 directs the computer to the READ statement, and the procedure is repeated until the computer is sent to Statement 545 to print the totals.

RANDOM NUMBERS

A computer may be used to simulate certain real situations by a random selection of acceptable inputs to a model. The generated outputs can then be analyzed to determine the reactions of the model. One way of doing this is to input a list of random numbers that represent chance events. The computer has the capability of generating pseudo-random numbers by using the function RND(0), which will generate a list of decimal numbers uniformly distributed between, but not including zero and one. The symbol within the parentheses in the RND(0) function is a zero. The statement A = RND(0) will assign a randomly selected value to A that is between, but not including, zero and one (.000001 to .999999).

An example of random selection of numbers using the function RND(0) is shown in the computer listing and printout below.

Example 7

```
10  FOR K = 1 TO 10
20  A = RND(0)
30  PRINT A
40  NEXT K
50  END

RUN
 .204935
 .229581
 .533074
 .132211
 .995602
 .783713
 .741854
 .397713
 .709588
 .67811
```

The program in Example 7 will print a list of ten 6-digit randomly selected decimal numbers, such as .204935, .229581, and .533074. The computer can also be instructed to generate random numbers that are between numbers other than zero and one.

```
10  K = 6 * RND(0)
```

Statement 10 will generate random numbers between, but not including, zero and six.

```
6 * .999999 = 5.99999          6 * .000001 = .000006
```

```
20  K = 10 * RND(0) -5
```

Statement 20 will generate random numbers between, but not including, –5 and +5.

```
10 * .999999 = 9.99999          10 * .000001 = .00001
9.99999 - 5  = 4.99999          .00001 - 5   = -4.99999
```

If the programmer wants the computer to generate randomly selected integer numbers zero through five, the following statement could be used.

```
30  K = INT(6 * RND(0))

     6 * .999999 = 5.99999 truncated = 5
     6 * .000001 = .000006 truncated = 0
```

The INT function would truncate the decimal part of the numbers.

```
40  K = 5 + INT(6 * RND(0))

     6 * .000001 = .000006 truncated = 0 + 5 =  5
     6 * .999999 = 5.99999 truncated = 5 + 5 = 10
```

The INT function would truncate the decimal part of the numbers, and the randomly generated numbers would include 5 through 10.

Each time a program containing the RND(0) function is run, the same sequence of random numbers will be generated. This is desirable when debugging a program. However, the programmer may want a different sequence of random numbers generated each time a program is run. Complete randomness can be obtained by the use of the RANDOMIZE statement. RANDOMIZE may be shortened to RANDOM. The statement should appear at the beginning of the program and must precede the RND function. It could appear in the program as 10 RANDOMIZE. No matter how many RND(0) functions appear in the program, only one RANDOMIZE command is required.

When a coin is flipped a number of times, the probability of flipping a head is equal to the probability of flipping a tail. This is simulated in the computer listing and printout in Example 8 by instructing the computer to generate random numbers 1 through 10 and then assigning numbers 1 through 5 to tails and 6 through 10 to heads.

Example 8

```
5   INPUT N! NUMBER OF FLIPS
10  RANDOMIZE
15  FOR X = 1 TO N
20  K = 1 + INT(10 * RND(0))
25  IF K <= 5 THEN 40
30  PRINT "HEADS"
35  GO TO 45
40  PRINT "TAILS"
```

```
45  NEXT X
50  END

RUN
? 6
HEADS
HEADS
TAILS
TAILS
HEADS
TAILS
```

If two coins are flipped simultaneously a number of times, the probability of flipping tails is equal to the probability of flipping heads. A computer listing and printout showing this simulation is shown in Example 9.

Example 9

```
10  INPUT N! NUMBER OF TIMES TWO COINS ARE FLIPPED SIMULTANEOUSLY
20  RANDOMIZE
30  FOR X = 1 TO N
40  A = 1 + INT(10 * RND(0))
50  B = 1 + INT(10 * RND(0))
60  IF A<= 5 THEN 100
70  PRINT "COIN A IS HEADS"
80  H = H + 1
90  GO TO 120
100 PRINT "COIN A IS TAILS"
110 T = T + 1
120 IF B<= 5 THEN 160
130 PRINT "COIN B IS HEADS"
140 H = H + 1
150 GO TO 180
160 PRINT "COIN B IS TAILS"
170 T = T + 1
180 NEXT X
185 PRINT
190 PRINT "TOTAL HEADS =" H
200 PRINT "TOTAL TAILS =" T
210 END

RUN
? 5
COIN A IS TAILS
COIN B IS HEADS
COIN A IS TAILS
COIN B IS HEADS
```

```
COIN A IS HEADS
COIN B IS TAILS
COIN A IS TAILS
COIN B IS TAILS
COIN A IS TAILS
COIN B IS HEADS

TOTAL HEADS = 4
TOTAL TAILS = 6
```

SUMMARY

1. Library functions are subprograms that have been stored in the library of the computer memory.
2. Library functions can be called by a user through his program.
3. User-defined functions are defined by the use of a DEF statement. The form of the statement is shown below.

```
10  DEF FNA = (expression)
```

   DEF and FN are required. Any numeric variable name may be substituted for A.
4. Although the DEF statement is non-executable and can be inserted anywhere in the program, it is usually placed at the beginning.
5. The word *argument* is used to describe the variable in the parentheses in the following library functions: SQR(X), SIN(X), and INT(X).
6. User-defined functions can also be used with arguments. The function can have up to 5 arguments.

```
10  DEF FNA(A)     10  DEF FNA(A,B,C)     10  DEF FNA (A,B,C,D,E)
```

7. The argument is called a *dummy argument* unless or until it is assigned a value that is used in the expression. The argument X in the following DEF statement is a dummy argument.

```
10  DEF FNB(X) = 4 * X **2
```

8. A subroutine is a series of statements that constitute a program that can be executed only when called by another program.
9. To transfer to a subroutine the statement GOSUB is used, followed by the statement number of the first statement of the subroutine.
10. All subroutines must have a RETURN statement as the last statement of the subroutine.
11. When the RETURN statement is executed, control is transferred to the statement immediately following the GOSUB statement.
12. A subroutine may contain one or more GOSUB statements.
13. The function RND(0) is used for generating random numbers.
14. Each time the *same* program is run using the function RND(0), the computer generates the same sequence of random numbers.
15. The statement A = RND(0) will assign a random number to A between, but not including, zero and one (.000001 to .999999).
16. Numbers other than between zero and one can also be generated. The following statement will generate random numbers between, but not including, zero and 10.

```
10  B = 10 * RND(0)
```

17. The following statement will generate randomly selected integer numbers zero through seven.

```
10  B = INT(8*RND(0))
```

18. To secure randomly selected integer numbers from 10 through 20, the following statement can be used.

```
10  B = 10 + INT(11 * RND(0))
```

19. If a programmer desires complete randomness of numbers, he uses the RANDOMIZE statement.
20. RANDOMIZE can be shortened to RANDOM.
21. The RANDOMIZE statement should appear near the beginning of the program and must precede the RND(0) function.

SELF-TEST

1. In the Statement 10 B = SQR(Y)
   a. What kind of function is SQR?
   b. What is the Y called?
   c. If Y has a value of 16, what value will be stored in B?
2. What statement will define a function that equals B times P divided by Y?
3. What statement will define the function FNB(X), where the function equals X raised to the third power times 9?
4. What statement will store the value in function FNB(X) in Y?
5. Is this a valid statement? 10 DEF FNB(D,F) = D * F **2
6. If there is a value of 8 stored in X, what value is stored in B after the following statement is executed? 10 B = INT(X*3.7)
7. The subroutine in a program begins with Statement 70. What should be written at Statement 10 to direct the computer to that subroutine?
8. What statement terminates a subroutine?
9. To what statement does the computer go when it terminates a subroutine?
10. What statements should be written to accomplish the following operations?
    a. A statement number 30 that will generate the same real random numbers between zero and one every time the program is run.
    b. A statement number 40 that will generate the same integer random numbers between zero and six.
    c. A statement number 50 that will generate the same integer random numbers including 5 and 10.
11. a. What statement is necessary to secure different random numbers every time a program is run?
    b. Where in the program *must* this statement appear?
12. What command at a statement number 10 will define a user-defined function FNB for the following formula? X * 9/Y
13. What statement will assign the function in number 12 to L?
14. a. What command at statement number 80 will define a user-defined function called FND, with a dummy argument X assigning the following formula? Y * (A – B) ** 2
    b.
    ```
    20  DEF FND(X) = X * B/Y
    25  B = 12
    ```

```
30  Y = 3
40  A = FND(2)
```

What is the value assigned to A at Statement 40?

15.
```
10  DEF FNH (P,R) = P * R/100

20  X = FNH(1000,7)
```

What is the value assigned to X at statement 20?

ASSIGNMENTS[1]

1. Random numbers may be used to create a dice game. The directions are listed below.
   a. There are 2 dice, each die having numbers 1 through 6.
   b. If the player makes a 2, 3 or 12 on the first throw, he loses; he is said to have shot "craps." The printout should show the number thrown.
   c. If he throws a 7 or an 11 on the first throw, he wins.
   d. If the player throws any other number he has a "point" to make. He must throw the dice until he does one of the following.
      1. Throws the same number, in which case he wins, keeps the dice, and starts over.
      2. Throws a 7 before he makes his point, in which case he loses and must pass the dice to the next shooter.
   e. In creating the game, the computer should print out what happened.
      1. "Craps—you lose—keep throwing."
      2. "You made a 7 or an 11 on first throw—you win—keep throwing."
      3. "You made your point—you win—keep throwing."
      4. "You did not make your point—you lose. Pass the dice to the next shooter."

   A flowchart, a computer listing, and a printout should be preprepared.
2. The Wilkens Company requires a chart of depreciation for the four items listed below. The output is to be as illustrated. The depreciation method is straight-line and the formula is: Depreciation = original price, minus scrap value, divided by number of

[1] The centering rules in Chapter 5 should be applied for Assignments 2 and 3.

years to be depreciated, or D = (OP–SV)/YD. Book value is found by subtracting the total number of years' depreciation from the original price. The name of the item, purchase price, scrap value, and number of years to be depreciated are to be printed once—on the first line with the first year's depreciation. The years are to be numbered, and the book value at the end of every year is to be printed. A subroutine is to be used to read in the data; figure out depreciation; print the name of the item, purchase price, scrap value, and number of years of depreciation; and establish the number of years for the FOR/NEXT loop that is to be used to finish the problem. The program will read in data and will also have an INPUT statement for the number of times through the loop. A flowchart, a computer listing, and a printout of the report should be prepared. The data to be used are shown below.

ITEM	PURCHASE PRICE	SCRAP VALUE	NO. OF YRS. TO BE DEPR.
WELDER	5000	500	9
LATHE	7500	300	9
JOINER	6000	500	11
PUNCH PRESS	5300	400	7

The printout should be in the form shown below.

```
                              WILKENS COMPANY

                          Depreciation Schedule
                          Straight-Line Method

                                 No. of Yrs
              Purch   Scrap        To Be                  Yrly        Book
  Item        Price   Value     Depreciated      Yr       Dep.        Value

Welder        5000     500          XX           X       XXX.XX      XXXX.XX
                                                 X       XXX.XX      XXXX.XX
                                                 X       XXX.XX      XXXX.XX
                                                 9       XXX.XX      XXXX.XX

Lathe         7500     300          XX           X       XXX.XX      XXXX.XX
                                                 X       XXX.XX      XXXX.XX
```

3. This problem appeared in a more simplified form at the end of Chapter 5. In this problem an INPUT statement is to be used to

input the *number* of departments to be involved and a READ statement is to be used to read in the data. The input printout should not appear in the middle of the output.

The Gillis Department Store wants a printout of all of the departments, their sales in hundreds, and their percentage of total sales. The percentage of sales is found by dividing the department's sales by the total sales. A flowchart, a computer listing, and a printout should be prepared.

```
                    GILLIS DEPARTMENT STORE

                    Listing of Total Sales
                             And
                     Percentage of Sales
                    First Quarter of 1981


                         Sales in        Percent of
    Department           Hundreds        Total Sales

         A                 414             XX.XX
         B                 540             XX.XX
         C                 819             XX.XX
         D                 711             XX.XX
         E                1121             XX.XX
         F                 650             XX.XX
         G                1280             XX.XX
         H                 418             XX.XX
         I                 990             XX.XX
         J                1070             XX.XX

    Total                 XXXX
```

4. This problem requires the use of principles in all of the previous chapters. The programmer for the Nelson Mfg. Co. is to print out a report in the format shown below.

```
                         NELSON MFG. CO.

                        EMPLOYEES' WAGES
                TWO WEEK PERIOD ENDING AUGUST 20, 1981

 Employee      Rate  Hrs  Exemp   Gross     Net      With     Pay

XXXXXXXXXX    X.XX   XX    X    XXXX.XX  XXXX.XX  XXX.XX  XXXX.XX
```

The withholding table on page 231 should be used for the information needed for the program. The computer should figure the gross salary, net salary (gross minus exemptions), withholding, and amount of the check. The data to be input is shown below. In the marital status column, zero signifies not married and one signifies married.

EMPLOYEES	RATE	HRS	MARITAL STATUS	NO. OF EXEMP.
C. ALLEN	4.76	80	0	1
B. BROWN	8.35	80	1	3
C. CARLSON	7.28	80	1	2
S. DODGE	5.25	80	0	1
V. JACKSON	5.50	80	0	1
L. MOORE	6.80	80	1	4
W. PEARSON	7.50	80	1	5
B. SMITH	9.00	80	1	4

FEDERAL INCOME TAX--WITHHOLDING INFORMATION*

Single Taxpayers: If net wages (allowing $23 for each claimed exemption) is not over $19**		Amount to be Withheld		Married Taxpayers: If net wages (allowing $23 for each claimed exemption) is not over $38**		Amount to be Withheld	
Over	But not over		of excess over	Over	But not over		of excess over
19	38	2.69 + 15%	19	38	76	5.38 + 15%	38
38	57	5.58 + 16%	38	76	114	11.15 + 16%	76
57	76	8.65 + 17%	57	114	152	17.31 + 17%	114
76	152	11.92 + 19%	76	152	304	23.85 + 19%	152
152	228	26.53 + 21%	152	304	456	53.08 + 22%	304
228	304	42.69 + 24%	228	456	608	86.92 + 25%	456
304	380	61.16 + 25%	304	608		125.38 + 28%	608
380	456	80.38 + 27%	380				
456	532	101.15 + 29%	456				
532	608	123.46 + 31%	532				
608		147.30 + 34%	608				

*This is not an official U.S. Government chart.
**No withholding has been deducted in these cases.

12

SEQUENTIAL AND RANDOM ACCESS FILES[1]

In this chapter the following topics will be discussed.

A. Using sequential files
   1. Assigning data file names
   2. Terminating a program
   3. Creating the data file
   4. Inputting from the data file
   5. Using transaction and master files
   6. Adding to the master file
   7. Eliminating a file

[1] This discussion pertains only to computers of the PDP 11/40 or higher series using the RSTS/E operating system.

8. Deleting a record from the master file
9. Retrieving a record from the master file
10. Updating the master file
11. Sorting the transaction file

B. Using random access files
   1. Creating a virtual array file
   2. Updating a virtual array file
   3. Adding to the virtual array file
   4. Deleting from the virtual array file

In previous chapters, the program and the data have been stored in a single file. The computer automatically stored the program and the data separately within that file. Only when the programmer typed SAVE was the whole file copied from main storage into auxiliary storage.

In this chapter, an entirely separate file is used to store the data in auxiliary storage. Other files are used to store the programs needed to enter the data into storage or to retrieve the data from storage. One program is used to write, or output, onto the data file in auxiliary storage. When a file is opened for output, it is opened to receive data. Another program is used to read, or input, because the data are brought out of auxiliary storage into main storage for use in the program. When a file is opened for input, it is opened to allow the data to be retrieved from the file, as demonstrated in the following diagram. However, one program might be used to open files for both input and output, provided the file is closed for either activity before opening it for the other.

Input/Output to a Data File

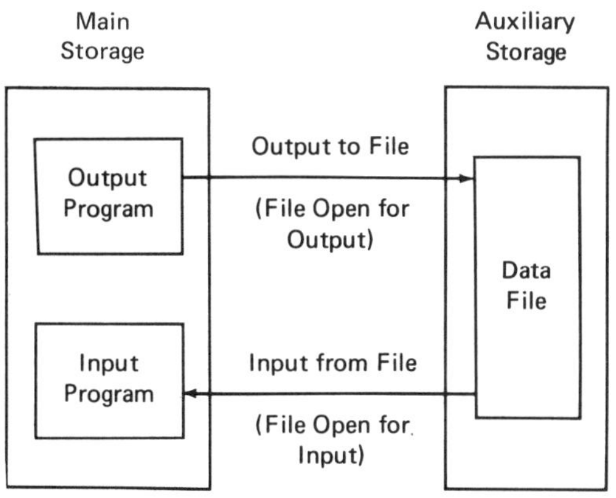

Sequential files are files that can be accessed only by starting from the beginning of the file every time the computer is directed to search for data. On the other hand, when searching for data in random access files, sometimes called direct access files, the computer goes directly to the data location. The first part of this chapter demonstrates the use of a sequential data file, because the syntax and programming are simpler. Random access files utilizing virtual arrays are presented in the last part of this chapter.

USING SEQUENTIAL FILES

ASSIGNING DATA FILE NAMES

The program and the file it manipulates cannot have the same name. In RSTS/E, when a program name is entered by the programmer, the system automatically gives it an extension of .BAS if no extension is entered with the program name. Although a program name must be different from the file name, it can be similar, as shown below.

Program Name:	CH5 (CH5.BAS)
Data File Name:	CH5.DAT

The rules for choosing a program file name are discussed in Chapter 2. However, the rules for choosing a data file name are slightly different.

1. The first part of the data file name is chosen in the same way as are program names (one to six characters, which must be letters or numbers).
2. A decimal point is inserted following that part of the name.
3. Then zero to three letters may be added after the decimal point. Since some combinations of letters are used for default extensions by the system, the authors recommend that .DAT be used to prevent problems because descriptive extensions can be useful to the programmer. The default file extensions, which should be avoided unless they apply to the specific file, are listed below.

.BAC	.LOG
.BAS	.LST
.BAK	.OBJ
.CBL	.RNO

.DOC	.SAV
.FOR	.TMP
.CMD	.TXT
.CTL	

PROBLEM 12-1

TERMINATING A PROGRAM

The first example of using sequential files will deal with Program CH5 shown in Figure 12-1 and is based on data from Chapter 5, Assignment 1.

```
10  ON ERROR GOTO 90
```

FIGURE 12-1

Problem 12-1—Inputting to the File

```
LIST
CH5       01:07 PM          10-Nov-81
10   ON ERROR GOTO 90
20   OPEN "CH5.DAT" FOR OUTPUT AS FILE 1
30   INPUT E$,S
40   P = S *.0275 \ F = S * .0585
50   PRINT #1, USING "\          \!###.##!#.##!##.##",E$,',',S,',',P,',',F
60   GO TO 30
70   CLOSE 1
80   GOTO 100
90   IF ERR= 11 AND ERL = 30 THEN RESUME 70 ELSE ON ERROR GOTO 0
100  END

Ready

RUN
CH5       01:07 PM          10-Nov-81
? BELLMAN,239.86
? BERRY,224.54
? CARTWRIGHT,205.78
? CARSON,196.93
? DILLON,216.45
? DOYLE,231.78
? ^Z
```

ON ERROR GOTO is a command to trap errors in the program. Any error detected in the execution of this program is directed to Statement 90.

```
90  IF ERR=11 AND ERL=30 THEN RESUME 70 ELSE ON ERROR GOTO 0
```

Statement 90 is used in place of a trailer constant and an IF statement to test for that trailer. Each diagnostic (error message) has a number, as listed in Appendix C. At Line 90 the computer is commanded to determine if the diagnostic is Error 11 (ERR=11), which is the error "End of file on device," and also to determine if the error occurred during the execution of Line 30 (ERL=30). The RESUME part of the statement transfers control to Line 70 to continue the program. The zero at the end of Statement 90 after the words ON ERROR GOTO directs control to the operating system, which aborts the program and prints out an error message. If the zero is omitted after the phrase ON ERROR GOTO, the computer assumes a zero.

```
30  INPUT E$,S
```

When the programmer is inputting data from the keyboard and comes to the end of the data, he depresses the Control Key and the letter Z simultaneously. As a result, the diagnostic "End of file on device" is caused. As a result of the ON ERROR GOTO in Statement 10 of this program, the CONTROL-Z will cause control to go to Line 90. This method of ending the program will operate when both conditions at Line 90 are true (the error number is 11 and the error occurred at Line 30). Statement 70 closes the file.

```
70  CLOSE 1
```

CREATING THE DATA FILE

Statement 20, which opens the file, allows data to be put into the file.

```
20  OPEN "CH5.DAT" FOR OUTPUT AS FILE 1
```

The file name must be placed in quotes. The word OUTPUT is used to open the file to print data on auxiliary storage. The file number is used within the program to reference the file. Only 12 file numbers can be used at the same time in a program. A file number can be used only for input or for output, not for both. However, once a file is closed, the file number used for the closed file may be used for some other file.

Statement 30 enables data to be entered from the keyboard, while Statement 40 computes the amount of pension and FICA.

```
30  INPUT E$,S
40  P = S * .0275\F = S * .0585
```

Statement 50 tells the computer to print the data obtained at Statements 30 and 40 on the file "CH5.DAT". The "#1" references the file "CH5.DAT". Then any input or output using the file will make reference to it by the number 1. The backslashes are used to store string data from E$. The exclamation points are to denote one-column fields into which anything can be printed. In this statement, the exclamation points are used to print commas to separate the data fields.

```
50  PRINT #1, USING "\          \!###.##!#.##!##.##",E$,',',S,',',P,',',F
```

This method of printing on the data file saves storage space, as it records the data fields close together. An important point in visualizing this method of storage is to picture data stored in the file as similar to data typed in DATA statements in previous chapters.

DATA STORED IN FILE "CH5.DAT"	DATA STATEMENTS IN A PROGRAM
`BELLMAN   ,239.86,6.60,14.03`	`60 DATA BELLMAN,239.86,6.60,14.03`
`BERRY     ,224.54,6.17,13.14`	`65 DATA BERRY,224.54,6.17,13.14`
`CARTWRIGHT,205.78,5.66,12.04`	`70 DATA CARTWRIGHT,205.78,5.66,12.04`
`CARSON    ,196.93,5.42,11.52`	`75 DATA CARSON,196.93,5.42,11.52`
`DILLON    ,216.45,5.95,12.66`	`80 DATA DILLON,216.45,5.95,12.66`
`DOYLE     ,231.78,6.37,13.56`	`85 DATA DOYLE,231.78,6.37,13.56`

Statement 60 returns control to Statement 30 so more data may be input from the keyboard as the program is run.

When the programmer types RUN, he then must input the data from the keyboard. The program is terminated when the CONTROL-Z is used. Since the computer is commanded by Statement 10 to catch each diagnostic (error message), the computer goes to Statement 90. Statement 90 sends control to Statement 70 because of the error caused by the CONTROL-Z. Any other error returns control to the operating system and aborts the program. Files must be closed before the program is ended.

INPUTTING FROM THE DATA FILE

In using files, the data is input to a program in main storage *from a file* in auxiliary storage with INPUT statements, rather than with READ and DATA statements as in previous chapters. Therefore, a program must be created to input the data from auxiliary storage. Because the computer stored the data in "CH5.DAT", Statement 30 in the program in Figure 12-2 opens the file "CH5.DAT" for input using File 1. The same file number used in opening a file for output is not necessarily used in opening the same file for input, although in Statement 30 the same file number is used.

```
30  OPEN "CH5.DAT" FOR INPUT AS FILE 1
```

Statements 40 to 130 print out the title and headings.

Statement 140 inputs the data from the file just as it would have with READ and DATA statements. The command INPUT #1 tells the computer to retrieve the data from the "CH5.DAT" file on FILE 1 and to store it in locations E$, S, P, and F.

```
140 INPUT #1, E$, S, P, F
```

Statements 150 through 200 cause a detail line to be printed, and Statement 210 sends the computer back to Statement 140 where another line of data is input. Looping will continue until there is no more data to be read. To catch errors, an ON ERROR GOTO statement is used at Line 10. When there are no more data in the file, control is sent to Statement 230, which in turn sends it to Statement 220 if the error was due to lack of data. Statement 220 closes the data file and sends control to Statement 240, which terminates the program.

```
220 CLOSE 1\GOTO 240
230 IF ERR=11 AND ERL=140 THEN RESUME 220 ELSE ON ERROR GOTO
240 END
```

When the programmer types RUN, the resulting printout is as shown at the bottom of Figure 12-2.

FIGURE 12-2

Problem 12-1—Program To Input from a Data File

```
LIST
CH5B     01:09 PM          10-Nov-81
10 ON ERROR GOTO 230
20 PRINT \ PRINT
30 OPEN "CH5.DAT" FOR INPUT AS FILE 1
40 PRINT;TAB(27); "KING NUT FACTORY"
50 PRINT
60 PRINT;TAB(20); "RECORD OF WEEKLY GROSS SALARY,"
70 PRINT;TAB(26); "PENSIONS, AND FICA"
80 PRINT
90 PRINT
100 PRINT;TAB(27); "WKLY GROSS"
110 PRINT;TAB(12); "EMPLOYEE"; TAB(29); "SALARY"; TAB(42); "PENSION";
120 PRINT;TAB(55); "FICA"
130 PRINT
140 INPUT #1, E$, S, P, F
150 PRINT;TAB(11); E$; TAB(29);
160 PRINT USING "###.##", S;
170 PRINT;TAB(43);
180 PRINT USING "#.##", P;
190 PRINT;TAB(55);
200 PRINT USING "##.##", F
210 GOTO 140
220 CLOSE 1 \ GOTO 240
230 IF ERR=11 AND ERL=140 THEN RESUME 220  ELSE ON ERROR GOTO 0
240 END

Ready

RUN
CH5B     01:09 PM          10-Nov-81


                          KING NUT FACTORY

                   RECORD OF WEEKLY GROSS SALARY,
                         PENSIONS, AND FICA


                          WKLY GROSS
           EMPLOYEE         SALARY       PENSION      FICA

          BELLMAN           239.86        6.60        14.03
          BERRY             224.54        6.17        13.14
          CARTWRIGHT        205.78        5.66        12.04
          CARSON            196.93        5.42        11.52
          DILLON            216.45        5.95        12.66
          DOYLE             231.78        6.37        13.56
```

USING TRANSACTION AND MASTER FILES

Businesses use files in most facets of their operations. To illustrate how files are used, a few business applications will be explained.

To keep accounts receivable up to date, a department store would use two files, a master file and a transaction file. The transaction file is used to record the daily purchases and payments. At the end of the month, the transactions in the transaction file are placed on the master file. Problems 12-4 and 12-5 show the addition to and deletion from records, a process called *updating*. A master file would be larger, but in Problem 12-3 six customer records are used to show how files are utilized. All that is done with these customer records is to add charges, deduct payments, compute finance charges, and record the payments due. A printout of a run of the program is shown below the program listing in Figure 12-3.

FIGURE 12-3

Problem 12-2—Opening a Master File

```
LIST
DPTSTR  05:07 AM           12-Feb-81
10  ON ERROR GO TO 50
15  OPEN 'DPMSTR.DAT' FOR OUTPUT AS FILE 1
20  PRINT 'N=CUST #;N$=CUST NAME; P=ACC.FIN. CHGE; B=BAL'
25  PRINT "ENTER CONTROL-Z TO TERMINATE"
30  INPUT N,N$,P,B
35  PRINT #1,USING "####!\        \!###.##!#####.##",N",",N$,",",P,",",
40  GO TO 20
45  CLOSE 1\GO TO 55
50  IF ERR=11 AND ERL=30 THEN RESUME 45 ELSE ON ERROR GO TO
55  END

Ready
```

```
RUN
DPMSTR          07:19 AM         12-Feb-81
N=CUST #;N$=CUST NAME;P=ACC. FIN. CHGE; B=BAL
? 4110,JOHNSON,5.21,455.21
N=CUST #;N$=CUST NAME;P=ACC. FIN. CHGE; B=BAL
? 4327,KARACHI,1.69,56.21
N=CUST #;N$=CUST NAME;P=ACC. FIN. CHGE; B=BAL
? 4415,KNOLLS,14.37,0
N=CUST #;N$=CUST NAME;P-ACC. FIN. CHGE; B=BAL
? 4832,LAWRENCE,3.43,90.43
N=CUST #;N$=CUST NAME;P=ACC. FIN. CHGE; B=BAL
? 5010,LOMBARDO,2.93,123.93
N=CUST #;N$=CUST NAME;P=ACC. FIN. CHGE; B*BAL
? 5212,MARTIN,0,38
N=CUST #;N$=CUST NAME;P=ACC. FIN. CHGE; B=BAL
?^Z
```

PROBLEM 12-2

Problem 12-2, shown in Figure 12-3, uses Statement 15 to name the master file "DPMSTR.DAT" and to open the file. Statement 30 allows the input of data from the keyboard, while Statement 35 prints the data on the file. The variables used are N for customer number, N$ for customer name, P for accumulated finance charge, and B for the balance.

PROBLEM 12-3

Occasionally, the contents of the master file might be checked. An example of a program that will list contents of a data file is shown in Problem 12-3 in Figure 12-4. That program causes a printout of the contents of the data file "DPMSTR.DAT".

PROBLEM 12-4

ADDING TO THE MASTER FILE

Sometimes master files are updated by the addition of new accounts. For illustrative purposes, the following two accounts will be added to master file "DPMSTR.DAT".

```
4385,KELLEY,2.49,104.89
4948,LITTLE,.67,55.47
```

Adding customers at the beginning or end of the file is simple, but to add within the file is more difficult. The program in Figure 12-5 demonstrates the procedure of adding within the file. The master file "DPMSTR.DAT" is opened for input to retrieve the data, and a new master file is opened for output to receive the data from the old master file as well as the additional customers. This file is named "DDSTR.DAT".

FIGURE 12-4

Problem 12-3—Printing the Contents of a Master File

```
DPSTRR                    12-Feb-81         07:18 AM

10  ON ERROR GO TO 80
15  PRINT\PRINT
20  OPEN "DPMSTR.DAT" FOR INPUT AS FILE 1
25  PRINT;TAB(37);"ACCUMULATED"
30  PRINT;TAB(39);"FINANCE";TAB(55);"AMT."
35  PRINT;TAB(8);"ACCT #";TAB(23);"NAME";TAB(39);"CHARGES";TAB(55);"OWED"
40  PRINT
45  INPUT #1,N,N$,P,B
50  PRINT;TAB(9);
55  PRINT USING "####",N;
60  PRINT;TAB(21);N$;TAB(39);
65  PRINT USING "###.##          #####.##",P,B
70  GO TO 45
75  CLOSE 1\GO TO 85
80  IF ERR=11 AND ERL=45 THEN RESUME 75 ELSE ON ERROR GO TO
85  END

RUN
DPSTRR  08:50 AM          13-Feb-81


                                     ACCUMULATED
                                       FINANCE          AMT.
        ACCT #          NAME           CHARGES          OWED

         4110         JOHNSON            5.21          455.21
         4327         KARACHI            1.69           56.21
         4415         KNOLLS            14.37            0.00
         4832         LAWRENCE           3.43           90.43
         5010         LOMBARDO           2.93          123.93
         5212         MARTIN             0.00           38.00
```

```
40  PRINT "CUSTOMERS TO BE ADDED"
50  PRINT "N=CUST #;N$=CUST NAME;P=ACC. FIN. CHGE;B=BAL"
60  PRINT  "INPUT -9,0,0,0 FOR LAST CUSTOMER"
70  INPUT N,N$,P,B
80  IF N=9 GO TO 150
85  IF S=1 GO TO 100
90  INPUT #1,N1,C$,P1,B1
```

A switch (S) is used in this problem. It is initialized to zero at Statement 5. After the customer number to be added is entered from the keyboard at Statement 70, control drops to Statement 80. At State-

FIGURE 12-5

Problem 12-4—Adding to the File

```
LIST
CH12     05:03 PM          15-Feb-81
5   S=0
10  ON ERROR GO TO 200
20  OPEN 'DPMSTR.DAT' FOR INPUT AS FILE 1
30  OPEN 'DDSTR.DAT' FOR OUTPUT AS FILE 2
40  PRINT 'CUSTOMERS TO BE ADDED'
50  PRINT  'N=CUST #;N$=CUST NAME; P=ACC.FIN.CHGE;B=BAL'
60  PRINT 'INPUT -9,0,0,0 FOR LAST CUSTOMER'
70  INPUT N,N$,P,B
80  IF N = -9 GO TO 150
85  IF S=1 GO TO 100
90  INPUT #1,N1,C$,P1,B1
95  S=1
100 IF N < N1 GO TO 130
110 PRINT #2,USING '####!\             \!###.##!#####.##'N1,',',C$,',',P1,',',B1
120 GO TO 90
130 PRINT #2,USING '####!\             \!###.##!#####.##',N,',',N$,',',P,',',B
140 GO TO 40
150 INPUT #1,N1,C$,P1,B1
160 PRINT #2,USING '####!\             \!###.##!#####.##',N1,',',C$,',',P1,',',B1
170 GO TO 150
180 IF N <> -9 GO TO 130
190 CLOSE  1, 2\GO TO 230
200 IF ERR=11 AND ERL=90 THEN RESUME 180
210 IF ERR=11 AND ERL=150 THEN RESUME 190
220 ON ERROR GO TO
230 END

Ready

RUN
CH12     11:44 AM          15-Feb-81
CUSTOMERS TO BE ADDED
N=CUST #;N$=CUST NAME;P=ACC. FIN. CHGE;B=BAL
INPUT -9,0,0,0 FOR LAST CUSTOMER
? 4385,KELLY,2.49,104.89
N=CUST #;N$=CUST NAME;P=ACC. FIN. CHGE;B=BAL
INPUT -9,0,0,0 FOR LAST CUSTOMER
? 4948,LITTLE,.67,55.47
N=CUST #;N$=CUST NAME;P=ACC. FIN. CHGE;B=BAL
INPUT -9,0,0,0 FOR LAST CUSTOMER
? -9,0,0,0
```

ment 80 the question is asked, "Does N = -9?" Unless all customers to be added have been entered, N does not equal -9, so control drops to Statement 85 where control is transferred to Statement 100 if S equals one. It will equal zero only the first time. If it does equal zero, control drops to Statement 90 where a record is input from the file. The switch prevents control from dropping to Statement 90 after a record is input from the keyboard if there is a record stored in memory and not entered in the file. Otherwise every time a record to be added is entered from the keyboard, a record would be entered from the file. If the previous record entered from the old file has not yet been entered on the new file, it would never be entered because a new record would take its place in memory. Switch S is set to one when a record is entered from the file.

Statement 70 allows the additional customers to be input from the keyboard. In previous chapters, dummy variables were used to determine when the trailer data were read. To show that technique in a program with input statements, it is used in this program at Statements 60 and 80. Even though the fields to be input are the same in both files, different variable names must be used. Variables N, N$, P, and B are used for the additions, and variables N1, C$, P1, and B1 are used in Statement 90 for the fields retrieved from the old master file.

Although it is not done in this program, the programmer might want to add some statements, after inputting the data for the customers to be added, for the purpose of verifying whether the data is correct as keyed. Statements 72, 74, and 76 *could possibly be added* to the program.

```
72  PRINT N,N$,P,B
74  INPUT "IS THE DATA ENTERED CORRECTLY--YES OR NO",Q$
76  IF Q$ = "NO" GO TO 40
```

Statement 72 would print out the data as entered. The programmer would look at the printout to check its accuracy. Statement 74 would ask, "Is the data entered correctly--yes or no". If the data were entered correctly, the operator would type "yes" and the program would execute as if these statements had not been added. If the operator types "no," control is sent to Statement 40 to reenter the data.

```
100  IF N < N1 GO TO 130
110  PRINT #2,USING "####!\              \!###.##!#####.##",N1,",",C$,",",P1,",",B1
120  GO TO 90
130  PRINT #2,USING "####!\              \!###.##!#####.##,N,",",N$,",",P,",",B
140  GO TO 40
```

Statement 100 asks if N, the number of the customer to be added, is less than N1, the customer number from the master file. For example, Customer 4385 must be placed between Customers 4327 and 4415. To do this, the computer retrieves a customer number from the master file and compares it with the one to be added. When the customer number (N1) is larger than the one to be added (N), the computer is directed to Statement 130, which prints the customer to be added on to the master file. The computer is then directed to go to Statement 40 where a new customer to be added is entered.

```
180 IF N <> -9 GO TO 130
190 CLOSE 1, 2\GO TO 230
200 IF ERR=11 AND ERL=90 THEN RESUME 180
210 IF ERR=11 AND ERL=150 THEN RESUME 190
220 ON ERROR GO TO
230 END
```

If the number of the customer to be added (N) is larger than the one retrieved from the file (N1), control drops to Statement 110 where it is directed to print the customer from the old file into the new file. When the last customer to be added has been printed on the new file and the computer asks for a customer to be entered at Statement 70 the operator enters -9,0,0,0. At Statement 80, when the computer tests what is stored in N and finds it to be a -9, control is directed to Statement 150.

```
150  INPUT #1,N1,C$,P1,B1
160  PRINT #2,USING "####!\          \!###.##!#####.##",N1,",",C$,",",P1,",",B1
170  GO TO 150
190  CLOSE 1,2\GO TO 230
200  IF ERR=11 and ERL=90 THEN RESUME 180
210  IF ERR=11 AND ERL=150 THEN RESUME 190
220  ON ERROR GO TO
230  END
```

Statements 150, 160, and 170 print the remainder of the old file on the new file. If there are no more data to be printed, the "End of file on device" error message sends control to Statement 10, which in turn sends control to Statement 200. When the conditions are tested at Statement 200 and the error line is not 90 (ERL=90), control drops to Statement 210. When the conditions there are tested and are found to be true (ERR=11 and ERL=150), control is transferred to Statement 190. The files are then closed and control is sent to Statement 230, which is the END statement.

When the last record on the old data file has been written on the new file and there is still a new record to be added to the file, an "End of file on device" error message is generated at Line 90. Statement 10 catches that error and directs control to Statement 200. When the conditions are tested and are found to be true (ERR=11 and ERL=90), then control is transferred to Statement 180.

If there is a -9 stored in N when Statement 180 is executed, control drops to Statement 190, which closes the files and sends control to Statement 230, which terminates the program. If N does not equal -9, in other words a new customer number (N) is to be added, control is directed to Statement 130 where the customer is printed on the file. Control goes back to Statement 40 where a new customer to be added is entered. This process continues until Statement 80 detects the trailer constant, which causes the program to end as explained earlier.

To place two statements checking for the diagnostic "End of file on device" in this program is very important, because there are two different input statements (the input statement entering new customers has its own method of terminating). The ON ERROR GO TO statement at Line 10 will cause any errors to be caught and will direct control to Line 200. If the error occurred on Line 90, then no more data are available from the file. The program resumes at Line 180. If the error occurred on Line 150, control resumes at Line 190. Any other errors will be processed by the operating system via Statement 220. The ON ERROR GO TO must be placed *after* the second "IF ERR=11" statement.

ELIMINATING A FILE

Although it may seem obvious, every time something is done to the master file a new file is created and the old file should be eliminated. However, before the old file is destroyed, the new one should be checked for accuracy.

The first master file was "DPMSTR.DAT" and the new one is "DDSTR.DAT". To check "DDSTR.DAT" for accuracy, the programmer brings a listing of Problem 12-3 from storage, as shown in Figure 12-4. This program is used to print out the contents of file "DPMSTR.DAT". The operator replaces Statement 20 OPEN "DPMSTR.DAT" FOR INPUT AS FILE 1 with Statement 20 OPEN "DDSTR.DAT" FOR INPUT AS FILE 1 and runs it to check whether the file is correct after the additions have been input. The run is shown in Figure 12-6. After noting that the file is correct, he then types KILL "DPMSTR.DAT". This command destroys that file. It is important to note that the file must be closed before it can be killed.

Another point worth noting is that any time a file is opened for output it destroys any other file by that name.

FIGURE 12-6

Printout of the Contents of the Master File "DDSTR.DAT"

```
DPSTRR  12:12 AM        15-Feb-81
```

ACCT #	NAME	ACCUMULATED FINANCE CHARGES	AMT. OWED
4110	JOHNSON	5.21	455.21
4327	KARACHI	1.69	56.21
4385	KELLEY	2.49	104.89
4415	KNOLLS	14.37	0.00
4832	LAWRENCE	3.43	90.43
4948	LITTLE	.67	55.47
5010	LOMBARDO	2.93	123.93
5212	MARTIN	0.00	38.00

PROBLEM 12-5

DELETING A RECORD FROM THE MASTER FILE

Sometimes it is necessary to delete a customer from a file. Mr. Knolls, Customer 4415, wrote and asked that his account be closed. The program shown in Figure 12-7 is designed to do that.

Again, two files must be opened. Statement 15 retrieves the data from an existing file, and Statement 20 opens a file to create a new master file.

FIGURE 12-7

Problem 12-5—Deleting a Record from the File

```
LIST
CH12D    02:42 PM          15-Feb-81
10  ON ERROR GO TO 65
15  OPEN "DDSTR.DAT" FOR INPUT AS FILE 2
20  OPEN "DDDSTR.DAT" FOR OUTPUT AS FILE 1
25  INPUT "CUSTOMER NUMBER TO BE DELETED";N1
30  INPUT #2, N,N$,P,B
45  IF N1=N GO TO 30
50  PRINT #1,USING "####!\            \!###.##!#####.##",N,",",N$,",",P,",",B
55  GO TO 30
60  CLOSE  1, 2\GO TO 70
65  IF ERR=11 AND ERL=30 THEN RESUME 60 ELSE ON ERROR GO TO
70  END
```

Statement 25 stores the number of the record to be deleted in N1. Statement 30 inputs data from the existing master file. Statement 45 compares the number of the data input from the file and the number stored in N1. If the two are not equal, the computer prints the retrieved record on the new master file. When the two are equal so that the customer to be deleted is found, the computer is sent back to retrieve another customer record. The PRINT USING statement is bypassed, so the customer is skipped, or deleted. The computer will then retrieve and print out the remaining customers on the new file.

PROBLEM 12-6

RETRIEVING A RECORD FROM THE MASTER FILE

Another use of the master file is shown in Problem 12-6. A customer, Mr. Lombardo, contacted the business office complaining that there was an error in his balance. To locate and print out the Lombardo record, the program listed in Figure 12-8 is used.

Statement 8 opens the file for input. Statement 12 causes the number of the customer to be retrieved to be entered from the keyboard. Statement 25 inputs the customer information from the file. At Line 30, if the customer number from the file is equal to the customer number entered from the keyboard, the computer is ordered to go to Statement 40. Statements 40, 45, 50, and 55 print out the customer record. If the customer number entered from the file is not equal to the one entered from the keyboard, the computer is commanded at Statement 35 to retrieve another customer from the file. The search continues until the customer is located.

In this problem, because only one customer is to be located, control drops to Statement 60 when that customer is located. However, if more than one customer is to be retrieved, a Statement 57 *would be inserted* into the program: 57 GOTO 10. If this statement is inserted to terminate the program, the operator depresses CONTROL-Z. A Statement 62 *would be added* to catch the CONTROL-Z.

```
62  IF ERR=11 AND ERL=12 THEN RESUME 60
```

UPDATING THE MASTER FILE

The transaction file is used to post daily business transactions, and once a month the transactions are transferred from the transaction file to the master file, a process called "Updating the Master File."

FIGURE 12-8

Problem 12-6—Retrieving a Record from the File

```
LIST
CHH12    02:57 PM          31-Jul-81
5    ON ERROR GO TO 65
8    OPEN 'DDDSTR.DAT' FOR INPUT AS FILE 1
10   PRINT 'CUSTOMER NUMBER TO BE LOCATED'
12   INPUT N1
14   PRINT;TAB(37);'ACCUMULATED'
16   PRINT;TAB(39);'FINANCE';TAB(55);'AMT.'
18   PRINT;TAB(8);'ACCT #';TAB(23);'NAME';TAB(39);
19   PRINT 'CHARGES';TAB(55);'OWED'
21   PRINT
25   INPUT #1,N,N$,P,B
30   IF N1=N GO TO 40
35   GO TO 25
40   PRINT;TAB(9);
45   PRINT USING '####',N;
50   PRINT;TAB(21);N$;TAB(39);
55   PRINT USING '###.##          #####.##',P,B
60   CLOSE 1\GO TO 70
65   IF ERR=11 AND ERL=25 THEN RESUME 60 ELSE ON ERROR GO TO
70 END

Ready

RUN
CHH12    02:57 PM          31-Jul-81
CUSTOMER NUMBER TO BE LOCATED
? 5010
                                          ACCUMULATED
                                            FINANCE         AMT.
        ACCT #          NAME                CHARGES         OWED

         5010          LOMBARDO               2.93          123.93
```

In previous examples, all of the string data have been one-word fields, which created no problems when writing on the files. The problem used in this section is more detailed, since each string will consist of more than one word. As stated earlier, data printed on the files must be input as if it were data in DATA statements, but without the statement numbers and the word DATA.

In the discussion in Chapter 3 dealing with strings, the point was made that string data with more than one word or with punctuation must be placed in quotes in DATA statements. When the programmer writes the statement printing data on a file, the data looks like the data fields printed in DATA statements. In other words, string fields with more than one word or with punctuation must have quotes around those fields. The commas with quotation marks around them act as separators and are placed on the files by the use of exclamation marks. The quotes to be placed around strings are enclosed within quotation marks and are also placed on the files by the use of exclamation marks.

To demonstrate the similarity between the DATA statement, Statement 20, and the statement printing on the data file, Statements 10 and 15, both kinds of statements are illustrated below.

```
20  DATA 1011, "J. H. JONES","PAYROLL",73.83

10  PRINT #1,USING "####!!\                  \!!",A,",",'"',N$,'"',",";
15  PRINT #1,USING "!\              \!!##.##",'"',D$,'"',",",B
```

In Statement 10, the crosshatches are filled by variable A. The first exclamation mark is filled by the comma separating the data fields, and the second exclamation mark is filled by the quote beginning the string field N$. The two backslashes and the spaces between them are for the string field filled by N$. The third exclamation mark is for the ending quote after the string field N$. The fourth exclamation mark is for the comma separating the fields.

In Statement 15, the first exclamation mark is for the quotes beginning the string field D$. The backslashes and the spaces between them are for the string field D$. The second exclamation mark is for the ending quote after the field D$. The third exclamation mark is for the comma separating the D$ and B fields. The crosshatches are for the field filled by the variable B. Therefore, if A = 1011, N$ = J. H. Jones, D$ = Payroll, and B = 73.83, the data printed on the file would appear as 1011,"J. H. JONES","PAYROLL",73.83.

PROBLEM 12-7

Master files contain a great deal of information, but only a small portion of it will be used in Problem 12-7. The B & B Department Store has several thousand credit customers. However, this problem will involve only five customer accounts from the many that actually exist in the department store's records. The data for these five customers are listed below.

CUST. NO.	NAME AND ADDRESS	ACCUMULATED FINANCE CHARGE	BALANCE
1003	Bob Anderson 343 Coronado Ave. Long Beach, Calif. 90804	8.95	35.58
1011	J. H. Hanover 1723 E. Fourth St. Long Beach, Calif. 90804	37.63	57.89
1234	Bob J. Jenkins 1334 E. Harding St. Long Beach, Calif. 90805	11.15	37.65
1718	Christopher L. Mullins 3022 E. Third St. Long Beach, Calif. 90804	25.93	86.58
1927	Roy H. Smith 190 Redondo Blvd. Long Beach, Calif. 90804	3.45	0.00

The program for Problem 12-7, shown in Figure 12-9, is used to open the master file for output to print the data on the file. This program is similar to the preceding programs used to open files for output,

FIGURE 12-9

Listing of Problem 12-7—Creating a Master File

```
LIST
66        03:20 PM          21-Mar-81

10   ON ERROR GO TO 140
20   OPEN 'BUS.DAT' FOR OUTPUT AS FILE 1
30   PRINT 'N=CUST #;N$=CUST NAME;S$=ST. ADDRESS;C$=CITY,ST.;';\
     PRINT 'P=ACC. FIN. CHGE;B=BAL'
40   PRINT 'ENTER CONTROL Z TO TERMINATE'
50   INPUT N,N$,S$,C$,P,B
80   PRINT #1,USING '####!!\                        \!',N,',',"',N$,'"';
90   PRINT #1,USING '!!\                        \!!',',',"',S$,'"',',';
100  PRINT #1,USING '!\                        \!!',"',C$,'"',',';
110  PRINT #1,USING '###.##!#####.##',P,',',B
120  GO TO 30
130  CLOSE 1\GO TO 150
140  IF ERR=11 AND ERL=50 THEN RESUME 130 ELSE ON ERROR GO TO
150  END
```

though the data in Problem 12-7 are more detailed. Statements 80, 90, 100, and 110 are used to print the data on the files. A semi-colon appears at the end of the PRINT USING Lines 80, 90, and 100 so that one line of printing will be entered on the file. Because the string data are more complex, quotation marks must be placed around the strings. Figure 12-10 is the run of the program, with the data input from the keyboard.

FIGURE 12-10

Run of Problem 12-7

```
RUN
66        03:22 PM          31-Jul-81
N=CUST #;N$=CUST NAME;S$=ST. ADDRESS;C$=CITY,ST.;P=ACC. FIN. CHGE;B=BAL
ENTER CONTROL Z TO TERMINATE
? 1003,'BOB ANDERSON','343 CORONADO AVE.','LONG BEACH, CA 90804',8.95,35.38
N=CUST #;N$=CUST NAME;S$=ST. ADDRESS;C$=CITY,ST.;P=ACC. FIN. CHGE;B=BAL
ENTER CONTROL Z TO TERMINATE
? 1011,'J. H. HANOVER','1723 E. FOURTH ST.','LONG BEACH, CA 90804',37.63,57.89
N=CUST #;N$=CUST NAME;S$=ST. ADDRESS;C$=CITY,ST.;P=ACC. FIN. CHGE;B=BAL
ENTER CONTROL Z TO TERMINATE
? 1234,'BOB J. JENKINS','1334 E. HARDING ST.','LONG BEACH, CA 90805',11.15,37.65
N=CUST #;N$=CUST NAME;S$=ST. ADDRESS;C$=CITY,ST.;P=ACC. FIN. CHGE;B=BAL
ENTER CONTROL Z TO TERMINATE
? 1718,'CHRISTOPHER L. MULLINS',' 3022 E. THIRD ST.','LONG BEACH, CA 90804',25.93,
,86.58
N=CUST #;N$=CUST NAME;S$=ST. ADDRESS;C$=CITY,ST.;P=ACC. FIN. CHGE;B=BAL
ENTER CONTROL Z TO TERMINATE
? 1927,'ROY H. SMITH','190 REDONDO BLVD.','LONG BEACH, CA 90804',3.45,0.00
N=CUST #;N$=CUST NAME;S$=ST. ADDRESS;C$=CITY,ST.;P=ACC. FIN. CHGE;B=BAL
ENTER CONTROL Z TO TERMINATE
? ^Z
```

The program in Figure 12-11 is created to print out the contents of the master file "BUS.DAT" created in Problem 12-7. The printout of the contents of File "BUS.DAT" is shown in Figure 12-12.

PROBLEM 12-8

Thousands of transactions take place daily in the B & B Department Store, but transactions affecting the five customers used in Problem 12-8 occur only a few days during the month. Transactions are given

FIGURE 12-11

Program To Print Out Contents of Master File "BUS.DAT"

```
68       03:52 PM          21-Mar-81
5    ON ERROR GO TO 60
10   OPEN 'BUS.DAT' FOR INPUT AS FILE 1
15   PRINT\PRINT;TAB(20);'LISTING OF CUSTOMER ACCOUNTS'
20   PRINT
22   INPUT #1,N,N$,S$,C$,P,B
25   PRINT;TAB(10);N$
30   PRINT;TAB(10);S$
35   PRINT;TAB(10);C$
40   PRINT\PRINT;TAB(40);'ACC. FIN. CHARGE';
42   PRINT;TAB(60);'BALANCE'
45   PRINT
50   PRINT;TAB(45);\PRINT USING '###.##',P;
52   PRINT;TAB(60);\PRINT USING '#####.##',B
53   GO TO 20
55   CLOSE 1\GO TO 65
60   IF ERR=11 AND ERL=22 THEN RESUME 55 ELSE ON ERROR GO TO
65   END
```

for five days, as listed below. In the transaction file, only the customer number and his payment or charge is listed.

B & B DEPARTMENT STORE TRANSACTIONS

	CUST. NO.	PAYMENT	CHARGE
Day 1	1011	10.00	0.00
	1718	10.00	0.00
Day 2	1003	10.00	0.00
	1234	10.00	0.00
Day 3	1003	0.00	15.75
Day 4	1011	0.00	8.93
	1234	0.00	25.63
	1718	0.00	11.93
Day 5	1011	0.00	15.65
	1718	0.00	22.35

A file must be created to act as a transaction file on which daily transactions are entered. The program to create the transaction file for the department store in this problem is listed in Figure 12-13.

FIGURE 12-12
Printout of Contents of Master File "BUS.DAT"

```
              LISTING OF CUSTOMER ACCOUNTS

BOB ANDERSON
343 CORONADO AVE.
LONG BEACH, CALIF. 90804

                              ACC. FIN. CHARGE    BALANCE

                                     8.95           35.38


J. H. HANOVER
1723 E. FOURTH ST.
LONG BEACH, CALIF. 90804

                              ACC. FIN. CHARGE    BALANCE

                                    37.63           57.89


BOB J. JENKINS
1334 E. HARDING ST.
LONG BEACH, CALIF. 90805

                              ACC. FIN. CHARGE    BALANCE

                                    11.15           37.65


CHRISTOPHER L. MULLINS
3022 E. THIRD ST.
LONG BEACH, CALIF. 90804

                              ACC. FIN. CHARGE    BALANCE

                                    25.93           86.58


ROY H. SMITH
190 REDONDO BLVD.
LONG BEACH, CALIF. 90804

                              ACC. FIN. CHARGE    BALANCE

                                     3.45            0.00
```

FIGURE 12-13

Problem 12-8—Opening and Using Transaction File

```
LIST
69       08:53 AM          31-MAR-81
10  ON ERROR GO TO 68
20  OPEN 'BUSTR.DAT' AS FILE 2,MODE 2
30  PRINT 'N1=CUST #, P1=PAYMENT,C1=CHARGE'
32  PRINT 'ENTER TRAILER CONSTANT AS 9999,0,0'
35  PRINT 'USE CONTROL Z TO TERMINATE'
40  INPUT N1,P1,C1
55  PRINT  2,USING '####!####.##!####.##',N1,',',P1,',',C1
60  GO TO 30
65  CLOSE 2 \ GOTO 70
68  IF ERR=11 AND ERL=40 THEN RESUME 65 ELSE ON ERROR GO TO
70  END
```

Statement 20 is different from any previous statement illustrated. One of the differences is that the new file "BUSTR.DAT" is opened for neither input or output. The computer checks for a file named "BUSTR.DAT". If one is not found, then the computer assumes that this file is meant to be opened for output. If it finds a file by that name, it then assumes this file is to be opened for input.

The next part of Statement 20 that is different is "MODE 2". If this part were not placed in the statement, each day's transactions would be printed over the previous day's transactions. "MODE 2" means "open for append" and permits each day's transactions to be added following the previous day's transactions, i.e., at the end of the file.

Statement 40 permits the operator to enter the customer number, payments, and charges for each transaction from the keyboard. Statement 55 causes the data to be printed on the transaction file.

The operator enters a data line, or trailer constant, consisting of "9999,0,0" after the last of the month's transactions. This line is to be used when updating the master file at the end of the month. When the transaction file is merged with the master file and the trailer constant is encountered, the remainder of the master file is recorded without searching for any more transactions.

To terminate the program, the operator enters a CONTROL-Z after the last of the day's transactions is entered. CONTROL-Z creates an "End of file on device" diagnostic, which is picked up by the computer at Statement 10. Then control is sent to Statement 68 which transfers control to Statement 65. The file is closed and the computer is directed to Statement 70, which terminates the program.

PROBLEM 12-9

To check whether the data is correctly entered, the program in Problem 12-9 is created, as shown in Figure 12-14. The output is illustrated below the program listing in the same figure. The printout is used for proofreading purposes, so the operator can check that the data have been entered correctly.

FIGURE 12-14

Problem 12-9—Checking the Contents of the Transaction File

```
LIST
 1     08:53 AM            31-Mar-81
10  ON ERROR GO TO 75
15  OPEN "BUSTR.DAT" FOR INPUT AS FILE 1
17  PRINT;TAB(20);"CUST #";TAB(33);"PAYMENT";
18  PRINT;TAB(47);"CHARGES"\PRINT
20  INPUT #1,N1,P1,C1
30  PRINT;TAB(21);\PRINT USING "####",N1;
35  PRINT;TAB(34);\PRINT USING "###.##",P1;
37  PRINT;TAB(48);\PRINT USING "###.##",C1
40  GO TO 20
70  CLOSE  1\GO TO 80
75  IF ERR=11 AND ERL=20 THEN RESUME 70 ELSE ON ERROR GO TO
80  END

READY

RUN
71        08:57 AM          31-Mar-81
                           CUST #       PAYMENT        CHARGES

                            1011          10.00           0.00
                            1718          10.00           0.00
                            1003          10.00           0.00
                            1234          10.00           0.00
                            1003           0.00          15.75
                            1011           0.00           8.93
                            1234           0.00          25.63
                            1718           0.00          11.93
                            1011           0.00          15.65
                            1718           0.00          22.35
                            9999           0.00           0.00
```

SORTING THE TRANSACTION FILE

Before the data from the transaction file can be merged with the master file to update it, the data in the transaction file must be sorted so that all of the data for each customer is grouped. Each computer usually has a sort program in its operating system, and the reference manual explains how to use it. The sort program used in Figure 12-15 is not a system sort, but it is shown here to indicate what such a program might look like.

FIGURE 12-15

Sort Program—Sorting Contents of Transaction File

```
LIST
70        08:23 AM          02-May-81
10   ON ERROR GO TO 200
20   DIM B(11,3),M(11,3)
30   OPEN 'BUSTR.DAT' FOR INPUT AS FILE 1
40   FOR X = 1 TO 11
50   INPUT #1,B(X,1),B(X,2),B(X,3)
60   NEXT X
70   CLOSE  1
80   FOR Y = 1 TO 11
90   L = 10000
100  FOR A = 1 TO 11
110  IF B(A,1) <L GO TO 140
120  NEXT A
130  GO TO 160
140  L1 = A\L = B(A,1)
150  GO TO 120
160  M(Y,1) = L\M(Y,2) = B(L1,2)\M(Y,3) = B(L1,3)
170  B(L1,1) = 10000
180  NEXT Y
190  ! DATA IS NOW SORTED INTO M
191  OPEN 'BUSTR1.DAT' FOR OUTPUT AS FILE 2
192  FOR A = 1 TO 11
193  PRINT #2,USING '####!###.##',M(A,1),',',M(A,2);
194  PRINT #2,USING '!#####.##',',',M(A,3)
195  NEXT A
196  CLOSE  2\GO TO 210
200  IF ERR=11 AND ERL=50 THEN RESUME 70 ELSE ON ERROR GO TO
210  END
```

In this program the data must first be stored in a matrix. This storage is caused by Statements 30 through 60. The file is read in and each line is placed into the matrix. At Statement 20, variable B is dimensioned to hold 11 lines maximum with three values per line. Statement 70 closes the transaction file. Then Statements 80 through 180 sort the data into a new matrix, Matrix M. The program starts with the outside loop of the sort at Statement 80. It begins searching for the smallest number in the file by working down from the largest number until the smallest number is located. The variable L is used to store the largest number. To begin the program, a number larger than any conceivable number that can be found in the file is stored in L at Statement 90. Statement 100 begins the inside loop of the sort.

Statement 110 tests if the first element of the old matrix is less than L. If it is, control is transferred to Statement 140. At Statement 140, the row number is stored in variable L1. The necessity for this is that when the smallest number in the file is found, it will be stored in the new matrix. Because only the first column of each row is being sorted to find the smallest number, space for the rest of the row must be available when the smallest number is found so that columns 2 and 3 of that row may be printed.

Also, as a result of the second statement in multiple Statement 140, the number that is smaller than what was stored in L is now stored in L. This process is continued until the smallest number in the old matrix is located and stored in L, the row location of that number is stored in L1, and the computer has run through the inner loop. Control is then sent to Statement 130, and in turn to Statement 160, where the smallest number is stored in the new matrix along with columns 2 and 3 of that row.

Statement 170 stores an abnormally large number in the old matrix at the corresponding location of the number being stored in the new matrix so that the computer will ignore that location in the next search of the old matrix.

Once the record is sorted, it must be placed on the file. Statements 191 through 195 cause that printing. Statement 196 closes the file and sends the computer to the END statement.

The program illustrated in Figure 12-16 is created to print out the contents of the matrix to make certain that the data are correctly sorted. The printout is illustrated in the same figure.

At the end of the month, a program is run that handles the billing of the customers and the updating of the master file. Many operations are performed at the end of the month in a large department store, but the next problem is set up to handle only a few of them, as listed below.

1. Because updating of a master file necessitates the creation of a new master file, customers that are inactive for this particular period must be picked up in sequential order and merged with the active ones in the new file.
2. Some customers have balances but do not have any transactions in the transaction file, which means they made no payment and

FIGURE 12-16

Program To Print Out Contents of Transaction File Sort

```
LIST
73        11:41 AM         31-MAR-81
10  ON ERROR GO TO 43
12  OPEN 'BUSTR1.DAT' FOR INPUT AS FILE 1
15  DIM M(11,3)
20  PRINT;TAB(20);'CUST #';TAB(33);'PAYMENT';
22  PRINT;TAB(47);'CHARGES'\PRINT
23  FOR A = 1 TO 11
24  INPUT #1,M(A,1),M(A,2),M(A,3)
25  PRINT;TAB(21);\PRINT USING '####',M(A,1);
30  PRINT;TAB(34);\PRINT USING '###.##',M(A,2);
35  PRINT;TAB(46);\PRINT USING '#####.##',M(A,3)
40  NEXT A
42  CLOSE  1\GO TO 45
43  IF ERR=11 AND ERL=24 THEN RESUME 42 ELSE ON ERROR GO TO
45  END

RUN
73        11:41 AM         31-MAR-81
                    CUST #       PAYMENT        CHARGES

                     1003         10.00           0.00
                     1003          0.00          15.75
                     1011         10.00           0.00
                     1011          0.00           8.93
                     1011          0.00          15.65
                     1234         10.00           0.00
                     1234          0.00          25.63
                     1718         10.00           0.00
                     1718          0.00          11.93
                     1718          0.00          22.35
```

are past due. Although there are no such customers in this problem, the program is set up to treat these customers.

3. This program is set up to print the return address of the company as well as the name and address of the customer. Addresses are

printed only once, despite the fact that there might be many transactions per customer during the month.

The program is listed in Figures 12-17 and 12-18. The following paragraphs explain how the program works.

```
10  ON ERROR GOTO 325
15  A,P,P3=1\P2,L=0
```

FIGURE 12-17

Program To Update Master File and To Do End of Month Billing

```
LIST
MERGE    11:09 PM          04-Dec-81
10   ON ERROR GO TO 325
15   A,P,P3=1\P2,L=0
20   OPEN 'BUS.DAT' FOR INPUT AS FILE 1
25   OPEN 'BUSTR1.DAT' FOR INPUT AS FILE 2
30   OPEN 'BUS1.DAT' FOR OUTPUT AS FILE 3
35   INPUT #1,N,N$,S$,C$,F,B
40   IF N1 = 0 GO TO 55
45   IF N<>N1 GO TO 165
50   GO TO 75
55   INPUT #2,N1,P1,C1
60   IF P2 = 0 GO TO 160
65   IF N1<>N2 GO TO 175
70   IF N<>N1 GO TO 165
75   IF A = 0 GO TO 135
80   PRINT;TAB(5);'B & B DEPARTMENT STORE'
85   PRINT;TAB(5);'1009 PINE AVE.'
90   PRINT;TAB(5);'LONG BEACH, CA 90801'
95   PRINT\PRINT
100  PRINT;TAB(30);N$
105  PRINT;TAB(30);S$
110  PRINT;TAB(30);C$
115  A=0\B1=B
120  PRINT\PRINT\PRINT;TAB(45);'BAL. FORWARD      $';
121  PRINT USING '###.##',B
125  IF P = 0 GO TO 295
130  PRINT;TAB(15);
135  IF C1 = 0 THEN PRINT 'PAYMENT--THANKS ';/
     PRINT USING '###.##',P1\L=L+1\GO TO 155
150  PRINT;TAB(15);;'CHARGE              ';\PRINT USING '###.##',C1
151  L=L+1\B1=B1+C1
152  GO TO 55
155  P3=0\B1=B1-P1\GO TO 55
160  P2=1\N2=N1\GO TO 65
165  IF B=0 GO TO 255
170  P=0\GO TO 80
```

FIGURE 12-18

Continuation of Program To Update Master File and To Do End of Month Billing

```
175 IF P3=1 THEN PRINT;TAB(45);'PAYMENT PAST DUE'\L=L+1\GO TO 205
180 F1=B*.015\B1=B1+F1\P5=B1*.10
185 F=F+F1
195 IF P5<10 THEN P5=10
200 IF B1<10 THEN P5=B1
205 H=6-L\IF H=2 THEN PRINT\PRINT
210 IF H=3 THEN PRINT\PRINT\PRINT
215 IF H=4 THEN PRINT\PRINT\PRINT\PRINT
220 IF H=5 THEN PRINT\PRINT\PRINT\PRINT\PRINT
225 L=0
230 IF B=0 OR P3=1 GO TO 300
235 PRINT\PRINT;TAB(5);'FIN. CHARGE';\PRINT USING '###.##',F1;
240 PRINT;'    MIN. PAYMENT ';\PRINT USING '###.##',P5;
245 PRINT;'      BAL. OWING ';\PRINT USING '#####.##',B1
250 PRINT\PRINT
255 PRINT#3,USING '####!!\                           \!',N,',',"',N$,'"';
260 PRINT#3,USING '!!\                     \!!',',',',"',S$,'"',',';
265 PRINT#3,USING '\                            \!!',C$,'"',',';
267 IF B=0 THEN B1=B
270 PRINT #3,USING '###.##!#####.##',F,',',B1
275 A,P=1
280 N2=N1
285 GO TO 35
295 PRINT\PRINT\PRINT;TAB(5);'PAYMENT PAST DUE'\L=L+3\GO TO 205
300 F1=B*.015\P6=B*.10\B1=B1+F1\P5=B1*.10
305 P5=P5+P6\IF P5<10 THEN P5=10\IF B1<10 THEN P5=B1
310 F=F+F1\P=0
315 GO TO 235
320 CLOSE 1,2,3\GO TO 335
325 IF ERR=11 AND ERL=35 THEN RESUME 320
330 IF ERR=11 AND ERL=55 THEN RESUME 180 ELSE ON ERROR GO TO
335 END
```

The variable A is used as an address switch to keep from printing the customer's and store's name and address for each transaction. The variable P is used as a past-due switch to enable the computer to differentiate between the past-due accounts and those that are not. P3 is also a switch, which is used to catch a customer that does not make a payment but has made a charge. These switches are initialized to one at Statement 15. Also, a first-data switch (P2) and a line counter (L) are initialized to zero. P2 is used only the first time through the program.

```
20 OPEN 'BUS.DAT' FOR INPUT AS FILE 1
25 OPEN 'BUSTR1.DAT' FOR INPUT AS FILE 2
30 OPEN 'BUS1.DAT' FOR OUTPUT AS FILE 3
```

Three files are opened in this program. Statement 20 opens the master file to allow for the retrieval of data. Statement 25 opens the transaction file to allow for retrieval of data, and Statement 30 opens a new master file 'BUS1.DAT' for access so that the data from both the old master file and the transaction file can be merged and printed onto a new master file.

```
35  INPUT #1,N,N$,S$,C$,F,B
40  IF N1 = 0 GO TO 55
```

Statement 35 commands the computer to input from the master file. The variable N is the customer number; N$ the customer name; S$ the street address; C$ the city, state, and ZIP code; F the accumulated finance charge to date; and B the balance of the account.

After a line of data has been input from the master file, control drops to the next statement, Statement 40, where the decision "IF N1=0 GO TO 55" is located. N1 is the variable in which the customer number from the transaction file is stored. The first time the computer goes through the program, it has not input from the transaction file when it reaches Statement 40. Therefore, N1 equals zero, so the computer transfers control to Statement 55. Statement 55 inputs from the transaction file. N1 is the customer number, P1 is the payment, and C1 is the charge.

```
55  INPUT #2,N1,P1,C1
60  IF P2 = 0 GO TO 160
160 P2=1\N2=N1\GO TO 65
```

The reason for the switch (P2) is to place the customer number from the transaction file (N1) into a comparison location (N2). As long as N1 and N2 are equal, transactions are printed on the customer's statement. When they become unequal, it signifies that a new customer's transaction has been read. The first thing that is done in Statement 160 is to change the P2 switch to one so control will not return to Statement 160, since the only time control goes to Statement 160 is when P2 equals zero. After changing P2 to one, the computer is told to make N2 equal to N1, and control is sent to Statement 65.

```
65  IF N1<>N2 GO TO 175
70  IF N<>N1 GO TO 165
75  IF A = 0 GO TO 135
```

Statement 65 tells the computer that if N1 does not equal N2, it is to go to Statement 175. As they are equal the first time, control drops to Statement 70, which transfers control to Statement 165 if N (customer from master file) does not equal N1 (customer from transaction file). If they are equal, control drops to Statement 75. Statement 75 tests if A (the address switch) equals zero and when it does, control is transferred to Statement 135, where the first transaction of the customer is input. However, A equals one the first time through, so control is transferred to Statements 80 through 110, which print the store's name and address as well as that of the customer.

```
115 A=0\B1=B
120 PRINT\PRINT\PRINT:TAB(45);'BAL. FORWARD      $';
121 PRINT USING '###.##',B
125 IF P = 0 GO TO 295
```

After the addresses are printed the computer executes Statement 115, which stores a zero in the address switch (A) to prevent the computer from printing the store's and customer's addresses again as long as the same customer is being processed. The old balance (B) is stored in another variable (B1) to be used in future accumulations of the new balance. Statements 120 and 121 print the words "BAL. FORWARD" and the old balance on the statement. Statement 125 tells the computer to go to Statement 295 if the past-due switch (P) equals zero. The past-due switch is set to zero when no transactions are made and the customer has a balance owing.

```
130 PRINT;TAB(15);
135 IF C1 = 0 THEN PRINT 'PAYMENT--THANKS ';\
    PRINT USING '###.##',P1\L=L+1\GO TO 155
150 PRINT;TAB(15);'CHARGE              ';\PRINT USING '###.##',C1
151 L=L+1\B1=B1+C1
152 GO TO 55
155 P3=0\B1=B1-P1\GO TO 55
```

If P does not equal zero, control drops to Statement 130 where printing of the transaction begins. At Statement 135, if there is a payment made (C1=0), then the printer is directed to print "PAYMENT--THANKS" and the amount of payment. Also, a one is added to the line counter. Control is then directed to Statement 155. At Statement 155 the payment switch (P3) is set to zero to indicate a payment has been made. This is necessary so that the customer is not processed as past due. The payment is subtracted from the new balance (B1) and control is sent to Statement 55 to input another transaction. If, at Statement 135, there is no payment (C1<>0), control drops to Statement 150 where "CHARGE" is printed at Tab 15, followed by the amount of the charge (C1). At Statement 151, a one is added to the line counter (L) and the charge is added to the new balance (B1). At Statement 152, control is sent to Statement 55 to input another transaction.

```
55  INPUT #2,N1,P1,C1
60  IF P2 = 0 GO TO 160
65  IF N1<>N2 GO TO 175
```

Statement 55 was explained earlier. It retrieves transactions from the transaction file. After the first transaction in this program has been processed, P2 will always be one, so at Statement 60 control will not be sent to Statement 160. At Statement 65 if a new customer number is entered from the transaction file (N1), the amount stored in N1 will not equal the amount in the comparison location (N2), because what is stored in N2 is the previous customer. Therefore, control is transferred to Statement 175.

```
175 IF P3=1 THEN PRINT;TAB(45);'PAYMENT PAST DUE'\L=L+1\GO TO 205
205 H=6-L\IF H=2 THEN PRINT\PRINT
210 IF H=3 THEN PRINT\PRINT\PRINT
215 IF H=4 THEN PRINT\PRINT\PRINT\PRINT
220 IF H=5 THEN PRINT\PRINT\PRINT\PRINT\PRINT
225 L=0
```

Because a new customer number has been input from the transaction file, the computer must finish processing the old customer. At Statement 175 if the old customer has not made a payment (P3=1), the printer prints "PAYMENT PAST DUE" and adds a one to the line counter (L). Then control is directed to Statement 205. At Line 205, a variable H is used to figure how many lines the printer is to skip to reach the total line, Line 7. Since six lines are available for entering transactions, the number of lines printed (L) is subtracted from six. Statements 205 through 220 tell the computer how many blank lines are needed to reach the last line, Line 7. Line 225 places a zero in the line counter for use in printing the next customer's statement.

```
230 IF B=0 OR P3=1 GO TO 300
300 F1=B*.015\P6-B*.10\B1=B1+F1\P5=B1*.10
305 P5=P5+P6\IF P5<10 THEN P5=10\IF B1<10 THEN P5=B1
310 F=F+F1\P=0
315 GO TO 235
```

The computer is still dealing with a past-due customer. Statement 230 asks if the old balance (B) equals zero or if no payment was made this month (P3=1). If either condition is true, control is transferred to Statement 300. Statements 300 through 310 compute the finance charge and the minimum payment. At Line 300 the finance charge (F1) is found by multiplying .015 times the old balance (B). Because the customer did not pay his minimum payment last month, that minimum payment (P6) is again computed by multiplying the old balance times .10. The new balance (B1) is found by adding the finance charge to the new balance. The new minimum payment is found by multiplying the new balance (B1) times .10. At Statement 305 the minimum payment for this month is found by adding this month's minimum payment (P5) to last month's minimum payment (P6) and stored in this month's payment (P5). If the minimum payment is less than $10, the payment becomes $10 because the store has established a $10 minimum payment. The next condition that is tested is if the new balance (B1) is less than 10. If it is, the amount owed is stored in P5. Naturally, if a customer owes only $5, for example, he is not going to be charged $10. Instead, the amount owed becomes the payment due.

Statement 310 adds this month's finance charge (F1) to the accumulated finance charge for the year (F). The past-due switch (P) is set to zero. Then Statement 315 sends control to Statement 235. Statements 235 through 245 print the finance charge, minimum payment, and balance owing on the last line of the statement. The computer then executes Statements 250 through 270, which print the customer's record on the new master file, "BUS1.DAT".

```
275 A,P=1
280 N2=N1
285 GO TO 35
```

Data are printed onto the new file in only two instances: when another customer appears from the transaction file, or when a customer is inactive, therefore having no balance or no transaction. When a customer has no balance and no transaction, no statement is printed. Subsequently, the computer is sent to the old master file to pick up another customer. Before this can be accomplished, the address switch (A) and the past-due switch (P) must be set to one as they were when the program began. These switches are set at Statement 275. Also, the number of the new customer from the transaction file is placed into a comparison location at Statement 280. Then the computer is sent by Statement 285 to Statement 35, which enters another line of customer data from the old master file.

```
45  IF N<>N1 GO TO 165
165 IF B=0 THEN B1=B\GO TO 255
```

Following the "yes" branch at Statement 45, if the customer number from the transaction file does not equal the number from the master file, control is sent to Statement 165. The reason these two do not agree is that the customer from the master file made no transaction during the month. At Statement 165, if there is no balance showing in the customer's account, the old balance is placed in the new balance and, as explained in the previous paragraph, control is sent to Statement 255 where the customer is printed on the file.

```
170 P=0\GO TO 80
```

If there is a balance, which means the customer did not pay on his account as he had no transactions, the customer is past due. Therefore, control drops to Statement 170, the past-due switch is set to zero, and control is transferred to Statement 80.

Statements 80 through 121 have been discussed before. They print both the customer's and store's names and addresses, set the address switch to zero, place the old balance into the new balance, and print "BAL. FORWARD".

```
125 IF P = 0 GO TO 295
295 PRINT\PRINT\PRINT;TAB(5);'PAYMENT PAST DUE'\L=L+3\GO TO 205
230 IF B=0 OR P3=1 GO TO 300
```

Statement 125 sends control to Statement 295 because P is equal to zero. At Statement 295 the printer prints two blank lines and "PAYMENT PAST DUE". Then the computer adds a three to the line counter. Control is then sent to Statement 205. Statements 205 through 225 have been discussed previously. They determine the number of blank lines before the last line. Control drops from Statement 225 to 230 where, because the old balance (B) is equal to zero, control is sent to Statement 300.

Statements 300 through 315 have been discussed before. They determine the finance charge and minimum payment for past-due accounts and send control to Statement 235.

Statements 235 through 285 have also been explained previously. These statements print the finance charge, the minimum balance, and the balance owing on the statement. The customer's record is printed on the new master file, the switches A and P are set to one, the new transaction customer number is placed into the comparison location, and the computer is sent by Statement 35 to the old master file to retrieve another customer.

```
65  IF N1<>N2 GO TO 175
175 IF P3=1 THEN PRINT;TAB(45);'PAYMENT PAST DUE'\L=L+1\GO TO 205
180 F1=B*.015\B1=B1+F1\P5=B1*.10
185 F=F+F1
195 IF P5<10 THEN P5=10
200 IF B1<10 THEN P5=B1
```

If the "yes" branch is followed from Statement 65, the new customer number from the transaction file (N1) does not equal the comparison customer number from that file (N2). As a result, control is sent to Statement 175. The "yes" part of this statement, P3 does equal one, meaning no payment was made on an old balance, was discussed earlier. The printer prints "PAYMENT PAST DUE", one is added to the line counter, and control is sent to Statement 205.

Statement 205 begins the process of figuring the finance charge and the minimum payment, and printing the finance charge, the minimum payment, and the balance owed on the statement. Finally, the customer's record is printed on the file.

At Statement 175 if P3 does not equal one, control drops to Statement 180 where the finance charge is computed, the finance charge is added to the new balance, and the minimum payment is calculated. At Statement 185 the finance charge is added to the accumulated finance charge for the year. Statement 195 states that if the payment is less than 10, the payment becomes 10. Statement 200 states that if the new balance is less than 10, then the minimum payment becomes the amount owed. Control then drops to Statement 205. Statements 205 through 285, which print the remainder of the statement and print the customer's record on the new master file, have been explained previously.

```
320 CLOSE 1,2,3\GO TO 335
325 IF ERR=11 AND ERL=35 THEN RESUME 320
330 IF ERR=11 AND ERL=55 THEN RESUME 180 ELSE ON ERROR GO TO
335 END
```

When Statement 35 is executed and there are no more records in the old master file, an "End of file on device" error is generated. Statement 10 traps the error and sends control to Statement 325, which checks for the error "End of file on device" (ERR=11) and also checks if that error occurred at Line 35 (ERL=35). Since both conditions are true, control is directed to Statement 320. Statement 320 closes all three files and sends control to Statement 335, which terminated the program.

When Statement 55 is executed and there are no more records in the transaction file, an "End of file on device" error is generated. Statement 10 traps the error and sends control to Statement 325, which checks for the error "End of file on device" (ERR=11) and also checks if that error occurred at Line 35 (ERL=35). Since the error occurred at Line 55, control drops to Statement 330. At Statement 330 both conditions are found to be true; (ERR=11) and (ERL=55), so control is transferred to Statement 180. Statements 180 through 285 print the remainder of the statement and print the customer's record on the new master file.

If any other error occurs, Statement 10 traps the error and sends control to Statement 325. That error would not satisfy the test IF ERR=11, so control drops to Statement 330. Here again the error would not pass the test if ERR=11, so the ELSE ON ERROR GO TO part of the statement transfers control to the operating system. The operating system prints a diagnostic and aborts the program.

When the updating is completed, the operator calls out the program that lists accounts, shown in Figure 12-11. Then he changes Statement 10 of that program to read 10 OPEN "BUS1.DAT" FOR INPUT AS FILE 1. When the program is run, a listing of the current status of the new master file after updating results. The printout of this program is shown in Figure 12-19. The billing statements are illustrated in Figure 12-20. Since Roy H. Smith had no old balance and no transactions, he was not sent a bill.

USING RANDOM ACCESS FILES

Two ways of storing and accessing files are treated in this chapter—sequential and random access. Sequential files are discussed in the first section of this chapter and random access in this section. Although two types of random access are available, virtual arrays are presented. A virtual array is a matrix, or table, that is maintained in auxiliary storage.

PROBLEM 12-10

CREATING A VIRTUAL ARRAY

The problem given in this discussion uses a virtual array file for a tool manufacturer. The file is updated when orders for stock are processed.

FIGURE 12-19

Printing Contents of Master File "BUS1.DAT"

```
              LISTING OF CUSTOMER ACCOUNTS

        BOB ANDERSON
        343 CORONADO AVE.
        LONG BEACH, CALIF. 90804

                                     ACC. FIN. CHARGE    BALANCE

                                          9.48            41.66


        J. H. HANOVER
        1723 E. FOURTH ST.
        LONG BEACH, CALIF. 90804

                                     ACC. FIN. CHARGE    BALANCE

                                          38.50           73.34


        BOB J. JENKINS
        1334 E. HARDING ST.
        LONG BEACH, CALIF. 90805

                                     ACC. FIN. CHARGE    BALANCE

                                          11.71           53.84


        CHRISTOPHER L. MULLINS
        3022 E. THIRD ST.
        LONG BEACH, CALIF. 90804

                                     ACC. FIN. CHARGE    BALANCE

                                          27.23           112.16


        ROY H. SMITH
        190 REDONDO BLVD.
        LONG BEACH, CALIF. 90804

                                     ACC. FIN. CHARGE    BALANCE

                                          3.45            0.00
```

Tool manufacturers usually make many items, but for demonstration purposes only eight items are used. A great deal of information is usually placed in a company's files, but only three kinds of information will be used in this program: the part number, the quantity on hand, and the price per item. The matrix to be created is shown below. As matrices are addressed by row and column, the part number corresponds to the row number.

To begin with, the data file must be opened. The data files for virtual arrays are opened in the same manner as sequential data files and are created in much the same way as are the arrays in Chapter 10.

PART #	STOCK ON HAND	PRICE
1	60	10.50
2	45	5.75
3	98	9.33
4	57	14.27
5	83	6.53
6	75	12.83
7	92	4.27
8	63	8.10

FIGURE 12-20

Monthly Billing Statements for B & B Department Store

```
B & B DEPARTMENT STORE
1009 PINE AVE.
LONG BEACH, CA 90801

                    BOB ANDERSON
                    343 CORONADO AVE.
                    LONG BEACH, CA 90804

                                        BAL. FORWARD      $ 35.38
     PAYMENT--THANKS  10.00
     CHARGE           15.75



FIN. CHARGE  0.53   MIN. PAYMENT  10.00     BAL. OWING    41.66
```

FIGURE 12-20

Monthly Billing Statements for B & B Department Store

```
B & B DEPARTMENT STORE
1009 PINE AVE.
LONG BEACH, CA 90801

                              J. H. HANOVER
                              1723 E. FOURTH ST.
                              LONG BEACH, CA 90804

                                                  BAL. FORWARD      $ 57.89
           PAYMENT--THANKS  10.00
           CHARGE            8.93
           CHARGE           15.65


FIN. CHARGE   0.87   MIN. PAYMENT  10.00     BAL. OWING     73.34

B & B DEPARTMENT STORE
1009 PINE AVE.
LONG BEACH, CA 90801

                              BOB J. JENKINS
                              1334 E. HARDING ST.
                              LONG BEACH, CA 90805

                                                  BAL. FORWARD      $ 37.65
           PAYMENT--THANKS  10.00
           CHARGE           25.63


FIN. CHARGE   0.56   MIN. PAYMENT  10.00     BAL. OWING     53.84

B & B DEPARTMENT STORE
1009 PINE AVE.
LONG BEACH, CA 90801

                              CHRISTOPHER L. MULLINS
                              3011 E. THIRD ST.
                              LONG BEACH, CA 90804

                                                  BAL. FORWARD      $ 86.58
           PAYMENT--THANKS  10.00
           CHARGE           11.93
           CHARGE           22.35

FIN. CHARGE   1.30   MIN. PAYMENT  11.22     BAL. OWING    112.16
```

Statement 20 in Figure 12-21 opens the file named 'KING.DAT '. Statement 25 is similar to other dimension statements except that it contains a file number immediately following DIM. The array is dimensioned larger than is currently needed to allow for future additions to the array.

When the computer reserves storage space in auxiliary storage, it appropriates a section of storage in which data may already be stored. To clear these storage locations, they must be initialized to zero. Statement 30 sets the *last* element to zero. To set the remaining locations to zero, one of two methods may be used. The method shown in Statements 30 and 35 is the most efficient. If the last element of the array is set to zero, the computer immediately sets the maximum size

FIGURE 12-21

Problem 12-10—Creating a Virtual Array

```
LIST
VA31      09:08 PM          04-Dec-81
20   OPEN 'KING.DAT' FOR OUTPUT AS FILE 1
25   DIM #1,P(10,3)
30   P(10,3) = 0
35   MAT P = ZER
45   FOR A = 1 TO 8
50   PRINT 'ITEM #, STOCK ON HAND, PRICE'
55   INPUT P(A,1), P(A,2), P(A,3)
60   NEXT A
65   CLOSE 1
70   END
```

```
RUN
VA31      08:45 PM          04-Dec-81
ITEM #, STOCK ON HAND, PRICE
? 1,60,10.50
ITEM #, STOCK ON HAND, PRICE
? 2,45,5.75
ITEM #, STOCK ON HAND, PRICE
? 3,98,9.33
ITEM #, STOCK ON HAND, PRICE
? 4,57,14.27
ITEM #, STOCK ON HAND, PRICE
? 5,83,6.53
ITEM #, STOCK ON HAND, PRICE
? 6,75,12.83
ITEM #, STOCK ON HAND, PRICE
? 7,92,4.27
ITEM #, STOCK ON HAND, PRICE
? 8,63,8.10
```

of the matrix instead of creating the matrix row by row as when the MAT = ZER Command is used by itself.[2] When the last element is set to zero and the MAT = ZER Command is used, execution time is reduced. Matrix commands are discussed in Appendix A, pages 312 through 323. The ZER Command is explained on page 321.

The other method of setting all locations to zero is listed below.

```
30  FOR A = 8 TO 1 STEP -1
32  FOR B = 3 TO 1 STEP -1
34  P(A,B) = 0
38  NEXT B
40  NEXT A
```

Statement 45 in Figure 12-21 is the beginning of the loop to designate rows. Statement 50 tells the operator what information is to be input. Statement 55 is the input statement permitting the operator to input from the keyboard. This program forces the operator to enter 8 lines of information. Statement 60 is the statement ending the loop, and Statement 65 closes the file. Statement 70 ends the program.

The program and printout in Figure 12-22 print out the contents of the virtual array named P. The reason for this program is to check for accuracy in that array.

ADDING RECORDS TO A VIRTUAL ARRAY FILE

The complete program to add records to a virtual array file is shown in Figure 12-23.

```
10  OPEN 'KING.DAT' FOR INPUT AS FILE 1
20  OPEN 'KONG.DAT' FOR OUTPUT AS FILE 2
```

In the following programs utilizing virtual arrays, a new file is created. Statement 10 opens the old file for input and Statement 20 opens the new file for output.

In this discussion the following two items will be added to the existing file.

ITEM #	QTY ON HAND	PRICE
9	50	17.23
10	75	8.97

[2] Some installations do not have the MAT package.

FIGURE 12-22

Printing Contents of Virtual Array P

```
LIST
VA32      09:04 PM          04-Dec-81
20   OPEN 'KING.DAT' FOR INPUT AS FILE 1
25   DIM #1,P(10,3)
30   PRINT\PRINT\PRINT;TAB(15);'QTY ON'
35   PRINT;TAB(8);'ITEM #';TAB(16);'HAND';TAB(25);'PRICE'\PRINT
40   FOR D = 1 TO 10
45   PRINT;TAB(9);
50   PRINT USING '##      ###        ##.##',P(D,1),P(D,2),P(D,3)
55   NEXT D
60   CLOSE 1
65   END
```

```
RUN
VA32      08:52 PM          04-Dec-81


              QTY ON
      ITEM #   HAND       PRICE

        1       60        10.50
        2       45         5.75
        3       98         9.33
        4       57        14.27
        5       83         6.53
        6       75        12.83
        7       92         4.27
        8       63         8.10
        0        0         0.00
        0        0         0.00
```

The two dimension statements, Statement 30 for the original file and Statement 40 for the new file, are shown below.

```
30   DIM #1,P(10,3)
40   DIM #2,P1(10,3)
```

To zero out the new array, Statements 50 and 60 are used.

```
50   P1(10,3)=0
60   MAT P1=ZER
```

To add to a virtual array file, the data in the original file must be entered into the new file. This is achieved by Statements 70, 80, and 90.

```
70   FOR A = 1 TO 8
80   P1(A,1)=P(A,1)\P1(A,2)=P(A,2)\P1(A,3)=P(A,3)
90   NEXT A
```

Statements 100 through 160 add the new data to the file.

```
100   A=A+1
110   INPUT 'ARE THERE ANY RECORDS TO BE ADDED'Q$
120   IF Q$ = 'YES' THEN 130 ELSE 170
130   PRINT 'THE FOLLOWING ITEMS ARE TO BE ADDED TO THE FILE'
140   PRINT 'ITEM #, STOCK ON HAND, PRICE'
150   INPUT P1(A,1),P1(A,2),P1(A,3)
160   GO TO 100
```

The new file can be sorted if the data to be added belong at the beginning or in the middle of the file. In this instance, the data entered belong at the end of the file, so the file need not be sorted.

The program to add to a virtual array file is shown in Figure 12-23.

FIGURE 12-23

Program To Add to a Virtual Array

```
LIST
100A      09:06 PM          04-Dec-81
10   OPEN 'KING.DAT' FOR INPUT AS FILE 1
20   OPEN 'KONG.DAT' FOR OUTPUT AS FILE 2
30   DIM #1,P(10,3)
40   DIM #2,P1(10,3)
50   P1(10,3)=0
60   MAT P1=ZER
70   FOR A = 1 TO 8
80   P1(A,1)=P(A,1)\P1(A,2)=P(A,2)\P1(A,3)=P(A,3)
90   NEXT A
100   A=A+1
110   INPUT 'ARE THERE ANY RECORDS TO BE ADDED'Q$
120   IF Q$ = 'YES' THEN 130 ELSE 170
130   PRINT 'THE FOLLOWING ITEMS ARE TO BE ADDED TO THE FILE'
140   PRINT 'ITEM #, STOCK ON HAND, PRICE'
150   INPUT P1(A,1),P1(A,2),P1(A,3)
160   GO TO 100
170   CLOSE 1,2
180   END
```

Figure 12-24 shows the execution of the program, allowing the operator to input the additional records from the keyboard.

FIGURE 12-24

Printout of the Program To Add to a Virtual Array

```
RUN
100A     08:54 PM          04-Dec-81
ARE THERE ANY RECORDS TO BE ADDED
? YES
THE FOLLOWING ITEMS ARE TO BE ADDED TO THE FILE
ITEM #, STOCK ON HAND, PRICE
? 9,50,17.23
ARE THERE ANY RECORDS TO BE ADDED
? YES
THE FOLLOWING ITEMS ARE TO BE ADDED TO THE FILE
ITEM #, STOCK ON HAND, PRICE
? 10,75,8.97
ARE THERE ANY RECORDS TO BE ADDED
? NO
```

Figure 12-25 shows the program that prints out the file and the resulting printout of the new file that contains the added records.

DELETING RECORDS FROM A VIRTUAL ARRAY FILE

When deleting a record from a virtual array file, two possible solutions are available. One solution is that the programmer may write a program that deletes the record and leaves a blank area of storage in the new file where the deleted record would have been stored. The other solution is that the programmer may enter only the records to be retained into the file starting at the beginning of the file and leaving the bottom portion of the file blank. The latter solution will be used in this explanation. Figure 12-26 shows the program that deletes from the file.

This program uses three FOR/NEXT loops. The first FOR/NEXT loop duplicates the old array into the new array. The second FOR/NEXT loop deletes the record from the new array and stores the remaining records in the new array one row higher than they were stored in the old array. This prevents any blank rows of storage in the middle of the array. The third FOR/NEXT loop zeros out the remainder of the array following the last record that was stored.

```
10  C=0
20  OPEN 'KONG.DAT' FOR INPUT AS FILE 1
30  OPEN 'GORRIL.DAT' FOR OUTPUT AS FILE 2
40  DIM #1,P(10,3)
```

FIGURE 12-25

Program To Print the New Array and Printout of the New Array

```
LIST
VA33     09:36 PM          01-Dec-81
20   OPEN 'KONG.DAT' FOR INPUT AS FILE 1
25   DIM #1,P(10,3)
30   PRINT\PRINT\PRINT;TAB(15);'QTY ON'
35   PRINT;TAB(8);'ITEM #';TAB(16);'HAND';TAB(25);'PRICE'\PRINT
40   FOR D = 1 TO 10
45   PRINT;TAB(9);
50   PRINT USING '##      ###       ##.##',P(D,1),P(D,2),P(D,3)
55   NEXT D
60   CLOSE 1
65   END

Ready

RUN
VA33     09:36 PM          01-Dec-81


              QTY ON
        ITEM #  HAND      PRICE

         1       60      10.50
         2       45       5.75
         3       98       9.33
         4       57      14.27
         5       83       6.53
         6       75      12.83
         7       92       4.27
         8       63       8.10
         9       50      17.23
        10       75       8.97
```

```
50   DIM #2,P1(10,3)
60   P1(10,3)=0
70   MAT P1=ZER
```

Statement 10 initializes counter C to zero. This counter will be used to determine how many records are deleted. Statements 20 and 30 open the files, Statements 40 and 50 dimension the arrays, and Statements 60 and 70 zero out the new array.

```
80   FOR A = 1 TO 10
90   P1(A,1)=P(A,1)\P1(A,2)=P(A,2)\P1(A,3)=P(A,3)
100  NEXT A
```

FIGURE 12-26

Program To Delete from a Virtual Array

```
LIST
101CCC   04:36 PM          03-Dec-81
10  C=0
20  OPEN 'KONG.DAT' FOR INPUT AS FILE 1
30  OPEN 'GORRIL.DAT' FOR OUTPUT AS FILE 2
40  DIM #1,P(10,3)
50  DIM #2,P1(10,3)
60  P1(10,3)=0
70  MAT P1=ZER
80  FOR A = 1 TO 10
90  P1(A,1)=P(A,1)\P1(A,2)=P(A,2)\P1(A,3)=P(A,3)
100 NEXT A
110 INPUT "ARE THERE RECORDS TO BE DELETED"Q$
120 IF Q$ = 'YES' THEN 130 ELSE 220
130 C=C+1
140 INPUT "ITEM # TO BE DELETED"N
150 X=1
160 FOR A = 1 TO 10
170 IF N = P1(A,1) THEN 200
180 P1(X,1)=P1(A,1)\P1(X,2)=P1(A,2)\P1(X,3)=P1(A,3)
190 X=X+1
200 NEXT A
210 GO TO 110
220 FOR Z = (A -(C-1)) TO 10
230 P1(Z,1),P1(Z,2),P1(Z,3) = 0
240 NEXT Z
250 KILL'KONG.DAT'
260 NAME 'GORRIL.DAT' AS 'KONG.DAT'
270 CLOSE 1,2
280 END
```

Statements 80, 90, and 100 comprise the FOR/NEXT loop that duplicates the old array into the new array.

```
110 INPUT "ARE THERE RECORDS TO BE DELETED"Q$
120 IF Q$ = 'YES' THEN 130 ELSE 220
130 C=C+1
140 INPUT "ITEM # TO BE DELETED"N
150 X=1
```

When Statement 110 is executed and the operator inputs "yes" from the keyboard, Statement 120 transfers control to Statement 130. Statement 130 increments the counter used to count how many records will be deleted. Statement 140 allows the operator to input, from the keyboard, the number of the item to be deleted. Statement 150 stores a one in the counter that will compute into which row the next record will be stored in the new array.

```
160 FOR A = 1 TO 10
170 IF N = P1(A,1) THEN 200
180 P1(X,1)=P1(A,1)\P1(X,2)=P1(A,2)\P1(X,3)=P1(A,3)
190 X=X+1
200 NEXT A
```

Statements 160 through 200 comprise the FOR/NEXT loop that deletes the record from the new array and stores the remaining records in the new array one row higher than they were stored in the old array. Statement 160 begins the FOR/NEXT loop. Statement 170 compares the number of the record to be deleted (N) with the number of the record stored at (A,1) of the array P1; and when they are equal, control is transferred to Statement 200. This prevents the record from being stored in the new array. When the records are not equal (it is not the record to be deleted), control drops to Statement 180, which stores the record to be added in the new array. Statement 190 adds one to the counter that is used to determine into which row in the new array the next record will be stored. Statement 200 is the last statement for the FOR/NEXT loop.

```
210 GO TO 110
110 INPUT "ARE THERE RECORDS TO BE DELETED"Q$
120 IF Q$ = 'YES' THEN 130 ELSE 220
```

After the new array has been completed, with the desired record deleted, control drops to Statement 210 which transfers control to Statement 110. When Statement 110 is executed, the operator responds from the keyboard with a "yes" or "no". Statement 120 determines if the response is "yes." If the response is "yes", control drops to Statement 130, which begins the sequence of statements that will delete another record. If the operator responds with "no," control is transferred to Statement 220.

```
220 FOR Z = (A -(C-1)) TO 10
230 P1(Z,1),P1(Z,2),P1(Z,3) = 0
240 NEXT Z
```

Statements 220, 230, and 240 comprise the FOR/NEXT loop that zeros out the remainder of the new array following the last record that was stored. In Statement 220, the FOR statement, the counter is initialized to the number of the row of the new array that is first set to zero.

That would be the row following the row where the last record was stored. (A–(C–1)) is the equation that determines that value. The variable A is the name of the counter in the FOR statement (Statement 160) of the FOR/NEXT loop that causes the records to be stored in the new array. The value stored in A is the maximum number of rows in the array, which is 10 in this problem. The variable C is the name of the counter that was used to determine how many records were deleted. The value one must be subtracted from the value stored in the C counter, and that result is subtracted from the value in counter A. For example, in this problem, 3 records will be deleted. This would cause counter C to store the value of 3. When 1 is subtracted from 3, the result is 2. When 2 is subtracted from 10, the result is 8. Therefore, the counter Z in statement 220 is initialized to 8. When the FOR/NEXT loop is executed, Rows 8, 9, and 10 will be initialized to zero. Rows 1 through 7 will contain the 7 records that remain after the 3 records were deleted.

```
250 KILL'KONG.DAT'
260 NAME 'GORRIL.DAT' AS 'KONG.DAT
270 CLOSE 1,2
280 END
```

Statement 250 destroys the old file in storage. Statement 260 renames the new file. The name given the new file is the name that was previously given to the old file. Statement 270 closes the files, and Statement 280 is the last statement of the program.

Figure 12-27 shows the execution of the program that deletes the records from the file, and Figure 12-28 shows the program that produces the printout of the file after the deletions. Figure 12-29 is the printout of the file after deletions.

FIGURE 12-27

Printout of the Program To Delete from a Virtual Array

```
RUN
101CCC   12:05 PM           02-Dec-81
ARE THERE RECORDS TO BE DELETED
? YES
ITEM # TO BE DELETED
? 2
ARE THERE RECORDS TO BE DELETED
? YES
ITEM # TO BE DELETED
? 5
ARE THERE RECORDS TO BE DELETED
? YES
ITEM # TO BE DELETED
? 7
ARE THERE RECORDS TO BE DELETED
? NO
```

FIGURE 12-28

Program To Print the New Array

```
LIST
VA33     09:00 PM          04-Dec-81
20   OPEN 'KONG.DAT' FOR INPUT AS FILE 1
25   DIM #1,P(10,3)
30   PRINT\PRINT\PRINT;TAB(15);'QTY ON'
35   PRINT;TAB(8);'ITEM #';TAB(16);'HAND';TAB(25);'PRICE'\PRINT
40   FOR D = 1 TO 10
45   PRINT;TAB(9);
50   PRINT USING '##      ###        ##.##',P(D,1),P(D,2),P(D,3)
55   NEXT D
60   CLOSE 1
65   END
```

FIGURE 12-29

Printout of the New Array After Deletions

```
Ready

RUN
VA33        09:01 PM            04-Dec-81


                    QTY ON
           ITEM #    HAND          PRICE

             1        60           10.50
             3        98            9.33
             4        57           14.27
             6        75           12.83
             8        63            8.10
             9        50           17.23
            10        75            8.97
             0         0            0.00
             0         0            0.00
             0         0            0.00
```

PROBLEM 12-11

UPDATING A VIRTUAL ARRAY

The following discussion concerns the original virtual array that was created in program VA31 shown in Figure 12-21.

Updating virtual arrays is simpler than updating sequential files. The only problem one might have is to type in the wrong row number.

To be sure the desired row number or record number is the one retrieved, some verification should be done. Statements 50 and 55 in Problem 12-11 shown in Figure 12-30 are written for that purpose. The printout of that program is shown in Figure 12-31. This program gets the record number to be updated as a result of Statement 35 and changes the price at Statement 70. This change will be on the file permanently when the file is closed at the end of the program.

FIGURE 12-30

Problem 12-11—Program To Update File 'KING.DAT'

```
LIST
VA6      01:41 PM          12-Dec-81
15   ON ERROR GO TO 85
20   OPEN 'KING.DAT' FOR INPUT AS FILE 1
25   DIM #1, P(10,3)
30   PRINT 'RECORD NUMBER TO BE UPDATED.  USE CONTROL Z TO TERMINATE'
35   INPUT A
45   PRINT USING '##    ###    ##.###',P(A,1),P(A,2),P(A,3)
50   PRINT 'VERIFY IF CORRECT NUMBER "YES" OR "NO"'
55   INPUT Q$
60   IF Q$ = "NO" GO TO 35
65   PRINT 'INPUT PRICE'
70   INPUT P(A,3)
75   GO TO 30
80   CLOSE  1\GO TO 90
85   IF ERR = 11 AND ERL=35 THEN RESUME 80 ELSE ON ERROR GO TO
90   END
```

FIGURE 12-31

Printout of Program To Update File 'KING.DAT'

```
RUN
VA6        01:44 PM           12-Dec-81
RECORD NUMBER TO BE UPDATED.  USE CONTROL Z TO TERMINATE
? 2
 2      45      5.75
VERIFY IF CORRECT NUMBER "YES" OR "NO"
? 'YES'
INPUT PRICE
? 6.00
RECORD NUMBER TO BE UPDATED.  USE CONTROL Z TO TERMINATE
? 3
 3      98      9.33
VERIFY IF CORRECT NUMBER "YES" OR "NO"
? 'YES'
INPUT PRICE
? 9.60
RECORD NUMBER TO BE UPDATED.  USE CONTROL Z TO TERMINATE
? 4
 4      57      14.27
VERIFY IF CORRECT NUMBER "YES" OR "NO"
? 'YES'
INPUT PRICE
? 14.62
RECORD NUMBER TO BE UPDATED.  USE CONTROL Z TO TERMINATE
? 5
 5      83      6.53
VERIFY IF CORRECT NUMBER "YES" OR "NO"
? 'YES'
INPUT PRICE
? 6.80
RECORD NUMBER TO BE UPDATED.  USE CONTROL Z TO TERMINATE
? 7
 7      92      4.27
VERIFY IF CORRECT NUMBER "YES" OR "NO"
? 'YES'
INPUT PRICE
? 4.58
RECORD NUMBER TO BE UPDATED.  USE CONTROL Z TO TERMINATE
? 8
 8      63      8.10
VERIFY IF CORRECT NUMBER "YES" OR "NO"
? 'YES'
INPUT PRICE
? 8.40
RECORD NUMBER TO BE UPDATED.  USE CONTROL Z TO TERMINATE
? ^Z
```

As a result of inflation, prices on six of the items in this program have gone up.

Item 2 raised to 6.00
Item 3 raised to 9.60
Item 4 raised to 14.62
Item 5 raised to 6.80
Item 7 raised to 4.58
Item 8 raised to 8.40

After the new prices are placed in the file, the operator then uses the program in Figure 12-22 to list the contents of the file so that they can be checked for accuracy. That printout is shown in Figure 12-32.

FIGURE 12-32

Contents of Updated Virtual Array P

ITEM #	QTY ON HAND	PRICE
1	30	10.50
2	0	6.00
3	98	9.60
4	25	14.62
5	73	6.80
6	75	12.83
7	72	4.58
8	63	8.40
0	0	0.00
0	0	0.00

PROBLEM 12-12

The program shown in Figure 12-33 is constructed to do three things. It fills customer orders. It also prints a notice to reorder when stock on hand consists of 50 or fewer of each item, though most companies would have a different reordering number for the various items. The program is also set up to fill customer orders partially when not enough items are on hand and to backorder for the rest of the order.

To show how the program works, two hypothetical orders will be

FIGURE 12-33

Program To Fill Orders, Backorder, and Notify of Need To Restock

```
LIST
VA7      08:48 AM         14-Dec-81
25  DIM#1,P(10,3)
30  OPEN 'KING.DAT' FOR INPUT AS FILE 1
32  PRINT 'NAME OF COMPANY ORDERING'
33  INPUT N$
35  PRINT 'INPUT RECORD OF ORDER TO BE FILLED'
36  PRINT 'INPUT -9 TO TERMINATE'
40  INPUT F
42  IF P(F,2) = 0 GO TO 77
45  IF F=-9 GO TO 95
50  PRINT 'AMOUNT OF ORDER'
55  INPUT G
60  IF P(F,2)>G THEN P(F,2)=P(F,2)-G\GO TO 70
65  IF P(F,2)<= G THEN X=G-P(F,2)\X=X*-1\GO TO 80
70  IF P(F,2)<=50 THEN PRINT 'ORDER PART #';P(F,1);'STOCK ON HAND ';P(F,2)
73  PRINT
75  GO TO 90
77  PRINT\PRINT'OUT OF STOCK OF ITEM #';P(F,1);'ORDER WILL BE BACKORDERED'
78  PRINT\GO TO 90
80  B=B-X\P(F,2)=P(F,2)-P(F,2)
81  PRINT
82  PRINT 'NOTIFY CUSTOMER HE WILL RECEIVE';B;'OF ITEM #';P(F,1)
83  PRINT '  REMAINING NO. OF ITEMS,';X;'WILL BE BACKORDERED'
84  PRINT '  ORDER PART #';P(F,1);'--STOCK ON HAND =';P(F,2)
85  PRINT
90  GO TO 35
95  CLOSE  1
100 END
```

treated, as shown in Figure 12-34. The first order is received from Industrial Hardware of Los Angeles and contains the items listed below.

30 of Item #1
50 of Item #2
10 of Item #5

The second order is received from Hardware Limited of San Diego and contains the items listed below.

20 of Item #2
32 of Item #4
20 of Item #7

FIGURE 12-34

Printout of Program To Fill Orders, Backorder, and Notify of Need To Reorder

```
RUN
VA7      08:47 AM          14-Dec-81
NAME OF COMPANY ORDERING
? "INDUSTRIAL HARDWARE OF LOS ANGELES"
INPUT RECORD OF ORDER TO BE FILLED
INPUT -9 TO TERMINATE
? 1
AMOUNT OF ORDER
? 30
ORDER PART # 1 STOCK ON HAND  30

INPUT RECORD OF ORDER TO BE FILLED
INPUT -9 TO TERMINATE
? 2
AMOUNT OF ORDER
? 50

NOTIFY CUSTOMER HE WILL RECEIVE 45 OF ITEM # 2
  REMAINING NO. OF ITEMS, 5 WILL BE BACKORDERED
  ORDER PART #2--STOCK ON HAND = 0

INPUT RECORD OF ORDER TO BE FILLED
INPUT -9 TO TERMINATE
? 5
AMOUNT OF ORDER
? 10

INPUT RECORD OF ORDER TO BE FILLED
INPUT -9 TO TERMINATE
? -9

READY

RUN
VA7      08:49 AM          14-Dec-81
NAME OF COMPANY ORDERING
? "HARDWARE LIMITED OF SAN DIEGO"
INPUT RECORD OF ORDER TO BE FILLED
INPUT -9 TO TERMINATE
? 2

OUT OF STOCK OF ITEM #2 ORDER WILL BE BACKORDERED

INPUT RECORD OF ORDER TO BE FILLED
INPUT -9 TO TERMINATE
? 4
AMOUNT OF ORDER
? 32
ORDER PART # 4 STOCK ON HAND  25

INPUT RECORD OF ORDER TO BE FILLED
INPUT -9 TO TERMINATE
? 7
AMOUNT OF ORDER
? 20

INPUT RECORD OF ORDER TO BE FILLED
INPUT -9 TO TERMINATE
? -9
```

The order from Industrial Hardware is filled first, followed by the order from Hardware Limited. When the order for Item #1 is filled, stock on hand drops below 50 and is listed to reorder. When Item #2 is ordered, the computer does three things: (1) it fills the order for 45 of the 50 items, (2) it backorders 5 items, and (3) it reorders the item. When the order of Item #5 is filled, the stock on hand is 73 items, which is above the reorder limit of 50.

The order from Hardware Limited is then filled. Because there is no longer any stock of Item #2, the computer prints a backorder notice. Item #4 is filled, but because the stock on hand is below 50, it is reordered. Then Item #7 is filled. The operator then inputs a -9 when item number is requested, and the program is terminated.

The operator wishes to verify the stock on hand after filling the orders, so he calls out and runs the program to print the contents of the virtual array. That program is shown in Figure 12-22. The printout is shown in Figure 12-35.

FIGURE 12-35

Contents of Virtual Array P After Filling Orders

ITEM #	QTY ON HAND	PRICE
1	30	10.50
2	0	6.00
3	98	9.60
4	25	14.62
5	73	6.80
6	75	12.83
7	72	4.58
8	63	8.40
0	0	0.00
0	0	0.00

USING STRING VIRTUAL ARRAYS

The array file 'KING.DAT' has only 3 columns and consists only of numbers. These contents are unrealistic because most companies have much more detailed information in the rows and also use string data. Therefore, two types of information will be added to the program: location and name.

String virtual array storages have one difference from other string arrays. The maximum number of characters in the string must be specified in the dimension statement and must be in powers of 2 up to 512. Therefore, the maximum length of the string will be one of the following: 2, 4, 8, 16, 32, 64, 128, 256, or 512. If the user decides to ignore the rules and specifies any other length, the computer will assume the next higher size. For example, if in Statement 25 in Figure 12-36, P$ is dimensioned P$(8) = 66, the computer would assume P$(8) = 128. The 8 in the parentheses would denote that 8 different lines of data can be stored, and each line has a maximum of 128 characters. If the user does not denote a length, the computer assumes 16 characters.

PROBLEM 12-13

Problem 12-13 uses the same item number, stock on hand, and price used in Problem 12-12. It also adds the description of the item and its location. The program is shown in Figure 12-36. When the program is run, the operator at the keyboard inputs the data. The printout of the program is illustrated in Figure 12-37.

FIGURE 12-36

Program To Add String Data to Virtual Array P

```
LIST
VA1       11:49 AM          14-Dec-81
20   OPEN 'STRING.DAT' FOR OUTPUT AS FILE 1
25   DIM#1,P(8,3),P$(8)=32, L$(8)=16
27   P$(8), L$(8) = " "\P(8,3)=0
30   MAT P = ZER
32   FOR A = 1 TO 8
34   P$(A), L$(A) = " "
36   NEXT A
40   FOR A = 1 TO 8
44   PRINT 'ITEM #, STOCK ON HAND, QUANTITY, DESCRIPTION, & LOC.'
47   INPUT P(A,1), P(A,2), P(A,3), P$(A), L$(A)
50   NEXT A
55   CLOSE  1
60   END
```

In the program in Figure 12-36, Statement 20 opens the file to receive the data. Statement 25 dimensions the various matrices to be used. The string matrices are set for the maximum length of the strings. Statement 27 sets the last element of each matrix to a blank. Statement 30 zeros out the Matrix P. Statement 32 is the beginning of the A loop used to clear the matrices P$ and L$, and Statement 36 is the end of that loop. Statement 40 is the beginning of the A loop used to input data.

FIGURE 12-37

Run of Program To Add String Data to Virtual Array P

```
RUN
VA1      08:56 PM          14-Dec-81
ITEM #, STOCK ON HAND, QUANTITY, DESCRIPTION, & LOC.
? 1,30,10.50,'HAMMER,CLAW, MET. HNDL, 16"','BIN A-2'
ITEM #, STOCK ON HAND, QUANTITY, DESCRIPTION, & LOC.
? 2,0,6.00,'HAMMER,CLAW,WOOD HNDL,14"','BIN A-8'
ITEM #, STOCK ON HAND, QUANTITY, DESCRIPTION, & LOC.
? 3,98,9.60,'SAW,CROSS-CUT,26"','RACK D-3'
ITEM #, STOCK ON HAND, QUANTITY, DESCRIPTION, & LOC.
? 4,25,14.62,'SAW,RIP,26"','RACK D-8'
ITEM #, STOCK ON HAND, QUANTITY, DESCRIPTION, & LOC.
? 5,73,6.80,'SAW,HVY DUTY HACK','RACK D-15'
ITEM #, STOCK ON HAND, QUANTITY, DESCRIPTION, & LOC.
? 6,75,12.83,'LEVEL,24"','BIN B-3'
ITEM #, STOCK ON HAND, QUANTITY, DESCRIPTION, & LOC.
? 7,72,4.58,'FILE KIT, 4 FILES','BIN C-8'
ITEM #, STOCK ON HAND, QUANTITY, DESCRIPTION, & LOC.
? 8,63,8.40,'SQUARE,STEEL,18"','BIN D-9'
```

Statement 44 is the print statement that tells the keyboard operator what data is to be printed and in what order. Statement 47 allows the operator to input a line of data. Statement 50 is the ending statement of the loop, Statement 55 closes the file, and Statement 60 terminates the program.

The program in Figure 12-38 is used to print out the contents of

FIGURE 12-38

Program To Print Out Contents of File 'STRING.DAT'

```
LIST
VA2      9:30 PM          14-Dec-81
10   OPEN 'STRING.DAT' FOR INPUT AS FILE 1
15   DIM#1,P(8,3),P$(8) = 32,L$(8) = 16
20   PRINT\PRINT;TAB(9);'STOCK ON'
25   PRINT 'ITEM #       HAND     PRICE              DESCRIPTION';
30   PRINT;TAB(60);'LOCATION'
35   PRINT
40   FOR A = 1 TO 8
45   PRINT;TAB(2);
50   PRINT USING '##          ###      ##.##     ',P(A,1),P(A,2),P(A,3);
55   PRINT;P$(A);TAB(60);L$(A)
60   NEXT A
65   CLOSE  1
70   END
```

the File 'STRING.DAT'. Once the file is opened for input at Statement 10 in this program, no other input statement is necessary to read the data as was necessary in sequential files. Once the file is opened, the data is available for retrieving. The printout that results from this program is shown in Figure 12-39.

FIGURE 12-39

Printout of Contents of File 'STRING.DAT'

ITEM #	STOCK ON HAND	PRICE	DESCRIPTION	LOCATION
1	30	10.50	HAMMER,CLAW, MET. HNDL,16"	BIN A-2
2	0	6.00	HAMMER,CLAW, WOOD HNDL,14"	BIN A-8
3	98	9.60	SAW,CROSSCUT,26"	RACK D-3
4	25	14.62	SAW,RIP,26"	RACK D-8
5	73	6.80	SAW,HVY DUTY HACK	RACK D-15
6	75	12.83	LEVEL,24"	BIN B-3
7	72	4.58	FILE KIT, 4 FILES	BIN C-8
8	63	8.40	SQUARE,STEEL,18"	BIN D-9

Ready

SUMMARY

1. When using a program to create a data file, different names must be used for the program and for the data file.
2. Data file names are made up of three parts: a name that consists of from one to six characters, a decimal point, and then zero to three characters following the decimal point–i.e., CH12.DAT.
3. There are two types of data files: sequential and random access.
4. Another method of terminating a program is through the use of an "ON ERROR GO TO" Command.
   - A. All error messages, or diagnostics, are assigned a number in the operating system.
   - B. The number eleven is assigned to the "End of File on Device" diagnostic.
   - C. To use this method, the program begins with the statement "ON ERROR GO TO ___", and the blank is filled with a statement number.
   - D. The statement to which the statement in C is sent would read as follows: "IF ERR=11 AND ERL=30 THEN RESUME 70 ELSE ON ERROR GO TO".

(1) The part of this statement "ERR=11" asks if the number of the diagnostic is "END OF FILE ON DEVICE."

(2) The part of this statement "ERL=30" asks if the error originated at Line 30 (the input line).

(3) The statement commands that if both conditions are true, "THEN RESUME 70", which causes the computer to resume executing at Line 70.

(4) The line at which the program resumes would be the one which closes the file—Statement 70 in this case.

(5) The part of the statement "ON ERROR GO TO" tells the computer to assume it is directed to zero. The zero directs control to the operating system, which aborts the program.

(6) When all of the data have been input, the operator depresses the "CONTROL" key and the letter Z simultaneously, which causes a diagnostic "End of File on Device".

5. To create a sequential file, the file must be opened for output.

```
20  OPEN "CH12.DAT" FOR OUTPUT AS FILE 1
```

"FILE 1" in this statement refers to channels. The channels can be numbered from 1 to 12.

6. To eliminate a file the command KILL followed by the program name is used. Also, a file is destroyed when a file by that same name is opened for output.

```
KILL "CH12.DAT"
```

7. Data is printed on the file by use of Print Using Statements.

```
50  PRINT #1, USING "!\                  \!!##.##!#.##!###",'"',E$,'"',",",S,",",P,",",F
```

A. The "PRINT #1" in Statement 50 tells the computer to print on FILE 1.

B. USING states that a PRINT USING format is being used.

C. The reason that exclamation marks are used is to place quotes around the string fields and to place commas (separators) between the fields. As a result of utilizing this format, storage space is saved because the fields are bunched.

8. A file must be closed before the program is terminated.
9. Once the file has been created, it can be accessed by opening the file for input.

```
10  OPEN "CH12.DAT" FOR INPUT AS FILE 1
```

10. To add data to a sequential file, the old file is opened for input and a new file must be created. Data are picked up from the old file and printed on the newly created file. Also, the additions are placed wherever they belong in the new file.
11. To delete data from a sequential data file, the old file is opened for input and a new file must be created. Data are picked up from the old file and printed on the new file, eliminating the data to be deleted.
12. To retrieve data from any file, that file is opened for input. The data to be retrieved is keyed by an operator, who specifies which record to get. The data are then compared with data input from the file. When the two are equal, the record is therefore found and is printed.
13. A statement that does not specify input or output may be used to open a file.

```
10  OPEN "BUS.DAT" AS FILE 1
```

The computer checks for a file named "BUS.DAT". If one is not found, the computer assumes this file is meant to be opened for output. If a file by that name is found, the computer assumes the file is opened for input.

14. A statement can be used to permit continued addition to a file without printing them over previous data. This is done by adding "MODE 2" at the end of the statement opening the file.

```
10  OPEN "BUS.DAT" AS FILE 1, MODE 2
```

15. Before a transaction file can be merged with a sequential master file, it must be sorted sequentially.
16. One of the ways to use random access files is by creating virtual arrays. Virtual arrays are matrices or tables.

17. Virtual arrays are opened in the same manner as are sequential files.
18. Virtual arrays must be dimensioned. Also, they must have the same file number in the dimension statement as is used when opening the file.

```
10  DIM #1,P(8,2)
```

19. Storage locations for arrays must be zeroed out before they are used. The most efficient way to clear out the storage is as follows. Note: Some installations do not have the MAT package.

```
15  P(8,2) = 0
20  MAT P = ZER(8,2)
```

20. Virtual arrays containing strings can also be created. They, too, must be dimensioned, but additional information must be supplied. The maximum length of the string must be stated, and the length must be in powers of 2 up to 512 (2, 4, 8, 16, 32, 64, 128, 256, or 512). If the length is stated in other than a power of 2, the computer assumes the next higher power. If no length is specified, the computer assumes 16.

```
10  DIM #1, P$(8) = 32, L$(8) = 16     (Correct dimensioning)

10  DIM #1, P$(8), L$(8) = 20          (Incomplete dimensioning)
10  DIM #1, P$(8) = 16, L$(8) = 32     (Computer-assumed dimensioning)
```

21. To add to a virtual array file, the data to be added is entered into memory. The computer, through a FOR/NEXT loop, checks every record currently stored in the file to see if the stored data is greater or less than the data to be added. If the data in the file is less than the data to be added, the record in the data file is printed on the new file. If the data in the file is greater than the data to be added, the record to be added is printed on the new file. This process continues until all records are placed on the new file.
22. To delete a record from a virtual array file, the data to be deleted is entered into memory. The computer, through a FOR/NEXT loop, compares every record in the file with the record to be deleted. If the record in the file is not the data to be de-

leted, it is entered on the new file. If the record is the one to be deleted, the computer retrieves another record from the file for comparison purposes. This causes the record to be deleted to be omitted from the new file.

SELF TEST

TRUE OR FALSE QUESTIONS

1. The following is a valid sequence.

```
NEW
NEW FILE NAME--LBE
10  ON ERROR GO TO 85
15  OPEN "LBE" FOR INPUT AS FILE 1
```

2. There are two types of data files: sequential and random access.
3. The number of the diagnostic "End of File on Device" is 12.
4. ERL means the line at which an error originated.
5. The command RESUME tells the computer to resume executing at the line closing the program.
6. Depressing the CONTROL key and the letter C simultaneously causes a diagnostic "End of File on Device".
7. A virtual array is a matrix or table.
8. This is a valid statement to dimension a virtual array: 10 DIM A(10,5).
9. To retrieve data from a file, the file must be opened for output.
10. The following is a valid statement.

```
20  OPEN "BABY.DAT" AS FILE 1
```

11. Opening a file for output destroys any other file by the same name.
12. The length of strings must be dimensioned and must be in powers of 3.

SHORT ANSWERS

13. Write a statement to open a sequential file for output that permits the addition of data to the file without printing over previous data.
14. Write a dimension statement for the virtual array A that has 5 rows and 4 columns.
15. Write a dimension statement for the following virtual arrays: L$ with a field width of 24 characters, M$ with a field width of 55 characters, and A$ with a field width of 39 characters.
16. What field length does the computer assume with the following dimension statement?

```
10  DIM #1, L$, B$(30), C$(120)
```

17. Finish the following statement.

```
PRINT #1, USING "###!\            \!!###",
```

18. Write a statement (10) to open the file BUSH.DAT for output.
19. Write a statement (20) to open the file BUSH.DAT for input.
20. Write a statement (30) to open the file BUSH.DAT for either input or output.
21. What is the total number of channels available for use when dealing with files?
22. Write a statement (80) to check for an "End of Device on File" diagnostic created at Statement 20 that will have the computer continue at Statement 70 or transfer control to the operating system to terminate the program.
23. Write a line that will command the computer to eliminate the file "RACK.DAT".
24. What are the various lengths of strings available for use when dealing with files?
25. Write statements that will zero out the virtual array P(9,4) in the most efficient manner.
26. If the length of a string is not dimensioned, what does the computer do?
27. If the length of a string is not dimensioned to the correct power, what does the computer do?

ASSIGNMENTS[3]

1. A sequential master file using the Pearlman Department Store's customers' numbers 1012, 1020, 1137, 1150, 1538, 1665, and 1842 should be created. These accounts are listed on pages 299 through 303.
   A. A program to list the contents of that master file should be created.
   B. A program to add customer numbers 1023, 1307, and 1443 to the file should be created.
   C. A program to delete customers 1020 and 1665 should be created.
   D. Listings for all of these created programs should be handed in, as well as printouts of the contents of the file after: (1) a master file has been created, (2) the customers have been added, and (3) the customers have been deleted.

2. A random access master file using the Pearlman Department Store's customers' numbers 1101, 1122, 1672, 1945, 2050, and 2452 should be created.
   A. A program that will list the contents of that master file should be created.
   B. A program to add to the file should be created.

      Customers' numbers 1420, 1742, 2145, and 2462 should be added to the file, and the contents of the file should be printed out.
   C. A program to delete from the file should be created.

      Customers' numbers 1122 and 2050 should be deleted from the file, and the contents of the file should be printed out.
   D. Listings for all of these programs—as well as printouts of the file after opening the file, adding to the file, and deleting from the file—should be handed in.

3. Pearlman Department Store bills customers once a month. A sample of their statement appears below.

[3] Long street addresses should be logically shortened, i.e., Beach (BCH.), Drive (DR.), Street (ST.), Number (#).

PEARLMAN DEPARTMENT STORE
4150 Lakewood Blvd.
Lakewood, CA 90712

Cheryl Adams
88 W. 49th Street
Long Beach, CA 90803

			Amt. Paid $________
Balance			XXX.XX
Payment—Thank you	XXX.XX		
Charge		XXX.XX	
Fin. Charge $XX.XX	Min. Payment $XXX.XX		Bal. Owed $XXX.XX

A. Pearlman's charges 1.5 percent a month on the old balance as a finance charge.

B. Minimum payment is determined by multiplying 15 percent times the new balance. When this minimum payment is calculated and it is less than $15, Pearlman's sets the minimum payment at $15. However, if the new balance is less than $15, then the payment is the amount of the new balance.

C. If an account has a balance and no payment was received, the statement is to have the words "Past Due" printed where the payment normally is printed.

The new finance charge is added to the balance, and 15 percent of the old balance is added to 15 percent of the new balance to compute the new minimum payment due; otherwise, the new balance is due if it is less than $30.

D. Using Pearlman Department Store's list of charge customers, the customers numbered 2015, 2168, 2521, 2618, 2643, and 3023 are to be used to open a sequential master file.

E. A transaction file is to be created using the transactions for the month listed below.

F. A program to update the master file from the transaction file and to do the monthly billing should be created.

TRANSACTIONS

CUSTOMER NUMBER	PAYMENT	CHARGE
2521	0.00	15.75
2618	11.89	0.00
2168	15.00	0.00
2643	15.00	0.00
2521	43.89	0.00
2618	0.00	17.09
2643	0.00	23.18
2521	0.00	27.87
2015	0.00	92.63
2618	0.00	47.92
2168	0.00	83.95
2618	0.00	72.00
2168	0.00	17.59
2015	0.00	27.60

G. Listings of all programs, and the printout of the contents of the master file when it was originally opened and after it has been updated, should be handed in. Also, printouts of the contents of the transaction file before and after the sort should be handed in.

PEARLMAN DEPARTMENT STORE
Charge Customers

NUMBER	NAME	ADDRESS	ACCUMULATED FINANCE CHARGE	BALANCE
1012	Cheryl Adams	88 W. 49th Street Long Beach, CA 90803	3.95	51.87
1020	Jose Anaya	7112 Stafford Ave. Huntington Park, CA 90255	17.63	49.73

NUMBER	NAME	ADDRESS	ACCUMULATED FINANCE CHARGE	BALANCE
1023	Ian Anderson	4201 E. 7th Street Long Beach, CA 90808	27.32	93.87
1101	Kurt P. Balliet	925 S. 3rd Street Calimesa, CA 92431	14.76	22.80
1122	Beckie Bencivengo	9562 Scotstoun Drive Huntington Beach, CA 92646	4.80	0.00
1137	Mary F. Boblak	6605 Via Canada Santa Ana, CA 92704	15.15	107.27
1150	Kimberly Bowan	910 N. Mountain View Santa Ana, CA 92704	11.19	58.15
1307	Eric DeWert	4672 Dogwood Ave. Seal Beach, CA 90740	9.13	47.23
1420	Paul Easterling	9827 Orcaan Ave. Los Angeles, CA 90045	32.15	210.86
1443	Antonio Egenias	666 Swallow Road Castle Lakes, CA 90074	7.12	0.00
1538	Bill Featherstone	1012 Locust Street Long Beach, CA 90803	22.59	84.74
1665	Brent Green	2272 Long Hill Rd. Long Beach, CA 90803	38.95	420.87
1672	Marvin Grogan	4034 Country Club Dr. Lakewood, CA 90712	34.27	354.25
1742	Ann Hitchcock	50 Glendora Long Beach, CA 90803	5.83	34.72
1842	David Inouye	1234 Easy Ave. Long Beach, CA 90810	29.67	11.82
1937	Jacquelyne M. Jervis	9634 Clancey Ave. Downey, CA 90240	9.65	0.00

NUMBER	NAME	ADDRESS	ACCUMULATED FINANCE CHARGE	BALANCE
1945	Mike Jett	1234 Easy Ave. Long Beach, CA 90810	23.54	85.38
1950	Lionel Johnson	5959 Overhill Dr. Los Angeles, CA 90043	19.54	33.72
2015	Christina Lang	4645 E. 59th Street Maywood, CA 90270	47.28	198.67
2050	Donna Lotta	55632 Wallingsford Los Alamitos, CA 90720	21.89	0.00
2145	Jack Meatof	401 Jackson Way Compton, CA 90241	15.82	45.39
2163	Debra Moskowitz	6811 E. 10th Street Long Beach, CA 90815	4.67	12.80
2168	Sandy Masuda	8585 Pierce Dr. Buena Park, CA 90620	0.00	21.67
2452	Douglas Polhemus	451 Haines Ave. Long Beach, CA 90814	9.45	56.58
2462	Rosemarie Quitasol	9064 Alder Lane La Palma, CA 90621	16.45	38.25
2521	Sheila Refoy	909 Sonora Rd. Costa Mesa, CA 92626	43.89	254.98
2612	Dennis Sakoda	777 Bellflower Blvd. Long Beach, CA 90815	5.34	15.90
2618	June Satogiwa	2173 Delta Ave. Long Beach, CA 90815	11.89	53.27
2643	Steve Sloan	3617 N. Rutgers Long Beach, CA 90818	16.37	92.45
2715	Robin Taub	5136 Kingspine Rd. Rolling Hills, CA 90274	12.87	32.78

NUMBER	NAME	ADDRESS	ACCUMULATED FINANCE CHARGE	BALANCE
3012	Matt Walker	3204 Cerro Vista St. SW Huntsville, AL 35805	11.93	113.98
3023	Janet Weagle	1256 Manhattan Beach Blvd. Manhattan Beach, CA 90266	35.79	54.32
3043	Leona Wendlandt	109 Peace Place Costa Mesa, CA 92626	0.00	34.56
3063	Sylvia Williams	2651 Wall Street Signal Hill, CA 90805	17.81	0.00
3068	Eric Wilson	1016 Ynez Ave. Redondo Beach, CA 90277	34.43	189.34
3142	April Yotsuya	7842 Rustle Drive Pico Rivera, CA 90660	21.89	56.98

POTENTIAL CUSTOMERS

1349	John Duran	1313 S. Harbor Blvd. Anaheim, CA 92680
1642	Mike Goodall	3272 Kempton Rd. Los Alamitos, CA 90720
1755	Kai-Chi Hsu	24201 Ambassador Pl Harbor City, CA 90710
2045	Demetres Lolis	6202 Oakbrook Street Long Beach, CA 90815
2175	Tom Mylow	7526 Freeman Ave. Long Beach, CA 90815
2550	Jim Richardson	10275 Slater #207 Fountain Valley, CA 92708

NUMBER	NAME	ADDRESS	ACCUMULATED FINANCE CHARGE	BALANCE
3042	Harry White	8892 Shoal Circle Huntington Beach, CA 92646		
3125	Dennis Yee	640 Prospect #2 Long Beach, CA 90814		

APPENDIX A

Many more statements and commands not explained in this text are available on the RSTS/E operating system. For advanced programming techniques, reference may be made to the manufacturer's *Basic-Plus Language Manual* and *Systems User's Guide* published by Digital Equipment Corporation. Some of the commands that are explained in this Appendix are the following.

A. The DELETE command
B. The RENAME command
C. Multiple STOP statements
D. The CONT command
E. Logout procedures
   1. The BYE/F command
   2. The BYE/N command
   3. The BYE/I command
F. The RUNNH command

G. Sorting techniques
H. Calculating the median
I. EDIT programs
J. Matrix commands
   1. The MAT READ statement
   2. The MAT PRINT statement
   3. The MAT INPUT statement
   4. Matrix addition and subtraction
   5. Matrix multiplication
   6. The ZER command
   7. The CON command
   8. The IDN command
   9. The TRN command
   10. The INV command

THE DELETE COMMAND

The user was previously instructed that to delete a line in his program, he should merely repeat the line number and then depress the RETURN key. However, if the program had been saved, he should repeat the line number, depress the RETURN key, and then type REPLACE.

The user may also delete lines by using the DELETE command. One line can be deleted by typing DELETE and then the line number to be deleted.

```
DELETE 20
```

If a number of lines are to be deleted, the word DELETE should be typed, followed by the beginning line number to be deleted and the last line number to be deleted. In the statement below, all lines from 50 through 70 would be deleted.

```
DELETE 50-70
```

THE RENAME COMMAND

The use of the RENAME command enables the programmer to keep the old program stored under the old name and also to have that same program stored under a new one. The word SAVE should be typed after the RENAME command.

To rename a program, the programmer must be currently working on it, or he must take it out of storage. In the following statement, the programmer was working on JOB 1 and renamed it MAGI.

```
RENAME MAGI
SAVE
```

MULTIPLE STOP STATEMENTS

When a programmer desires to test a program, he can facilitate debugging by placing a number of STOP statements throughout his program. Each time the computer encounters a STOP statement as the program is executed, it causes the program to stop and prints the following message.

```
STOP AT LINE 80
```

The computer stops at Line 80 because Statement 80 contains a STOP command—80 STOP.

After the programmer has examined the program to that point and made any changes, if any needed to be made, he would then type CONT and the program would continue with the next statement.

THE CONT COMMAND

When the program has been halted through the use of a STOP statement or CTRL/C command, the programmer can restart the program most of the time by typing CONT and depressing the RETURN key. The program will continue with the statement following the one that was last executed. If the execution cannot continue, the computer will print the following message.

```
CAN'T CONTINUE
```

LOGOUT PROCEDURES

The operator should log out before he leaves the terminal. To log out, the user must be in the BASIC system. If he is using another system

(EDITOR or Mail), he can return to BASIC by typing EXIT, followed by a carriage return. The READY message will confirm that the operator is once more in BASIC.

Throughout the text, the user was shown how to exit the terminal with the BYE command. When using the BYE command, there is always a message following the command. The reader was told to type YES or Y for normal logout, as shown below:

```
BYE
CONFIRM: Y
```

THE BYE/F COMMAND

If the programmer wants a fast logout without any message, he types BYE/F. The BYE/F command suppresses the message normally printed out after logging off. The computer prints a number of blank lines and then an underscore.

THE BYE/N COMMAND

When the programmer types BYE and the computer types CONFIRM, the programmer types N if he wishes to exit one program and start another one without being logged out.

```
BYE
CONFIRM: N
```

The BYE/N command logs the user out of the program but does not log him off the computer. The computer prints a number of blank lines and then prints READY.

THE BYE/I COMMAND

The BYE/I command is used to delete programs that have been saved. After the programmer types BYE/I, the computer will list the name of the first program in his file, followed by a question mark. The programmer presses the RETURN key if he does not want to delete the program. If he does want to delete the program, he will type K, which means "kill", and press the RETURN key. The computer will then list the name of the second program in his file, followed by a question mark. The process continues until the names of all saved programs have been listed. An example appears below.

```
BYE\I
LINDA .BAS      1      60      26-JAN-81   ? K
RAND1 .BAS      3      60      07-FEB-81   ?
RON   .BAS      1      60      16-FEB-81   ? K
```

THE RUNNH COMMAND

Throughout the text, the examples used the RUN command when programs were executed. The computer always prints a header with that command. If the programmer does not desire a header, he types RUNNH.

SORTING TECHNIQUES

Sometimes it is desirable to sort data so they can be listed in either increasing or decreasing order. This might apply to any group of data that is to be arranged in sequential order. An example might be a payroll listing, in which the employee payroll number is used to list the employees in increasing order from the lowest payroll number to the highest payroll number.

An illustration of sorting will be shown and explained, since an example will aid in clarifying the logic used in a sorting program.

The object of the following program is to sort a group of test scores and arrange them in order from the highest to the lowest score. Students' names and test scores will be printed as shown in the listing below the program.

```
5   DIM N$(40), T(40)
10  FOR A=1 TO 40
15  READ N$(A), T(A)
20  IF T(A) > 100 THEN 30
25  NEXT A
30  L = A - 1
35  K = 1
40  FOR A = 2 TO L
45  IF T(A) > T(K) THEN K = A
50  NEXT A
55  IF T(K) < 0.0 THEN 85
60  PRINT N$(K), T(K)
65  T(K) = -9.0
70  GO TO 35
75  DATA BETTY, 70.5, SUE, 66.5, MARY, 92.3, BECKY, 99.9
80  DATA JOYCE, 89.5, HOLLY, 42.6, JANE, 80.6, JUDY, 110.0
85  END
```

```
READY

RUNNH

BECKY          99.9
MARY           92.3
JOYCE          89.5
JANE           80.6
BETTY          70.5
SUE            66.5
HOLLY          42.6
```

The statement at Line 5 reserves 40 storage locations for the students' names and 40 storage locations for the test scores. The loop is entered at Line 10 to read the data into the arrays.

To determine when all the legitimate test scores have been read, a number that is larger than any possible test score is used as the last test score. After this is read, Line 20 causes the system to jump out of the loop and to Line 30. L in Line 30 represents the number of test scores after the last test score (the dummy test score 110.0) has been subtracted from the number of test scores that were read.

```
40  FOR A = 2 TO L
45  IF T(A) > T(K) THEN K = A
50  NEXT A
```

Line 45 compares T(A), which is T(2), with T(K), which is T(1). If T(A) is larger than T(K), then T(K) becomes T(2). The next time through the loop T(A), which is T(3), is compared with T(K), which is T(2). Again, if T(A) is larger than T(K), then T(K) becomes T(3). If T(A) is not larger than T(K), then T(K) remains as it is. After the system has looped through all the test scores, T(K) will represent the largest score.

```
55  IF T(K) < 0.0 THEN 85
60  PRINT N$(K), T(K)
65  T(K) = -9.0
70  GO TO 35
```

Line 55 tests to determine if T(K) is less than 0. If it is, the system will go to the END statement. Line 60 prints the name and score of the student that achieved the highest test score. Line 65 changes the test score to -9. This eliminates the test score from again being found to be the highest score in the array.

The system returns to Line 35, where K is again set equal to 1 and the sorting continues. This time the second highest score is found to be the highest because the previously high score has been changed to -9. When all the scores have been sorted, printed, and changed to -9, the system makes one last sort and finds the largest score to be -9. Line 55 then directs the system to the END statement.

This type of sorting program would be too costly in terms of machine time if long arrays were to be sorted. Many computer manufacturers have developed efficient sorting routines for their own computers. These routines are given in the manufacturer's manuals.

CALCULATING THE MEDIAN

The median of a group of numbers is the middle value in order of size if the count of the numbers is odd, or the mean of the two middle values if the count of the numbers is even.

First, the numbers have to be sorted and arranged in ascending or descending order. A sorting program has been illustrated and explained earlier in this appendix. By adding Statements 7, 61, 62, and 80 through 115 to the sorting program, the median of the group of test scores can be calculated. The END statement in the original program was numbered 85. It is changed to 120 in this new program. The revised program and printout are shown below.

```
5   DIM N$(20),T(20),S(20)
7   N=0
10  FOR A = 1 TO 40
15  READ N$(A),T(A)
20  IF T(A) > 100 THEN 30
25  NEXT A
30  L = A-1
35  K=1
40  FOR A = 2 TO L
45  IF T(A) > T(K) THEN K = A
50  NEXT A
55  IF T(K) < 0.0 THEN 80
60  PRINT N$(K),T(K)
61  N=N+1
62  S(N) = T(K)
65  T(K) = -9.0
70  GO TO 35
75  DATA BETTY,70.5,SUE,66.5,MARY,92.3,BECKY,99.9
76  DATA JOYCE,89.5,HOLLY,42.6,JANE,80.6,JUDY,110.0
80  LET H = N/2
```

```
85  IF H <> INT(H) THEN 100
90  LET M = (S(H)+S(H+1))/2
95  GO TO 110
100 LET H = (N+1)/2
105 LET M = S(H)
110 PRINT
115 PRINT "THE MEDIAN IS" M
120 END

READY

RUN

BECKY              99.9
MARY               92.3
JOYCE              89.5
JANE               80.6
BETTY              70.5
SUE                66.5
HOLLY              42.6

THE MEDIAN IS 80.6
```

The sorting program arranges the test scores in descending order. After each score is printed, it is assigned to the S array at Statement 62. At Statement 80 the number of scores is divided by 2 and the result is tested at Statement 85 to determine whether the number of scores is odd or even. If there is an odd number of scores, Statement 100 adds 1 to the number of scores and divides by 2 to determine the position of the middle score. The result is then used as a subscript in the S array to assign this score to the median. If there is an even number of scores, Statement 90 adds the two middle scores and divides by 2 to get the mean of the two scores. The resulting figure represents the median.

EDIT PROGRAMS

Most time-sharing systems have system programs (i.e., public programs) that allow the programmer to manipulate files almost as easily as one would proofread an essay. The programmer can, by a few simple commands, strike out and add to a file of any kind very easily. The file is loaded into the EDIT program and modified by the programmer by manipulating the EDIT program. The EDIT program is valuable because it is used when a particular system does not allow a programmer to retrieve a file that is exclusively alphanumeric directly into main storage.

EDIT programs go under various names, depending on the system. Some examples are EDIT, EDITOR, XEDIT, etc. System manuals present explanations of the EDIT programs available for particular computers.

MATRIX COMMANDS

This section contains a discussion of some of the most commonly used matrix commands.

THE MAT READ STATEMENT

One of the most frequently used matrix commands, the MAT READ statement, is used to read in an entire array or matrix with one command rather than with loops. As a result, each element of the matrix does not have to be subscripted to enter it into the matrix.

Normally the matrix is dimensioned. If it is not dimensioned, it is assumed to consist of 10 rows, or 10 rows and 10 columns. Enough data to fill the matrix *must* be supplied or an OUT OF DATA message is printed.

The MAT READ statement causes the data to be entered row by row. In other words, all of the columns in the first row are entered first, then all of the columns in the second row, etc. By using subscripts, the programmer can secure an element from a matrix that was filled by a MAT READ statement.

```
10  DIM A(4,4),B(4)
15  MAT READ A,B
20  PRINT A(2,1),B(2)
25  DATA 2,4,6,8,10,12,14,16,18,20,22,24,26,28,30,32
38  DATA 100,101,102,103
40  END
```

In this program the computer would store the data as illustrated below.

A				B
2	4	6	8	100
10	12	14	16	101
18	20	22	24	102
26	28	30	32	103

The program would be printed as shown below.

```
LIST
MATR     15:12              05-FEB-81
10  DIM A(4,4),B(4)
15  MAT READ A,B
20  PRINT A(2,1),B(2)
25  DATA 2,4,6,8,10,12,14,16,18,20,22,24,26,28,30,32
38  DATA 100,101,102,103
40  END

READ

RUN
MATR     15:12              05-FEB-81
 10            101
```

A MAT READ statement is also used to redefine a matrix. A matrix can be redefined as long as the new dimensions do not exceed those previously allocated in the dimension statement.

```
10  DIM A(4,4),B(2,4)
15  MAT READ A(2,4),B(2,2)
20  PRINT A(2,1),B(2,2)
25  DATA 2,4,6,8,10,12,14,16,18,20,22,24,26,28,30,32
28  DATA 50,54,58,62,66,70,74,78
30  END
```

Statement 15 redefined Matrix A and Matrix B in the program. The printout would be as follows.

```
LIST
MATR     15:21              05-FEB-81
10  DIM A(4,4),B(2,4)
15  MAT READ A(2,4),B(2,2)
20  PRINT A(2,1),B(2,2)
25  DATA 2,4,6,8,10,12,14,16,18,20,22,24,26,28,30,32
28  DATA 50,54,58,62,66,70,74,78
30  END

READY

RUN
MATR     15:21              05-FEB-81
 10             24
```

THE MAT PRINT STATEMENT

The MAT PRINT statement allows a matrix to be printed without referencing each element of the matrix. In BASIC-PLUS, if there is more than one matrix to be printed, there must be a MAT PRINT statement for every matrix. On some computers, one statement will print all of the matrices. A very important point is that if a comma is placed after the variable, the computer prints an element in each print zone, row by row. In the absence of any punctuation, the computer places each element in the first print zone in each row. If a semi-colon follows the variable, the elements are printed in packed format, row by row.

An example of the use of the MAT PRINT statement with commas after the variable is shown below.

```
LIST
MATR       15:21             05-FEB-81
10  DIM A(4,4),B(4)
15  MAT READ A,B
20  MAT PRINT A,
25  MAT PRINT B,
27  DATA 2,4,6,8,10,12,14,16,18,20,22,24,26,28,30,32
28  DATA 5,10,15,20
30  END

READY

RUN
MATR       15:21             05-FEB-81
 2              4              6              8

 10             12             14             16

 18             20             22             24

 26             28             30             32


 5              10             15             20
```

The printout of the same program with semi-colons following the variables in Statements 20 and 25 is shown below.

```
READY

RUN
MATR    15:22              05-FEB-81

 2  4  6  8

 10  12  14  16

 18  20  22  24

 26  28  30  32


 5  10  15  20
```

The printout of the same program with no punctuation following the variables in Statements 20 and 25 is shown below.

```
READY

RUN
MATR        15:23              05-FEB-81
 2
 4
 6
 8
 10
 12
 14
 16
 18
 20
 22
 24
 26
 28
 30
 32

 5
 10
 15
 20
```

THE MAT INPUT STATEMENTS

The use of the MAT INPUT statement permits the operator to input the data at the terminal. By using the LINE FEED key, data can be input on succeeding lines.[1] The RETURN key is depressed when the data that has been typed is to be entered into the system.

An example of a program using MAT INPUT statements is shown in the computer listing and printout below.

```
READY

LIST
MATR      15:25             05-FEB-81
10  DIM A(4,4)
15  MAT INPUT A
20  MAT PRINT A,
25  END

READY

RUN
MATR      15:25             05-FEB-81
? 2,4,6,8,10,12,14,16,18,20,22,24,26,28,30,32
 2               4               6               8

 10              12              14              16

 18              20              22              24

 26              28              30              32
```

The MAT INPUT statement continues to accept data until the entire matrix is read or until the RETURN key has been depressed. After the data has been input, the number of input rows is contained in the variable NUM, the number of columns in the variable NUM2.

An example of a listed program and printout in which the operator entered only part of the dimensioned matrix is shown below. The printout shows how many rows (NUM) and how many columns (NUM2) were entered.

```
LIST
MATR      15:29             05-FEB-81
10  DIM A(50,4)
15  MAT INPUT A
20  PRINT NUM;
22  PRINT NUM2
25  END
```

[1] Appendix B, page 326, contains a short discussion of the LINE FEED key.

```
READY

RUN
MATR      15:29              05-FEB-81
? 2,4,6,8,10,12,14,16,18,20,22,24
 3  4
```

According to this printout, there were three input rows (Num=3) and four input columns (NUM2=4).

The two variables, NUM and NUM2, can be used in the program. When the following statement is added to the previous problem, the computer will multiply the number of rows by the number of columns.

```
23  B = NUM * NUM2
```

The printout would be as shown below.

```
LIST
MATR       15:30             05-FEB-81
10  DIM A(50,4)
15  MAT INPUT A
20  PRINT NUM;
22  PRINT NUM2
23  B = NUM * NUM2
24  PRINT B
25  END

READY

RUN
MATR       15:30             05-FEB-81
? 2,4,6,8,10,12,14,16,18,20,22,24
 3  4
 12
```

MATRIX ADDITION AND SUBTRACTION

If certain rules are followed, addition and subtraction can be accomplished by the use of MAT statements.

1. The number of rows and columns must be the same in all matrices used in the adding or subtracting operation.
2. Only *one* operation can be done in each statement.
3. The word MAT must precede the variable in which the operation

is to be stored to differentiate from a normal assignment statement.

In addition to these rules, the same variable can be used on both sides of the equal sign only in simple addition and subtraction operations. Scalar addition or subtraction of a matrix cannot be done.

The following program listing and printout demonstrate both addition and subtraction.

```
LIST
MATR        15:35                05-FEB-81
10  DIM A(1,4),B(1,4),X(1,4),Y(1,4)
20  MAT READ A,B
25  DATA 2,4,6,8,20,40,60,80
30  MAT X=A+B
32  MAT Y=B-A
34  MAT PRINT X;
36  MAT PRINT Y
38  END

READY

RUN
MATR        15:35                05-FEB-81
 22  44  66  88

 18  36  54  72
```

The following program demonstrates the use of the same variable on both sides of the equal sign. The computer will store the sum of A plus B in A.

```
10  DIM A(1,4),B(1,4),Y(1,4)
20  MAT READ A,B
25  DATA 2,4,6,8,20,40,60,80
30  MAT A=A+B
32  MAT Y=B-A
34  MAT PRINT A;
36  MAT PRINT Y
38  END

READY
```

```
RUN
MATR      15:36              05-FEB-81
 22  44  66  88
 18  36  54  72
```

MATRIX MULTIPLICATION

To accomplish multiplication using matrices, the following rules must be applied.

1. The number of rows in the first matrix must be equal to the number of columns in the second matrix, and the receiving matrix must have dimensions large enough to contain the number of rows in the first matrix added to the number of columns in the second one.
2. The same variable cannot be on both sides of the equal sign.
3. Only one operation can be done in each statement.
4. The word MAT must precede the variable in which the operation is to be stored to differentiate from a normal assignment statement.
5. Scalar multiplication can be accomplished by placing a constant, variable, or formula in parentheses: 20 MAT A=(5)*B or 20 MAT A=(K)*B or 20 MAT A=(X*Y**D)*B.

The program listing and printout shown below demonstrate matrix multiplication.

```
LIST
MATR       15:36              05-FEB-81
10  DIM A(4,3),B(3,4),S(4,4)
15  MAT READ A,B
20  MAT X=A*B
22  DATA 2,4,6,1,3,5,8,10,12,7,9,11
23  DATA 10,20,30,40,50,60,70,80,90,100,110,120
25  MAT PRINT X;
30  END

READY

RUN
MATR       15:30              05-FEB-81

760  880  1000  1120
600  700  790  880
1660  1960  2260  2560
1510  1780  2050  2320
```

To illustrate how the computer does matrix multiplication, the preceding problem will be used. The following schematically illustrates numbers stored in A, B, and X.

A			B				X			
2	4	6	10	20	30	40	760	880	1000	1120
1	3	5	50	60	70	80	600	700	790	880
8	10	12	90	100	110	120	1660	1960	2260	2560
7	9	11					1510	1780	2050	2320

The computer multiplies A(1,1) times B(1,1); A(1,2) times B(2,1); and A(1,3) times B(3,1), and adds the products of the three operations to secure the number stored in X(1,1). The complete process of filling Matrix X is diagrammed in Figure A-1.

FIGURE A-1

Filling Matrix X

```
2 x 10 =   20     2 x  20 =  40     2 x  30 =  60     2 x  40 =  80
4 x 50 =  200     4 x  60 = 240     4 x  70 = 280     4 x  80 = 320
6 x 90 =  540     6 x 100 = 600     6 x 110 = 660     6 x 120 = 720
          760               880              1000              1120

1 x 10 =   10     1 x  20 =  20     1 x  30 =  30     1 x  40 =  40
3 x 50 =  150     3 x  60 = 180     3 x  70 = 210     3 x  80 = 240
5 x 90 =  450     5 x 100 = 500     5 x 110 = 550     5 x 120 = 600
          610               700               790               880

 8 x 10 =   80     8 x  20 = 160     8 x  30 = 240     8 x  40 = 320
10 x 50 =  500    10 x  60 = 600    10 x  70 = 700    10 x  80 = 800
12 x 90 = 1080    12 x 100 =1200    12 x 110 =1320    12 x 120 =1440
          1660              1960              2260              2560
```

The same problem using scalar multiplication would require that Statement 20 be changed to read: 20 MAT X=(2)*A.

```
LIST
MATR      15:45             05-FEB-81
10  DIM A(4,3),B(3,4),X(4,4)
15  MAT READ A,B
20  MAT X=(2)*A
```

```
22  DATA 2,4,6,1,3,5,8,10,12,7,9,11
23  DATA 10,20,30,40,50,60,70,80,90,100,110,120
25  MAT PRINT X;
30  END

READY

RUN
MATR       15:45                  05-FEB-81
 4  8  12
 2  6  10
 16  20  24
 14  18  22
```

THE ZER COMMAND

In a statement such as 10 MAT A=ZER, all of the elements in the matrix are set to zero. If Matrix A were 2 x 2, a PRINT statement would cause the following printout when Statement 10 is used.

```
0  0
0  0
```

A matrix can be redefined with the ZER command.

```
10  DIM A(5,5)
20  MAT A=ZER
25  MAT PRINT A;.
30  END
```

The preceding program would cause the following printout.

```
RUN
NONAME    13:39              08-FEB-81
0    0    0    0    0
0    0    0    0    0
0    0    0    0    0
0    0    0    0    0
0    0    0    0    0
```

THE CON COMMAND

The CON command causes all of the elements in the matrix to be set to one. As with the ZER command, the matrix can be redefined with this command.

```
10  DIM A(5,5)
15  MAT A=CON
20  MAT PRINT A;
25  MAT A=CON(3,3)
30  MAT PRINT A;
35  END
```

The printout for this program appears below.

```
RUN
CON        15:40              05-FEB-81
  1    1    1    1    1
  1    1    1    1    1
  1    1    1    1    1
  1    1    1    1    1
  1    1    1    1    1

  1    1    1
  1    1    1
  1    1    1
```

THE IDN COMMAND

Through the use of the IDN command, a square matrix, which *must* be square to use IDN, is set to zero except at the diagonal, which consists of ones. The matrix may be redefined through the use of the IDN command.

```
10  DIM A(5,5)
15  MAT A=IDN
20  MAT PRINT A;
25  MAT A=IDN(3,3)
30  MAT PRINT A;
35  END
```

The printout illustrating the results of this command appears below.

```
RUN
IDN        15:42              05-FEB-81
  1    0    0    0    0

  0    1    0    0    0

  0    0    1    0    0
```

0	0	0	1	0
0	0	0	0	1

1	0	0
0	1	0
0	0	1

THE TRN COMMAND

The TRN command interchanges the rows and columns of a matrix. The receiving matrix must have compatible dimensions. Also, the variable being transposed must be placed in parentheses.

```
10  MAT M=TRN(A)
```

If A is 4 x 4, the variable M must be at least 4 x 4. The variable M may have larger dimensions, in which case it is redimensioned with the TRN command. For example, in Statement 15 in the following example, the variable M would be redimensioned to 5 x 5.

```
10  DIM M(10,10),A(5,5)
15  MAT M=TRN(A)
```

If Matrix A were 3 x 6, the receiving matrix would have to be 6 x 3 or larger. It would be redimensioned to 6 x 3 in Statement 15 below.

```
10  DIM M(6,6),A(3,6)
15  MAT M=TRN(A)
```

THE INV COMMAND

Because the INV command is used in linear programming and structural analysis, and requires an understanding of matrix algebra, it will not be described here. If the programmer needs this command, it is available, and he should read a book on matrix algebra for an explanation of the function.

APPENDIX B

A few of the program statements used in the textbook are compatible with only the RSTS/E operating system. These statements are explained in this appendix.

PRINT USING STATEMENTS

The PRINT USING statements, sometimes called image statements, explained in Chapters 4, 5, and 7 are not compatible with all systems. Various types of PRINT USING statements are used in other systems. The manufacturer's manual should be consulted for the types of statements to be used on each particular computer.

ASSIGNMENT STATEMENTS

A single statement may be used to assign the same value to several variables. The following statement would set the three variables to zero on the RSTS/E operating system. The TRS-80 does not have this capability.

```
30  A, T1, B1 = 0
```

MULTIPLE STATEMENTS

On the RSTS/E operating system, several statements may be written on a single line, provided each statement except the last is followed by a colon or a backslash. This capability is not available on all systems.

```
30  A = 5:T1 = 0:B1 = 50
```

or

```
30  A = 5\T1 = 0\B1 = 50
```

COMMENT STATEMENTS

On the RSTS/E operating system, an exclamation mark is used to indicate a comment on the same line and following a statement. The computer ignores everything following the exclamation mark, even though the comment will show on the listing.

```
15  X = B!  THIS PLACES THE BONUS IN X
```

Other systems use an apostrophe (single quote) in the place of the exclamation mark.

```
15  X = B  'THIS PLACES THE BONUS IN X
```

THE PRINTING OF DATES

As explained in Chapter 7, the current date can be printed by the RSTS/E operating system by using the following statement. The symbol inside the parentheses is a zero.

```
30  PRINT DATE$(0)
```

Systems manuals should be consulted for the various methods of printing dates in other systems.

IF-THEN-ELSE STATEMENTS

The IF-THEN-ELSE statements explained in Chapter 6 are not available on most systems.

THE LINE FEED KEY

The line feed key may be used on the RSTS/E operating system to continue a statement from one line to another. The RETURN key generates an end-of-statement character; the LINE FEED does not. On other systems, the line feed key is used only to advance one line per depression of the key.

APPENDIX C

The computer can transmit a large number of error messages, but only the most frequently encountered diagnostics are presented in this section. Each diagnostic has a number assigned to it, as designated in the following list.

5	?Can't find file or account
11	?End of file on device
28	?Programmable ∧C trap
45	?Virtual array not yet open
50	%Data format error
55	%Subscript out of range
57	?Out of data at line XX

?Can't Find File or Account

The file number or account number used by the programmer could not be found.

?End of File on Device

The programmer attempted to input beyond the end of a data file, or a source file called into core has no END statement in the program.

?Programmable ∧C Trap

The operator typed a CTRL/C while an ON ERROR GOTO statement was being executed, and the CTRL/C was trapped as an error.

?Virtual Array Not Yet Open

The programmer attempted to use a virtual array before the file containing the array was opened.

%Data Format Error

Data in the program was presented in an illegal format.

%Subscript Out of Range

The program referenced an array element that was beyond the number of elements dimensioned.

?Out of Data at Line XX

The READ statement requested more data than existed.

INDEX